The Professional
Product Owner

The Professional Product Owner

LEVERAGING SCRUM AS A COMPETITIVE ADVANTAGE

Don McGreal

Ralph Jocham

✦Addison-Wesley

Boston • Columbus • Indianapolis • New York • San Francisco • Amsterdam • Cape Town
Dubai • London • Madrid • Milan • Munich • Paris • Montreal • Toronto • Delhi • Mexico City
São Paulo • Sydney • Hong Kong • Seoul • Singapore • Taipei • Tokyo

Many of the designations used by manufacturers and sellers to distinguish their products are claimed as trademarks. Where those designations appear in this book, and the publisher was aware of a trademark claim, the designations have been printed with initial capital letters or in all capitals.

The authors and publisher have taken care in the preparation of this book, but make no expressed or implied warranty of any kind and assume no responsibility for errors or omissions. No liability is assumed for incidental or consequential damages in connection with or arising out of the use of the information or programs contained herein.

For information about buying this title in bulk quantities, or for special sales opportunities (which may include electronic versions; custom cover designs; and content particular to your business, training goals, marketing focus, or branding interests), please contact our corporate sales department at corpsales@pearsoned.com or (800) 382-3419.

For government sales inquiries, please contact governmentsales@pearsoned.com.

For questions about sales outside the U.S., please contact intlcs@pearson.com.

Visit us on the Web: informit.com/aw

Library of Congress Control Number: 2018934196

To my incredibly patient, supportive, and awesome wife Marita; also, to my little M&M's, Meagan and Molly, for being constant sources of laughter, love, and inspiration.
—Don

To my family—thanks for your understanding and lasting support. All of this, the travels, the long hours, would not have been possible without you. Natacha, you are the best and I love you. Noémie and Anaïs, thanks for keeping me down to earth. You are the best daughters I could wish for.
—Ralph

CONTENTS

FOREWORD

COMMUNICATION, INTENTIONALITY, AND FULFILLMENT

You may have something you want done. You may have a vision you want
fulfilled (a new way for people to travel between two places); a product you
want created (a water slide at a lake, or a quantum computer); an improvement
that you want to make to something (customer service is quicker, more
effective, friendlier). Regardless, you are a person who has the authority and
resources to try to get what you want. But you find it very, very hard.

Your skill is visioning what you want. Your skill is not necessarily building
what you want (even if you could, you don't have time to do so).

You just have to tell someone what you want, fund and provision them
adequately, and the result will be great (or at least satisfying).

We assume when we communicate with other people that they understand what
we mean. Not necessarily so. You may be inarticulate or incomprehensible.
The people you communicate with may be dunderheads.

Even more distressing, we assume that we know what we mean, even though we may not have thought it through accurately or completely. Our attempted communication may be premature. But, who has time to wait?!

This book presents a method of communicating our desires, cogently, coherently, and with a minimum of fuss and bother. Otherwise, we can alienate our allies, waste our capital, and cause irreparable damage. I know.

A great strength of Scrum is your ability to frequently check the clarity of what is being communicated, as well as how well the others perceive what you are communicating.

Frequent inspection of the clarity of communications and the consequences is important. It is particularly important at the start of an endeavor when we are just learning how to communicate what the results may be. As we get better at communicating, the communications become more precise. With less effort, we learn how to determine the unknown and turn it into clarity, and we get the results we desire.

As the person who wants something, when you use Scrum to improve communications and the outcomes, your role is called the Product Owner. Don McGreal and Ralph Jocham have written this book to help you use Scrum to do so. They should know because they have done it.

—Ken Schwaber

INTRODUCTION

This book describes how to effectively manage man-made products, mostly software products. But it just as easily could address other man-made products such as electrical grids, nuclear power plants, apple orchards, nano-robots, even storm-drainage systems. Anything envisioned, created, sustained, and eventually retired or replaced by people is within our purview.

We specifically address complex products, where more is unknown about their context than is known. The product's creator—its Product Owner—perceives a space of ideas and conceives something that others might find valuable or useful.

Take as an example the first version of iOS developed for the iPhone. As this product was being conceived and created, more was unknown than known, and a certain degree of success and failure was involved. The Product Owner brought the vision to a small group of people who had expertise in the necessary technology, market, and products. This group employed empiricism and small self-organizing teams to manage the creation and development of iOS, to control the risk, and to create value.

Sometimes an idea isn't ready for prime time. The technology might not be adequate for the vision, or the people may not be adequately skilled. However, the risk is controlled through short cycles of experimentation.

This process is called Scrum,[1] a framework for creating and then further developing complex products. Scrum identifies the Product Owner as the person who brings the product to life, from vision to creation, and who remains responsible for the product's viability as it develops and continues through its life cycle. A Product Owner is the one person who is accountable for a product at any point in time.

A product does things, performs functions, or causes change or results. A product's life cycle includes the following components:

- **Creation**—A product is envisioned and parts of it come to life, so it has some of the capabilities and can perform some of the functions that have been envisioned for it.
- **Emergence**—As the product is used and time passes, new capabilities and functions appear. These may be created for it or may be appended to it by interfaces to other products.
- **Maturity**—The product reaches maturity when fully capable, as envisioned and as emerged, as shaped by marketplace forces, new technologies, and the capabilities of its Product Owners.
- **Senescence**—Over the hill, the product is still used but has been eclipsed by newer, easier, more appealing products that have more or fewer capabilities, at greater or lesser prices, but are preferred by the marketplace and are more valuable.

A product could be a computer, software the computer is operating, a security system, a camera, a car, a workflow system, just-in-time-inventory software, a rocket, or a business function that uses one or more of the above and performs a function for an organization.

---

1. "Scrum Guides," Scrum.org, accessed March 4, 2018, http://scrumguides.org.

Examples of notable products and Products Owners include the following:

- Self-landing rockets—*Elon Musk*
- Electric cars—*Elon Musk*
- iPhones—*Steve Jobs*
- Polaroid camera—*Edwin Land*
- Model T car—*Henry Ford*
- Scrum—*Ken Schwaber and Jeff Sutherland*

These Product Owners were visionaries, people who imagined different methods of doing things, envisioned products to accomplish these things, and then caused these products to emerge. For these products to be remembered, their Product Owners had to guide them to maturity in the marketplace, where they proved themselves useful to people or organizations.

Scrum helps Product Owners during the visionary phase by simplifying demands on them. Product Owners who can excite, can envision, can cause the product to emerge are sometimes less skilled at managing and administering the product as it matures. That requires a person trained in more traditional skills such as manufacturing, inventory, marketing, sales, support, service, and invoicing. A Product Owner who has both sets of skills is the professional Product Owner.

Most of us are familiar with Product Owners who oversee products in the mature phase of their life cycles. To the extent that they are working closely with their stakeholders and are imbued with the vision, they are successful. Product Owners who also run the business, respond to market forces, and help the product morph as new technologies and ideas emerge help it to become more useful.

Senescence is a difficult part of the product life cycle. We have all seen products from IBM, CDC, Xerox, Kodak, Motorola, Nokia, Blackberry, Wang, DEC, and other organizations that reach this point in their life cycles. To the extent that these products are gracefully ridden into their graves, they sustain the organizations that hosted them through maturity. Now they are on life support. If they have been successfully carried through maturity, they may have provided an opportunity for new visionaries to come up with new products that can sustain the organization. Usually not.

This book describes how a person acting in the role of Product Owner can use Scrum to envision, emerge, and mature a product. Throughout the life cycle, the product is passed from person to person. In our view, it has to be passed from one accountable individual to the next accountable individual. That single person, the Product Owner, is responsible for everything that happens regarding the product, its value to its host organization, and to those who use it.

The Product Owner causes the product to live and grow in many different ways, such as development, partnerships, and interfaces. However, this one individual is the "buck stops here" person; he or she alone, not a committee or group, fulfills this function.

We have a great example of this in the United States with the Affordable Care Act (ACA) and the healthcare.gov site. When it was time for ACA to come to life, it didn't. It didn't respond on the Internet, it would not allow people to register, it confabulated data. And who was responsible for this disaster, this embarrassment? Nobody was sure.

> *A successful child has many parents. A failure has none.*
>
> —based on Tacitus, Agricola, ca. 98 AD

Eventually, the Secretary of Health, Education, and Welfare said that she was responsible, but she meant only that she was in the wrong place at the wrong time – not the Product Owner.

If you have a product at some point in its life cycle, and you want to use Scrum to create more value in it for its users, you will be its Product Owner. This book aims to tell you how to do so.

This book is part of a series of books by Scrum.org known as the professional series. This series was founded on a uniform set of values that bind the people involved in work, so that they can trust each other, minimize waste, and succeed.[2]

How to Read This Book

This book is laid out in a way that assumes you have some Scrum knowledge. If you are new to Scrum, we suggest you look first at Part II.

We reference the official *Scrum Guide* by Ken Schwaber and Jeff Sutherland (creators of Scrum) throughout the book and have made every effort to stay consistent with its language. For example, we capitalize official Scrum terms for roles, artifacts, and events the same way the *Scrum Guide* does.

Each chapter is relatively independent. Chapters are grouped into three parts:

- *Part I: Strategy*—This part has very little to do with Scrum itself. Instead our focus is proper agile product management and maximizing the ROI of a product. We introduce the three Vs (vision, value, validation) as a way to achieve this.
- *Part II: Scrum*—This part starts by defining empirical process control and how Scrum is a tool for managing complexity and continuous delivery of value. With help from the *Scrum Guide,* we define each role, artifact, and event with particular attention to the Product Owner role.
- *Part III: Tactics*—Part III introduces more concrete practices and tools for managing Product Backlogs and release plans, and concludes by examining what it means to be a professional Product Owner.

Each chapter begins with a short quiz. The intent is to set the stage for the chapter by inviting you to think independently about the core topics. We review the quiz at the end of the chapter to determine whether your thinking has changed at all—consider it Test-Driven Reading.

---

2. Other publications can be found or referenced at http://scrum.org.

Along the way, we share personal anecdotes from relevant experiences. These blurbs have one or both of our faces alongside them. Just like this one.

We put a lot of thought and practice into the Scrum.org Professional Scrum Product Owner course we both teach and maintain. We feel that this book is a perfect companion to that course as it contains all the same information and much more.

We sincerely hope that you enjoy reading it as much as we do teaching, discussing, coaching, and writing about these topics.

—Don and Ralph

Register your copy of *The Professional Product Owner* on the InformIT site for convenient access to updates and/or corrections as they become available. To start the registration process, go to informit.com/register and log in or create an account. Enter the product ISBN (9780134686479) and click Submit. Look on the Registered Products tab for an Access Bonus Content link next to this product, and follow that link to access any available bonus materials. If you would like to be notified of exclusive offers on new editions and updates, please check the box to receive email from us.

ACKNOWLEDGMENTS

Don and Ralph would like to thank Scrum.org for all its support with this book, in particular Ken Schwaber, David West, Kurt Bittner, and Eric Naiburg.

Another big thank you to everyone who took the time to review our book and provide invaluable feedback, especially Ken Howard, Lois Wortley, and Hiren Doshi.

Don would like to thank Improving for the support and encouragement for writing this book. It is a great example of how the power of trust changes everything. Improving is not just a company, it is a family.

Ralph and Don would like to thank Chrisitan Botta of Visual Braindump for the awesome drawings, including our mugshots. They're really us! ; -)

About the Authors

Don McGreal, in his role as VP of Learning Solutions at Improving (improving.com), is a hands-on agile consultant and instructor. He specializes in agile coaching at the enterprise and product management levels within larger organizations.

Don is a Scrum.org Professional Scrum Trainer who has authored and taught classes for thousands of software professionals around the globe. He is also cofounder of TastyCupcakes.org, a comprehensive collection of games and exercises for accelerating the adoption of agile principles.

Don is an Irish French-speaking Canadian living in Texas.

Ralph Jocham is a German citizen who spent the last 20 years collecting professional software and product development experience in France, the United Kingdom, the United States, and now Switzerland. He became an agile evangelist in 2000 and perfected his approach at ThoughtWorks.

Ralph is also Europe's first trainer with Scrum.org and has taught thousands of professionals around the globe. When not busy running his company, effective agile (effectiveagile.com), or helping all kinds of enterprises in Europe, he enjoys teaching at universities.

Ralph nevertheless finds time to spend quality time with his family on a regular basis, treating them to home-cooked international fine cuisine and going on long walks with the family dog.

Both Don and Ralph are course stewards for the Scrum.org Professional Scrum Product Owner course taught around the world.

STRATEGY

I

AGILE PRODUCT MANAGEMENT

We didn't do anything wrong, but somehow, we lost.

—Nokia CEO, Stephen Elop

QUIZ

To set the stage for this chapter, try answering each of the following statements with Agree or Disagree. Answers appear at the end of the chapter.

Statement	Agree	Disagree
Schedule, budget, and scope are the best ways to measure project success.	☐	☐
Product management is an essential practice for Product Owners.	☐	☐
A Product Owner should act as a proxy between the business and technology.	☐	☐
A Product Owner establishes a vision for a product.	☐	☐
Scrum provides all the tools necessary for successful product management.	☐	☐
Every development effort has a product.	☐	☐

PRODUCT MINDSET VERSUS PROJECT MINDSET

A *project* starts with an idea. If the idea sounds promising, a project can be initiated to make it a reality.

Important projects require organization and accountability. This is where a *project manager* comes in. A project manager is someone skilled in managing tasks and people, but not necessarily knowledgeable or passionate about the domain.

This project manager gathers enough information to create a plan. The plan will outline in detail the scope of the initiative over several project milestones and estimate how much time and money will be needed to complete it all. That manager then asks for resources (including people), forms a team around the project, and keeps each team member on task to ensure a successful outcome. Success is ultimately measured by how closely the project manager sticks to the initial plan—*scope, time, budget.*

This seems perfectly reasonable—at first.

But what about projects that remain on time, on budget, and within scope, and yet still do not succeed? For years, Nokia led the market in producing mobile phones. It delivered phone after phone on tight schedules. It knew how to run a project, and each individual project likely succeeded. But what about the company's phones? Is Nokia still around? Yes, as a department of Microsoft. What is interesting is that Microsoft paid more for Skype ($8.6 billion), a few hundred person services company, than it did for Nokia ($7.2 billion), a company that at one point had vast infrastructure, millions in hardware assets, and 100,000 employees.

If you or your company think in terms of projects and less in terms of products and value, the tide of fortune can turn rather quickly.

Interestingly, the word "project" used to mean to do something before (pro-) acting (-ject). In the 1950s, project management became more mainstream with the introduction of several techniques within the engineering and defense industries. This expanded the definition of "project" to include both planning and execution and has since expanded to hundreds of techniques across many other industries.

Don't worry, this is not a project management book. However, an understanding of the current state of project management should provide some context for why we wrote it.

This *project mindset* (see Figure 1-1) defines success from the "inside out," using internal measurements that are more about task management and about how accurately the initial plan was followed.

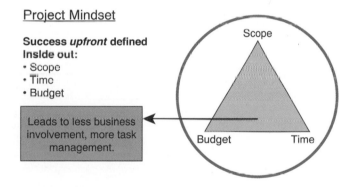

Figure 1-1 Visual representation of a project mindset

What is the alternative?

What do your customers value? Projects or products? The objective is not to deliver projects but to deliver value through *products*—products that ultimately lead to higher revenue and lower costs for your organization. Products that are so great that your customer base will grow and existing customers will stick around.

So forget about projects. Approach your idea and its business case as a product. Give your product idea to a capable team and introduce them to meaningful business targets such as user adoption, sales, and stakeholder satisfaction. Impress on the team that the only way to influence targets like these is to release something of value as soon as possible and validate your business assumption.

Now that the team has the proper mindset, the next question should be: "What can we ship first that will have the biggest impact on our targets?"

Suddenly, delivery and business start to align and bridge their communication gap.

This *product mindset* (see Figure 1-2) is an "outside in" approach that uses external measurements to actively guide the development of the product to maximize value.

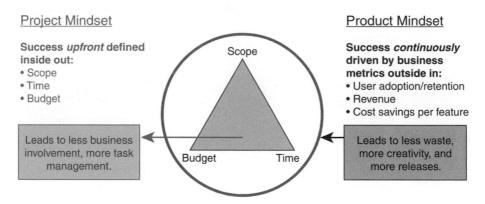

Figure 1-2 Product versus project mindset

A product mindset:

- encourages more frequent releases, which results in earlier feedback from the marketplace;
- communicates objectives instead of tasks; teams get more creative with their solutions and take more ownership over their plans; and
- eliminates waste by depending less on task assignment, reporting, and management decisions.

Contrast this with the project mindset, which leads to:

- less business involvement;
- more handoffs;
- more task management; and
- more people management.

But what if there isn't a product?

Read on. Later in this chapter, we make the case that software development always involves a product.

WHAT IS PRODUCT MANAGEMENT?

Figure 1-3 shows the different layers of planning within an organization that develops products of any kind. At the core of any Scrum-based approach is a *daily plan* within a *Sprint plan*. (Sprints and Sprint Planning are described in Chapters 5 and 6.) Both these plans belong to the Development Team that is doing the work. They have autonomy in developing a plan on how to best meet the Sprint Goal and inspect and adapt that plan every day.

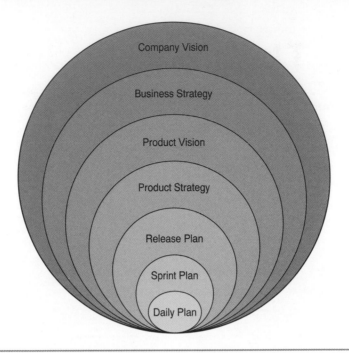

Figure 1-3 The different layers of planning

The two outside planning layers are the overall *company vision* and *business strategy*. Both are typically owned by an executive team or CEO, who establishes and communicates a company-wide vision and promotes an overall strategy under that vision.

In between the larger organizational goals and the work that Development Teams do day-to-day is a gap (see Figure 1-4).

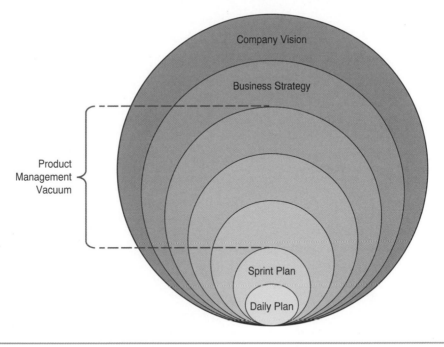

Figure I-4 The Product Management Vacuum

We call this the Product Management Vacuum, and it is a major motivation for writing this book.

THE PRODUCT MANAGEMENT VACUUM AND THE THREE VS

The thing about any vacuum is that it has an innate need to be filled.

If you are not careful, the Product Management Vacuum will get filled with meaningless busy work and extensive task management, often guided by project metrics as described earlier. All the layers of budgeting, project charters, handoffs, and tasks breakdown mask the true intention of the initiative. You run the risk of being busy without a clear direction.

The bigger the vacuum:

- the more disconnected the technology groups are from the business;
- the less engaged the people on the ground become;
- the more reliance there is on project and task management;
- the more hierarchies and handoffs emerge;
- the more complexity is introduced;
- the harder it is to shift directions when the business climate changes;
- the more "busy work" is created;
- the more waste and rework occurs; and
- the less value is delivered to customers.

True product management is about embodying agility throughout the whole organization from the top down to the bottom and thereby filling the Product Management Vacuum. Done right, this creates a true competitive advantage.

To fill the vacuum the right way, use the three Vs shown in Figure 1-5. Figure 1-6 represents how the three Vs fill the vacuum.

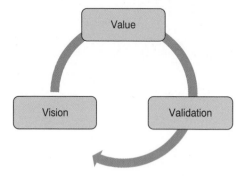

Figure 1-5 The three Vs

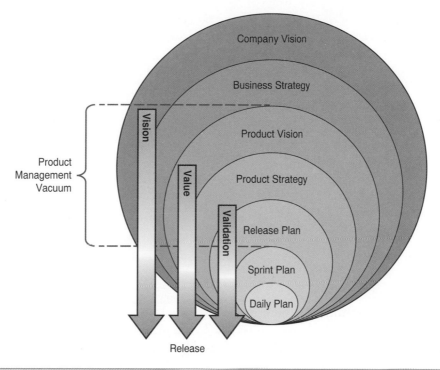

Figure 1-6 How Vision, Value, and Validation fill the Product Management Vacuum

Let's take a brief look at each of the Vs.

VISION

Vision creates *Transparency*.

The successful Product Owner establishes a clear product vision for her team, much like a military commander establishes clear intent for his subordinates. Doing so allows subordinates to act without direct orders if necessary to carry out the commander's intent.

From the book *Auftragstaktik: The Basis for Modern Military Command?* by Major Michael J. Gunther:

> The use of mission tactics [*Auftragstaktik*] allow[s] subordinate commanders . . . to interpret how best to achieve the commander's intent based upon their understanding of the tactical situation. . . . *The success of the doctrine rests upon the recipient of orders understanding the intent of the issuer and acting to achieve the goal even if their actions violate other guidance or orders they have received.*[1]

Self-organization does not just happen. Much like in the military, the two main ingredients are shared vision and clear boundaries.

In the context of product development, the boundaries are provided by Scrum and the vision is provided through the Product Owner's strong leadership and communication.

The product vision anchors everything in the process. This vision creates transparency because it forms the basis for all following conversations, leading to a common understanding for why you are building the product and what your customers' needs are. According to Richard Hackman, 30 percent of a team's success depends on how it was launched.[2] A great and well-communicated vision is paramount for a successful launch.

You need to communicate the product vision again and again to keep everyone on board and honest. Never forget that this vision represents the voice of the customer. If you stop listening to your customers, the resulting product will be of less value or even alienate them.

---

1. Michael J. Gunther, *Auftragstaktik: The Basis for Modern Military Command?* (Fort Leavenworth, KS: School of Advanced Military Studies, U.S. Army Command and General Staff College, 2012), 3 (emphasis added).
2. J. Richard Hackman, *Leading Teams: Setting the Stage for Great Performances* (Boston, MA: Harvard University Press, 2002).

I too often see the term "resources" used for human beings. These resources are given a catalog of requirements to implement and rarely have any idea about why. They lack the context of the vision and therefore are deprived of situational awareness. They fulfill exactly what was specified but often still miss the goal.

Making the connection to the product's (or even the organization's) vision helps team members make goal-driven commitments and feel like they are a part of something bigger than themselves. So how do you create a clear vision? Techniques are explored in Chapter 2, "Vision."

VALUE

Defining **value** provides you with something to *Inspect*.

Imagine the vision as a long thread. Value is the individual pearls you attach as you progress. Vision provides a foundation and direction, but without the pearls attached to it, there is no value. A Scrum Team's job is to identify and then attach pearls (value) to the thread (vision).

The first pearl could be either a large business initiative or a smaller distinct feature. Aim for the most valuable item first and attach it completely before moving on to the next one. In other words, always be in a position to deliver value.

"If you could have only one thing, what would it be?" is often a good opening question when identifying the most valuable.

> *If everything is important, then nothing is.*
>
> —Patrick Lencioni[3]

---

3. *Silos, Politics, and Turf Wars: A Leadership Fable about Destroying the Barriers That Turn Colleagues into Competitors* (San Francisco: Jossey-Bass, 2002).

Once you get this answer, often after persistent digging, try to truly under-stand the other person's view; try to grasp the underlying *why*. You might even go so far as to question the product's utility. Eventually, when you have narrowed it down and are convinced, go ahead and define how the value will manifest. Would a process take fewer clicks? How many? Will the behavior of a user change? How? Will a transaction be faster? How much faster? You need to provide more leadership than simply saying "let's do this!" If you are not able to quantify success or to prove the realization of value, then the chances of being on the wrong track are rather high. Do not forget that the only real proof, though, is through the customer. Everything before is nothing but a hypothesis.

> *I like the idea that through the functionality we develop, we actually improve the world. It might not be world peace we reach, but we make a positive impact on someone's life—even if it is just one click less in a process.*
>
> *Ralph*

So how do you measure value? Techniques are explored in Chapter 3, "Value."

VALIDATION

Validation causes *Adaptation*.

Most business assumptions are plainly wrong.[4] They look good on paper but do not hold up in the real world. Each valuable idea has to be validated as soon as possible. One place this is done in Scrum is the Sprint Review. The Sprint Review is the chance for all stakeholders to review the current state of the product and to get an insight into next steps. The closer the reviewers are to actual customers and the closer the Increment is to being released, the more realistic the feedback and subsequent adaptations.

---

4. Ronny Kohavi et al., "Online Experimentation at Microsoft" (ThinkWeek paper, Microsoft Corp., Seattle, WA, 2009).

Even if the Sprint Reviews go well and everyone seems happy, you still do not have true validation until the product or feature is in production and used. In Scrum, "Done" means the Increment is potentially releasable. However, to have ultimate validation and reduce the overall product risk, you need to establish a feedback loop with the marketplace. For this you need to release as frequently as the business can support.

The two core feedback loops in Scrum are on the process side and the product side:

- *Process* validation is about inspecting and adapting *how* the Scrum Team is working.
- *Product* validation is about inspecting and adapting *what* the Scrum Team is building.

Validation in the context of product management and the three Vs is about the latter: product validation.

Chapter 4, "Validation," describes this in more detail.

PRODUCT MANAGEMENT AND SCRUM

Building products requires that you consider a series of strategic activities. Consider the following list:

- Analyzing the industry and competition
- Maximizing ROI
- Forecasting and assessing feasibility
- Developing product strategy
- Planning releases
- Identifying customers and their needs
- Roadmapping the product
- Auditing results
- Creating outbound messaging

- Sustaining the product
- Executing the release
- Creating the business case
- Identifying product requirements
- Launching the product
- Developing customer retention strategy
- Defining product features and initiatives
- Retiring the product
- Marketing and branding

How many of these fit squarely in the realm of Scrum? Maybe three or four, but not many.

The world of product management is a lot bigger than Scrum, as suggested in Figure 1-7, which quite possibly explains why there is such a large Product Management Vacuum in the software industry.

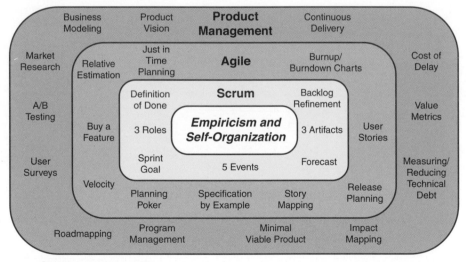

Figure 1-7 Scrum is augmented by many, many practices. (Figure © 1993-2016 Scrum.org. All rights reserved.)

This is where the Product Owner comes in. A Product Owner is one of the three Scrum roles. Although most product management activities are not part of the Scrum framework, as shown in Figure 1-8, a good Product Owner will take them on to fill the Product Management Vacuum.

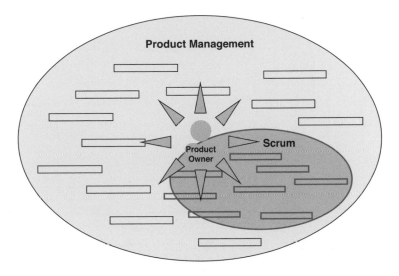

Figure 1-8 Product Ownership is agile product management leveraging Scrum.

In other words, a good Product Owner is an agile Product Manager.

When I work with an organization to identify ideal candidates for the Product Owner role, I first ask about the strategic activities above and who does them. If the organization already has a Product Manager who does many of these activities, then I consider them an ideal candidate for Product Owner. If nobody is doing these activities or that person is not willing or able to commit to a Product Owner role, then I insist on empowering our Product Owner to **own** these activities as a way of elevating the role beyond the tactical to the strategic.

An empowered and entrepreneurial Product Owner fills the Product Management Vacuum, as shown in Figure 1-9.

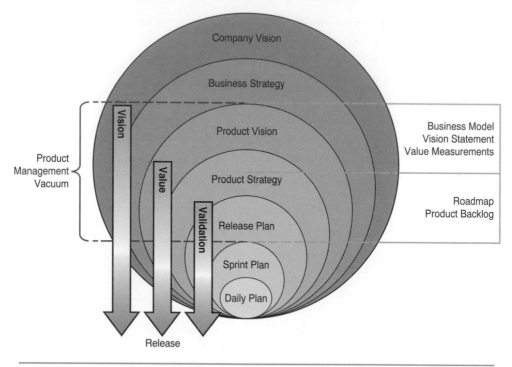

Figure 1-9 The Product Owner and the Product Management Vacuum

THE PRODUCT OWNER

Who should play the role of Product Owner?

Later in this book, more time is spent on the specific tasks and responsibilities of a Product Owner. This chapter stays at a more strategic level.

In Scrum, you need a Product Owner. But it obviously takes more than just filling the role. The effectiveness of that role, and of the overall Scrum implementation, depends a lot on the type of person in that role (see Figure 1-10).

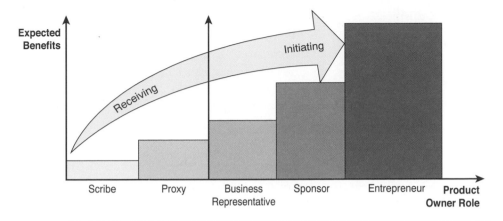

Figure 1-10 Product Owner role types by expected benefits

A **scribe** is likely someone on the technology side who has been tasked with capturing requirements for the Development Team. This person is often seen as the team's secretary and is asked to write everything down during meetings with the business. He has little to no decision-making ability, which severely impacts his effectiveness as a Product Owner and causes delays.

A **proxy** is still likely to come from the technology side but is seen as a representative of the business, maybe even for a particular product manager on the business side. She often has a business analyst or system analyst title. The problem is that a proxy creates an unnecessary indirection between the Development Team and the real influencers.

What is a likely response from the proxy whenever the team has a question for her? "Let me go ask," resulting in more delays.

Could the proxy get protective of her role and shut down any direct communication between the team and the business? Very likely. You surely see it all the time.

Both the scribe and proxy are on the receiving side of what goes into the product. They get told what to do. At best, they work out the details.

A **business representative** is someone from the business side rather than the technology side. This role is a clear improvement over the proxy role, as it demonstrates a commitment from the business toward the product. In contrast to the proxy Product Owner, this role provides more direct access to domain knowledge and stakeholder expectations. However, there may still be decision-making delays, as the business representative often has limited autonomy over product management.

A business **sponsor** is a big improvement on the Product Owner role. A sponsor is someone who spearheaded the initial business case and acquired the budget. Consequently, he has the trust and the mandate to make financial and product decisions on the spot. This creates fewer hiccups, less context switching, and largely improved flow. The Development Team can then focus more and get more things done sooner.

The ultimate Product Owner is an **entrepreneur**. This is someone who is spending her own money to fund the development of the product. This gives her complete responsibility over all product management decisions for both business and IT strategy. Now while this may not be a realistic situation for many organizations, an entrepreneurial mindset is still something that Product Owners should assume. They should expect to see a return on investment (ROI) as though their own money was at stake.

The business representative, sponsor, and entrepreneur are more on the initiating side of the product. Because of their deeper business understanding and their two-way communication, they develop a stronger customer empathy. This empathy allows them to initiate rather than simply receive the right requirements.

Keep in mind that the closer a Product Owner is to a sponsor the further he may disengage from the Development Team. Finding ways to maintain that sense of connection with the product vision becomes even more important and is what is expected of an entrepreneurial Product Owner.

Figure 1-11 provides a summary of this discussion of Product Owner roles types.

	Scribe	Proxy	Business Representative	Sponsor	Entrepreneur
Vision	None	Low	Medium	High	High
Decision Making	None	Low	Medium	High	High
Domain Knowledge	Low	Low	High	High	High
Budget	None	None	Low	High	High
Development Team Involvement	High	High	Medium	Low	High
Business Involvement	Low	Med	High	High	High
Accountability	None	Low	Medium	High	High

Product Owner   Product Owner Domain   Development Team Domain

Figure 1-11 Summary of Product Owner role types

I often find myself writing these five Product Owner role types down when talking to organizations. I like to ask them where they see their Product Owners. Not surprisingly, they are more often than not closer to the scribe and proxy roles. This then turns into a discussion of more practical actions a Product Owner could do to move up the list. Could a scribe start to be more representative of the business people? Could a proxy start learning more about the business side? Could a business representative ask to be more involved with budgeting and strategic direction? If the answer is no to any of these questions, then we should ask ourselves if we have the right person in the Product Owner role.

Don

DEFINING A PRODUCT

What is a product? On the surface, this question seems simple. But it's not.

> A product is anything that can be offered to a market that might satisfy a want or need.[5]

Companies sell many products—retail, financial products, seats on planes, cars.

In the world of software development, you make products too:

- Some are straight commodities—word processors, games, operating systems.
- Others are channels to other products—online retail, travel booking websites, mobile banking apps, search engines.

When this book refers to products, generally it means software products. However, many of the concepts discussed apply well beyond the realm of software.

To start, here are some assertions:

1. There is always a product. It may not always be obvious, but it is there and it needs to be identified.

   AND

2. Every product has a *customer* who is a:

   a. *Consumer:* Anyone who gets value from your product, whether or not they pay for it

   b. *Buyer:* Anyone who pays for your product, whether or not they use it

   c. *Both*

   AND

---

5. Philip Kotler, Linden Brown, Stewart Adam, Suzan Burton, and Gary Armstrong, *Marketing*, 7th ed. (Frenchs Forest, New South Wales: Pearson Education Australia/Prentice Hall, 2007).

3. Every product has a *producer* who receives a core benefit through:

   a. Revenue increase

   b. Cost decrease or avoidance

   c. Societal benefit

What happens far too often is that smaller areas of functionality or even smaller technical components are considered products, with no clear customer or value proposition.

I had in one of my Product Owner trainings a participant who introduced himself as "My name is . . . and I am the Product Owner for testing." Normally I am known for being swift with my words, but in this case I was speechless.

Ralph

Another common pattern is Conway's Law:

> Organizations which design systems . . . are constrained to produce designs which are copies of the communication structures of these organizations.[6]

The result of Conway's Law is a series of interconnected "systems" built by different departments (or hierarchies) within an organization with little focus on the actual product or on who the customer even is.

This is the reason Scrum names the role *Product* Owner and not System, Feature, or Component Owner.

The best approach is to think about the product from a customer's perspective. Which customer needs are you addressing? What do customers expect? What product improvements will make customers' lives easier?

---

6. Melvin E. Conway, "How Do Committees Invent?" *Datamation* 14, no. 5 (1968): 28–31.

Ralph

Don

When we work with companies to define their products, we emphasize that this is ultimately a business decision. Let's align our technology groups based on the products our business wants the end-customers to see.

For example, Company A may have a strategic direction of presenting their customers with a series of products to fulfill their needs, while Company B decides it would rather present its customers with one larger product. Both are valid options, and neither should be constrained by the technical software delivery structure. This needs to remain a strategic business choice, and technology should be able to adapt as seamlessly as possible.

This bridges the chasm between business and technology.

When you think of a car, what is the product? The engine, the entertainment system, the steering, the air conditioning, the car itself? What exactly is the product?

As stated above, start with the customer. Who is the consumer and who is the buyer?

If you are buying the car for yourself, then you are both the buyer and the customer. If you are a parent buying a car for your child, you are the buyer but the child is the consumer.

Car companies must design products with both in mind. Cars must include airbags and safety ratings for the parent and fun colors and multimedia systems for the teen.

But you can look at it from a different angle: The car company is the buyer as well as the consumer for components within the car. The products are the engines, entertainment systems, air bags, and so on that are produced by vendors or even internal groups.

So, to know your product, you need to know the consumer and buyer—your product's customers.

Getting back to software, Table 1-1 presents some realistic examples. See whether these assertions still hold true.

Table 1-1 Product Examples

Producer	Description	Buyer	Consumer	Producer Benefit
Microsoft	Professional office software for daily or occasional office work	Enterprise ———— Individual user	Employee ———— Individual user	Revenue (licensing)
Technology Department within an organization	Replace legacy backend system with updated web service API	Technology Department	Individual programmers	Cost savings (lower mainte-nance costs)
Wikipedia	Nonprofit encyclopedia with volunteer contributors	Donors	Information seekers	Social benefit (free informa-tion)
Call Center	A system for customer service agents to log calls	Call Center	Customer service agents in Call Center	Cost savings (shorter call times)
QA Department	Creating auto-mated tests for development teams	QA Department	Internal Development Teams	Cost savings (better quality)
Business Analyst Group	Creating docu-ments to hand over to IT for implementation	Business Department	IT Development Department	Revenue (salary)
Amazon.com	Retail website	Individuals	Individuals	Revenue (sales)
Facebook	Social media	Advertisers	Individuals	Revenue (advertising sales)

After you have identified your product, the next question is, "Is it a viable product?"

A viable product is one where the stated producer benefit comes to fruition. This means that you should have ways to measure the benefit along the way. Chapter 3, "Value," explains more about how to do this. For now, consider this a major responsibility of a Product Owner for maximizing ROI.

The preceding examples of the separate automated testing and business analysis groups rarely produce a viable ROI.

Admittedly, you will see examples of initiatives that have failed, time and time again. Is the automated testing group developing a product? Sure. But is the stated benefit of better quality even viable? Will the other Development Teams embrace testing environments that they did not develop themselves? Who will maintain this testing system after its implementation? The ROI is rarely there unless these efforts live with the Development Teams themselves. Regardless, it is important to understand the cost and perceived benefit and set up a feedback mechanism to ensure that the product is still viable.

An important takeaway when defining your product is to go as high as possible without losing sight of your core objectives. You have to find the right value area from the customer's point of view. What does the customer need, and what is the customer willing to pay for? What provides value?

Coming back to the car example, would you buy a steering wheel or a seat? You most likely want a usable product, a complete car in this case. This product provides a benefit to you as a consumer.

If you structure your teams below the value areas, you will see too many Product Owners, with all the resulting coordination overhead. Imagine having a separate Product Owner for each car component with no real centralized vision for the whole car as one product (see Figure 1-12).

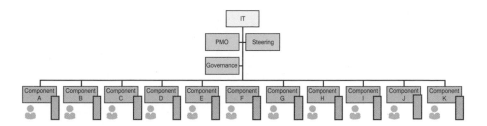

Figure 1-12 A Product Owner for each car component

Now when you add a new feature or large initiative for a value area, it needs to be broken down into units of work for each of the affected components. This creates enormous overhead, with many dependencies to be managed and resulting in skill shortage, timing, quality and integration issues. To handle all these dependencies, you will likely need to find a "feature" owner to take care of all the coordination and to be accountable for the feature. Some call this role a project manager (see Figure 1-13).

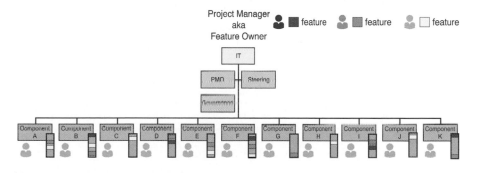

Figure 1-13 Project managers are feature owners.

The problems mentioned above can lead to the following:[7]

1. **Sequential life cycle**

    The dependencies from the various components need to be aligned, which requires a plan taking handoffs into account. Once Component B is completed, it is handed over to Component F, and so on.

---

7. Cesário Ramos, "Scale Your Product NOT Your Scrum," Scrum.org (February 2016).

2. **Unnecessary dependency management, coordination, and overhead management complexity**

   In a plan-driven approach, all the coordination of the dependencies is left to managers, many of whom are nontechnical. By instead providing a clear goal and leaving the implementation details to feature teams, you get commitment and working functionality more quickly for review.

3. **Working on low-value features**

   The feature is composed of functionality of various degrees of value, from very low to very high. Since the whole feature is being decomposed and top-down managed and coordinated in the components, there is no feedback to identify high- or low-value functionality.

4. **Handoffs, information scatter, and high inventory**

   Individual feature activities need to be completed before the next activity can start. Communication and knowledge transfer at those handoffs is done by documents and specification. All those interim activities lead to high inventory, spread-out information, and too many handoffs.

5. **Loss of customer and whole-product focus**

   When work is organized by activities to be completed by all those component teams, naturally the customer becomes secondary. There are enough dependencies, challenges, and other obstacles to manage that a customer, especially a customer providing feedback, can quickly become a nuisance.

6. **Opaque measure of progress**

   The sequential approach means you lose the feedback, which then means you are stuck measuring progress toward your plan instead of toward your value goals.

7. **Inventing work**

   What do you do when your component team runs out of work? You need to justify its existence. So you come up with "important stuff" that needs to be done so that you can justify your team's payroll.

8. **Bad quality**

   Since you focus on each component's quality, you lose sight of the final overall feature quality. Those local optimizations are known to cause problems for the real goal. Also, technical problems between those components are often not addressed correctly for lack of time. Remember the plan to be followed? This leads to technical quality issues in the long run.

Instead of thinking in components, you need to think in terms of one (larger) product. This can go a long way. A Product Owner should be able to handle a fairly large number of Development Teams for a single product.

Remember, the ideal Product Owner is an entrepreneur—a single voice for the vision of the product, regardless of its size. A company has just one CEO, whether it has 100 or 100,000 employees.

This is referred to as the Santa Claus rule. No matter how busy Santa gets, he does not bring on other Santas. How does he cope? Elves.

As products scale, Product Owners should find themselves less involved with the day-to-day tactics of product development and more involved with strategy and direction. They can get help (elves) from teams, stakeholders, assistants, and so on for the more tactical work. As Santa, you can delegate responsibility, but you still remain accountable for the success of Christmas.

If this is not sufficient, then split the product into value domains on the right level of abstraction (see Figure 1-14). This also requires that you set up cross-functional feature teams underneath your product accordingly. The resulting intercommunication is essentially the steering committee, Project Management Office (PMO), and governance in one body. This addresses the problems mentioned previously.

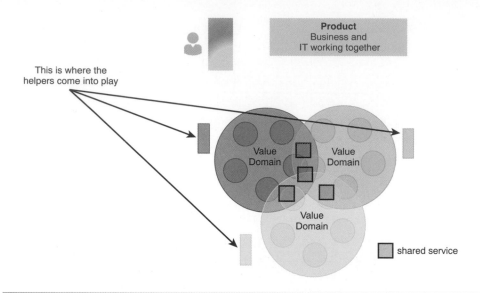

Figure 1-14 Independent customer-focused value domains, sharing common services

 I had a client who had several Product Owners for a large product. The client's solution was to allow each one to select something from his list for the next Sprint, round-robin style. While this may seem fair at first, is it the right strategic solution for the organization? Are the Development Teams truly working on the most valuable features? Who ultimately decides which features are best, regardless of how many voices there are? That person is the real Product Owner.

The shared services between the value domains represent dependency management and integration on a technical level. With today's continuous integration, infrastructure as code, and test automation, this area is well understood. Coordination on a technical level is far more predictable. You either have a working product or you do not.

QUIZ REVIEW

Compare your answers from the beginning of the chapter to the ones below. Now that you have read the chapter, would you change any of your answers? Do you agree with the answers below?

Statement	Agree	Disagree
Schedule, budget, and scope are the best ways to measure project success.		✔
Product management is an essential practice for Product Owners.	✔	
A Product Owner should act as a proxy between the business and technology.		✔
A Product Owner establishes a vision for a product.	✔	
Scrum provides all the tools necessary for successful product management.		✔
Every development effort has a product.	✔	

VISION

Whatever you can do or dream you can, begin it. Boldness has genius, and magic and power in it. Begin it now.

—Goethe

QUIZ

To set the stage for this chapter, try answering each of the following statements with Agree or Disagree. Answers appear at the end of the chapter.

Statement	Agree	Disagree
A product vision will emerge over time.	☐	☐
Every Scrum Team member should have a clear understanding of who the customers are and how the product generates revenue.	☐	☐
Most great products are created by happenstance.	☐	☐
A good vision should be free of emotion.	☐	☐
Agile is all about getting started; the right product will emerge eventually.	☐	☐
It is an advantage to have a technically minded Product Owner.	☐	☐

Let's start this chapter by looking at a couple of example vision statements from fictitious companies.

- AnyThreeNow.com, a global mail order service company "Anyone should be able to purchase anything, anytime from anywhere and get it in less than a day."
- ChaufR.me, a globally operating taxi service "We get you to your destination safely and reliably—as if your parents were driving you. Peace of mind with no wallet required."

What makes a vision compelling? Let's borrow a definition from Ari Weinzweig, co-founder of Zingerman's:

> A vision is a picture of the success of a project at a particular time in the future. A vision is not a mission statement. We see [the vision] as being akin to the North Star, a never-ending piece of work that we commit to going after for life. It also isn't a strategic plan—which is the map to where we want to go. A vision is the actual destination. It's a vivid description of what "success" looks and feels like for us—what we are able to achieve, and the effect it has on our staff.[1]

For Zingerman's, an effective vision needs to be:

- **Inspiring**
  All who help to implement it should feel inspired.
- **Strategically sound**
  That is, you have a decent shot at making it happen.
- **Documented**
  You need to write your vision down to make it work.
- **Communicated**
  Not only do you have to document your vision, but you have to tell people about it too.

This chapter introduces some practices that help create a strong vision.

---

1. Ari Weinzweig, "Why and How Visioning Works," Zingerman's, accessed February 16, 2018, https://www.zingtrain.com/content/why-and-how-visioning-works.

BUSINESS MODELING

You have a product idea. But where do you start?

Even if you already have a product, do you and the rest of your organization truly understand your customers, their needs, and your value propositions? Do you know how you will make money? What about costs?

In much the same way a business does, you need to invest in the right business model for your product. A business model describes the rationale of how an organization creates, delivers, and captures value.[2] You can apply that same rationale to a product.

Many templates and tools exist for creating business models. One of the more popular tools to engage all participants in a structured way is the Business Model Canvas,[3] a single diagram that describes your business

BUSINESS MODEL CANVAS

The Business Model Canvas is divided into nine areas. A group of stakeholders walks through each area while brainstorming both existing and future items.

I like to have people stand around a large canvas or whiteboard and add items on sticky notes that can easily be reorganized. I use a separate color for existing items to clearly distinguish our current situation from where we hope to go. Another tip: taking some time to organize the items in order of importance within each area can also generate some interesting discussions.

Don

The Business Model Canvas is shown in Figure 2-1. Below it, each area is described in the same order you should work through them with your stakeholders. The first five are linked to revenue (producer benefit). The last four are more about identifying costs.

---

2. Alexander Osterwalder et al., *Business Model Generation* (self-published, 2010).
3. "The Business Model Canvas," Strategyzer, assessed February 17, 2018, https://strategyzer.com/canvas/business-model-canvas.

KEY PARTNERS	KEY ACTIVITIES	VALUE PROPOSITIONS	CUSTOMER RELATIONSHIPS	CUSTOMER SEGMENTS
• Who are our partners? • Who are our key suppliers? • Which key resources are we acquiring from our partners? • Which key activities do our partners perform? **MOTIVATION FOR PARTNERSHIP** *Optimization and economy* *Reduction of risk and uncertainty* *Acquisition of particular resources and activities*	• What key activities do our value propositions require? • Our distribution channels? • Customer relationships? • Revenue streams? **CATEGORIES** *Production* *Problem Solving* *Platform/Network*	• What value do we deliver to the customer? • Which one of our customers' problems are we helping to solve? • What bundles of products and services are we offering to each segment? • Which customer needs are we satisfying? • What is the minimum viable product? **CATEGORIES** *Newness* *Performance* *Customization* *"Getting the Job Done"* *Design* *Brand/Status* *Price* *Cost Reduction* *Risk Reduction* *Accessibility* *Convenience/Usability*	• How do we get, keep, and grow customers? • Which customer relationships have we established? • How are they integrated with the rest of our business model? • How costly are they? **EXAMPLES** *Personal Assistance* *Dedicated Personal Assistance* *Self-Service* *Automated Services* *Communities* *Co-Creation*	• For whom are we creating value? • Who are our most important customers? • What are the customer archetypes? **EXAMPLES** *Mass Market* *Niche Market* *Segmented* *Diversified* *Multi-sided Platform*
	KEY RESOURCES		**CHANNELS**	**CHANNEL PHASES** *1. Awareness - How do we raise awareness about our company's product and services?* *2. Valuation - How do we help customers evaluate our organization's Value Proposition?* *3. Purchase - How do we allow customers to purchase specific products and services?* *4. Delivery - How do we deliver a Value Proposition to customers?* *5. After Sales - How do we provide post-purchase customer support?*
	• What key resources do our value propositions require? • Our distribution channels? • Customer relationships? • Revenue streams? **TYPES OF RESOURCES** *Physical* *Intellectual (brand, patents, copyrights, data)* *Human* *Financial*		• Through which channels do our customer segments want to be reached? • How do other companies reach them now? • Which ones work best? • Which ones are most cost-efficient? • How are we integrating them with customer routines?	

COST STRUCTURE		REVENUE STREAMS	
• What are the most important costs inherent to our business model? • Which key resources are most expensive? • Which key activities are most expensive? **SAMPLE CHARACTERISTICS** *Fixed Costs (salaries, rents, utilities)* *Economics of Scale* *Variable Costs* *Economics of Scope*	**IS YOUR BUSINESS MORE** *Cost Driven (leanest cost structure, low price value proposition, maximum automation, extensive outsourcing)* *Value Driven (focused on value creation, premium value proposition)*	• For what value are our customers really willing to pay? • For what do they currently pay? • How are they currently paying? • How would they prefer to pay? • How much does each Revenue Stream contribute to overall revenues?	**TYPES** *Asset Sale* *Usage Fee* *Subscription Fees* *Lending/Renting/Leasing* *Licensing* *Brokerage Fees* *Advertising* **FIXED PRICING** *List Price* *Product Feature Dependent* *Customer Segment Dependent* *Volume Dependent* **DYNAMIC PRICING** *Negotiation (bargaining)* *Yield Management* *Real-Time-Market*

Figure 2-1 Business Model Canvas

1. **Customer Segments**

   Start here. Who will get value from your product? Individual users, groups, personas, or any relevant stakeholders. Who is your buyer? Who is your consumer?

2. **Value Propositions**

   First understanding who your customers are makes it easier to identify the value propositions for each. What are their needs, and how does your product address them?

3. **Channels**

   You can have the greatest value propositions in the world, but if nobody knows about them, there is no value. Channels are how you intend to get your value propositions to your customers. Advertising? Word of mouth? Search engine? Training? For software products, identifying these is important as they may result in Product Backlog items that are often forgotten.

4. **Customer Relationships**

   This is about retaining your customers and possibly introducing them to additional value propositions. How do you keep them coming back for more? Should you put a loyalty program in place? Maybe a newsletter? Much like with channels, identifying these may introduce commonly forgotten Product Backlog items.

5. **Revenue Streams**

   How do your value propositions generate revenue? What and how much are your customers willing to pay for? Licensing? Membership fees? Advertising? Not every value proposition needs to generate revenue; however, everyone involved with the creation of the product must understand how it eventually makes money.

6. **Key Activities**

   Now that you have identified all the elements for generating revenue, you need to uncover the activities you will have to make an investment in. What will you need to do to make these value propositions a reality? This involves due diligence activities such as market research, legal feasibility, and possibly even patent registration.

7. **Key Resources**

   After identifying what you need to do (key activities), turn your attention to what you need to have. This includes people with the right skills, equipment, offices, tools, and many more.

8. **Key Partners**

   To better focus on your customers and value propositions, there are some things you simply should not do yourself even if you have the ability and money to do them. This is where partnerships come in handy. List them here. Think of hardware providers, service providers, distributors, and similar partners.

9. **Cost Structure**

   Now that you have a better idea of key activities, resources, and partners, you should have an easier time identifying the major investments needed to make this product a reality. Take this opportunity to make these costs explicit.

In addition to using the Business Model Canvas, you might consider other tools in the same space, such as the Lean Canvas[4] (a variation of the Business Model Canvas) or the Value Proposition Canvas[5] (by Strategyzer, the Business Model Canvas people).

Remember that the main objective of any of these tools is to explore your problem space and to generate discussion among stakeholders. You should not necessarily expect to have a clear vision after this. However, a good business model can provide you with the data necessary to craft that vision. Figure 2-2 presents an example Business Model Canvas for Uber.

---

4. Ash Maurya, "Why Lean Canvas vs Business Model Canvas?," *Love the Problem* (blog), February 27, 2012, https://leanstack.com/why-lean-canvas/.

5. "The Value Proposition Canvas," Strategyzer, assessed February 17, 2018, https://strategyzer.com/canvas/value-proposition-canvas.

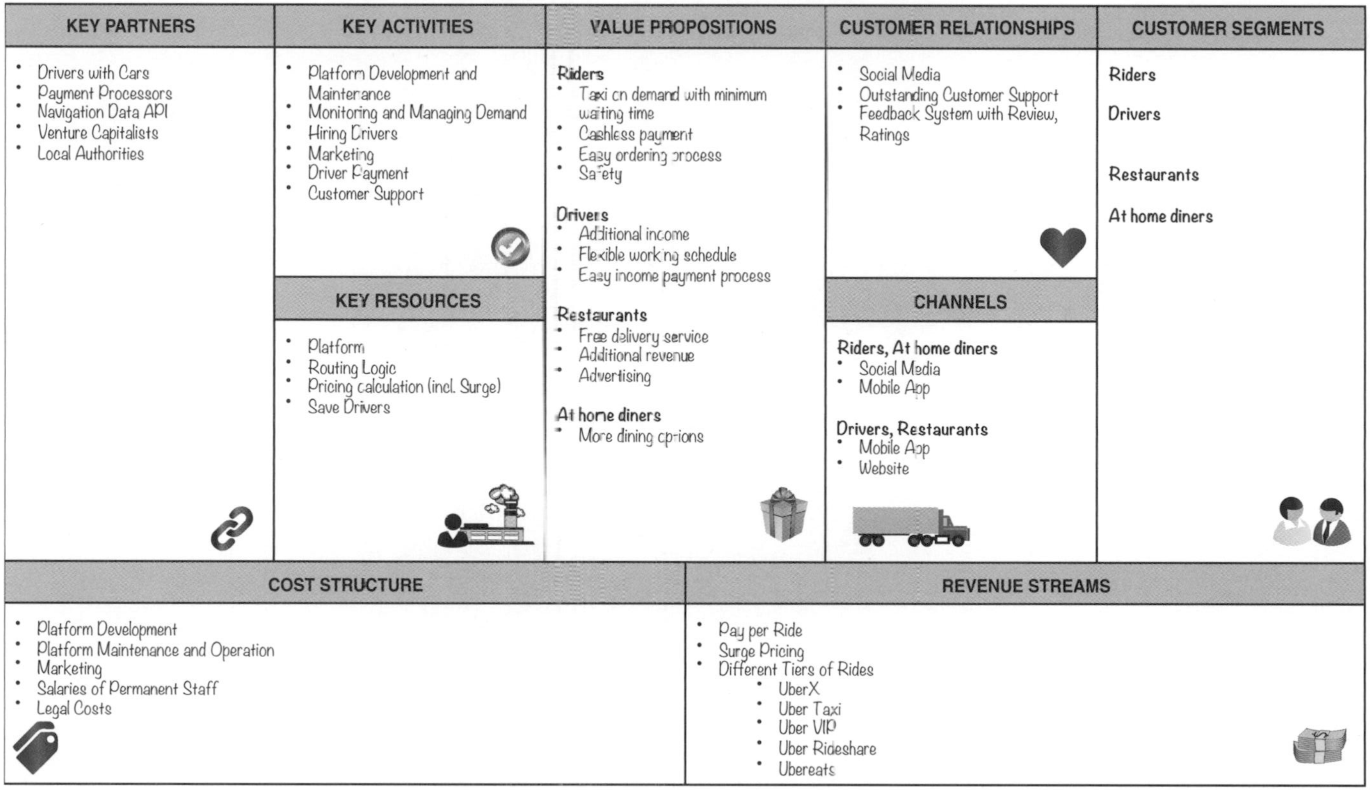

KEY PARTNERS	KEY ACTIVITIES	VALUE PROPOSITIONS	CUSTOMER RELATIONSHIPS	CUSTOMER SEGMENTS
• Drivers with Cars • Payment Processors • Navigation Data API • Venture Capitalists • Local Authorities	• Platform Development and Maintenance • Monitoring and Managing Demand • Hiring Drivers • Marketing • Driver Payment • Customer Support	**Riders** • Taxi on demand with minimum waiting time • Cashless payment • Easy ordering process • Safety **Drivers** • Additional income • Flexible working schedule • Easy income payment process **Restaurants** • Free delivery service • Additional revenue • Advertising **At home diners** • More dining options	• Social Media • Outstanding Customer Support • Feedback System with Review, Ratings	• Riders • Drivers • Restaurants • At home diners
	KEY RESOURCES • Platform • Routing Logic • Pricing calculation (incl. Surge) • Save Drivers		**CHANNELS** **Riders, At home diners** • Social Media • Mobile App **Drivers, Restaurants** • Mobile App • Website	

COST STRUCTURE	REVENUE STREAMS

• Platform Development
• Platform Maintenance and Operation
• Marketing
• Salaries of Permanent Staff
• Legal Costs
	• Pay per Ride
	• Surge Pricing
	• Different Tiers of Rides
	  • UberX
	  • Uber Taxi
	  • Uber VIP
	  • Uber Rideshare
	  • Ubereats

Figure 2-2 Example of the Business Model Canvas for Uber

PRODUCT VISION

Visions are tricky. Their purpose is to rally a group of people around a common goal. This is hard to do in a concise way, and many times you end up with some boilerplate buzzwordy statement that does not resonate with anyone (see Figure 2-3).

> "We continually foster world-class solutions as well as to quickly create principle-centered sources to meet our customer's needs."

> "Our challenge is to assertively network economically sound methods of empowerment so that we may continually negotiate performance-based solutions."

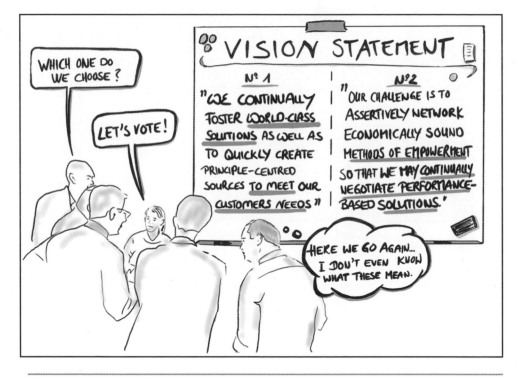

Figure 2-3 Boilerplate product vision statement

Boilerplate statements like these tend to get ignored. A good vision needs to be Focused, Emotional, Practical, and Pervasive.

FOCUSED

Focus involves much more than keeping your vision statement small and concise. Your vision needs to make it crystal clear who the target customer segment is and what your top value proposition is. If you take the time to create a business model, it will provide you with a good place to start crafting a vision. Your business model outlines all possible customers and the value propositions to them. Now you need to make some tough decisions about which ones are the most important.

You do this in much the same way marketing groups approach advertising. They realize that they cannot be all things to all people. Otherwise, they lose focus on what, who, and where to promote their products.

Product Box

Take, for instance, a popular cereal brand called Ceralios by United Good Cereal (UGC). They have many customer segments: young kids, teenagers, college students, parents, health-conscious people, older people—all valid and all pay to use the product. However, UGC simply cannot spend time and energy marketing their product as everything to everyone. The company needs to make decisions. Which television shows should it advertise with? What time of day should it advertise? What shelf should it place its product on in supermarkets?

Take a good look at the box design shown in Figure 2-4 and assess which customer segment was selected as its focus. What is the top value proposition represented by the box design?

Figure 2-4 Ceralios product box

The box is simple, with muted coloring, a focus on whole grain, and a heart-shaped bowl. Is this for kids? No. It was designed for adults and promotes a value proposition of heart health. The box has only seconds to grab a food shopper's attention away from the hundreds of competing products around it.

UGC just needs that one customer segment to pause long enough to pick up the box, maybe turn it around for more information, and then make a decision to buy.

Contrast this product box with the one shown in Figure 2-5.

Figure 2-5 Crunchy Flakes product box

Which target customer was this box designed for? Brighter colors, cartoon character, no real emphasis on health. It is obviously targeting kids, and the value proposition is much more about fun. Are these any healthier than the previous product which had a focus on heart health? Not necessarily. In fact, what is in the box is kind of irrelevant. Crunchy Flakes has clearly chosen its target customers, who it hopes will point out this box to their parents in the store.

Just like UGC and many cereal brands like them, you can take the same approach for your products. In fact, creating an actual box for your software product, even if it will never be shipped in one, isn't a bad idea. A popular technique along these lines is the Innovation Games Product Box.[6]

With the Product Box game, supply a group of stakeholders with a blank box and some artistic supplies (colored markers, stickers, magazines, etc.) and ask them to design a box for their product.

The front of the box needs to have the following:

- Product name
- Image
- Obvious target customer
- Obvious value proposition for the target customer

On the back and sides of the box, game players can add more details about the features and possibly information relevant to different customers. However, the front provides the focus necessary so that the vision is clear.

An important activity for the end of the Product Box activity is to have a representative stand up and pitch his box (and product) to potential stakeholders. The resulting pitch and box produce an effective vision.

---

6. "Collaboration Framework: Product Box," Innovation Games, accessed February 17, 2018, http://www.innovationgames.com/product-box/.

Figure 2-6 shows some examples from Product Owner trainings. The left-hand box touts photo sharing for prisoners and their families, and the right-hand box advertises crowdsourced funding for schools.

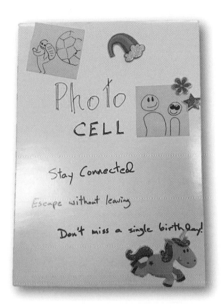

Figure 2-6 Product box examples from Professional Scrum Product Owner training

Elevator Pitch

Another common visioning tool that can complement the Product Box is the Elevator Pitch template, made popular in Geoffrey Moore's *Crossing the Chasm*.[7]

---

7. Geoffrey A. Moore, *Crossing the Chasm: Marketing and Selling Technology Products to Mainstream Customers* (New York: Harper Business, 1991).

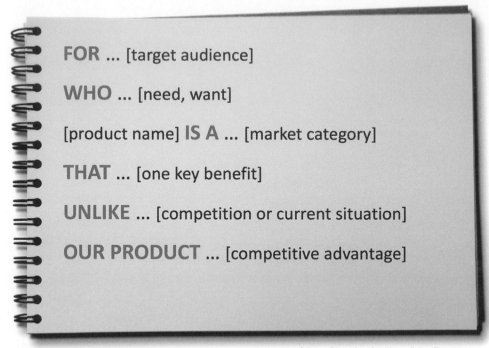

FOR ... [target audience]

WHO ... [need, want]

[product name] IS A ... [market category]

THAT ... [one key benefit]

UNLIKE ... [competition or current situation]

OUR PRODUCT ... [competitive advantage]

* From "Crossing the Chasm" Geoffrey Moore

Figure 2-7 Elevator Pitch template

As you can see in Figure 2-7, the Elevator Pitch template focuses on a single target customer and a single value proposition (one key benefit).

The Elevator Pitch template is a good place to start. It ensures you have all your bases covered. However, given that it is a template, it can often feel a little bland and a little long. So, once you've filled in the blanks, take some time to distill it into one or two sentences and find a way to make it a little more *practical* and a little more *emotional*.

PRACTICAL VERSUS EMOTIONAL

A good vision becomes much more memorable when your audience can imagine themselves doing something (practical) and when it tugs on their heart strings (emotional).

Imagine you have a product that creates efficiencies in an accountant's workflow.

An initial stab at a vision statement could produce something like this:

It is our business to seamlessly optimize CPA workflow management.

Beautiful, right?

Where would you place the preceding vision on the graph in Figure 2-8?

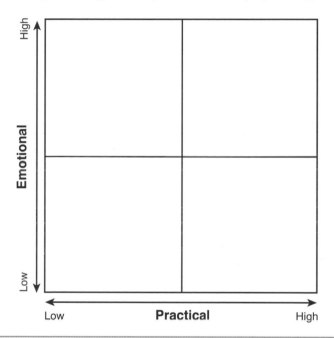

Figure 2-8 2 Brains: Tell It and Sell It, 2×2 graph

We have room for improvement. Our original vision statement is not very practical or emotional. In what ways will the product optimize the workflow? Will it make it simpler? Will it automate it? Will it speed it up? Which is most important to the target customer segment?

You can make the vision more practical by providing target customers with something they can actually imagine happening. How about this:

Our product speeds up your CPA workflow.

This version of the vision is now practical, but is it emotional?

To inject emotion into a vision, ask yourself how your customer would feel if you were to accomplish "speeding up the workflow." Happy? Accomplished?

If you simply went with "Our workflow management product will make you happy," then you lose the practical aspect of the vision (top left part of the quadrant).

You need to make it both practical *and* emotional. Ask yourself, "What is it about my product that makes target customers happy?" Maybe they won't have to deal with so much red tape. Maybe they will get home sooner to their families.

Consider a vision statement like that in Figure 2-9:

Our product speeds up the mundane tasks at work so that you can spend more time at home with family.

This statement is both emotional and practical and consequently provides more focus for your teams and stakeholders.

This 2×2 technique is called 2 Brains: Tell It and Sell It,[8] from the book *Gamestorming*.[9]

---

8. "2 Brains: Tell It and Sell It," *Gamestorming*, assessed February 17, 2018, http://gamestorming.com/games-for-design/2-brains-tell-it-sell-it/.
9. David Gray, Sunni Brown, and James Macanufo, *Gamestorming: A Playbook for Innovators, Rulebreakers, and Changemakers* (Beijing: O'Reilly, 2010).

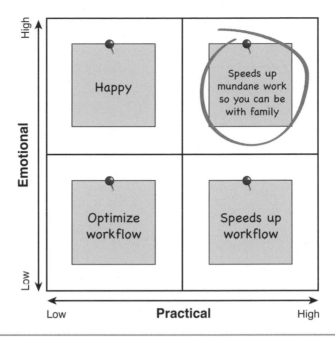

Figure 2-9 Emotional and practical vision

PERVASIVE

If a tree falls in a forest and no one is around to hear it, does it make a sound?

You may have crafted the best vision statement in the world, but if nobody ever hears it, it obviously is not much use. This happens way too often, when a small number of people who understand the vision just assume that everyone else does too. They show frustration when decisions are made that do not reflect the vision. They often chalk it up to lack of buy-in, initiative, or competence. They underestimate the importance of creating a disciplined practice of constantly reinforcing vision, even when it seems redundant to them.

As a Product Owner, it is your responsibility to communicate the vision and ensure it is well understood and adhered to. Fortunately, Scrum builds in many opportunities to do this.

VISIONING WITH SCRUM

Sprint Planning offers an excellent opportunity to remind your team of the vision. Kicking off with a reminder of the vision and how the top of the Product Backlog fits into it is a must. This also helps the Scrum Team come up with a more effective Sprint Goal.

The *Sprint Review* is an opportunity to reinforce the vision not just with your team, but with your stakeholders.

The *Sprint Retrospective* is your opportunity to inquire about the effectiveness of your vision communications. Consider asking the following questions in the retrospective:

- Is everybody on the team comfortable with the vision?
- Is our vision still relevant?
- Which actions from the last Sprint reflect the vision? Which do not?
- Do our stakeholders understand the vision? Which ones do not?
- What are some ways to improve our vision communication?

Disclaimer: I have found that all this constant droning on about the product vision can annoy my team and stakeholders. Lots of eye rolling. But I've learned not to feel bad about it. I now own it. This is often what is needed to keep the vision front and center in everyone's minds. I compare this to a parent constantly repeating the same messages about safety, grades, cleaning up, and so on. It eventually does sink in, and the children preach the same messages to their kids later in life. Another tactic to communicate the vision and ensure it is well understood and adhered to is to find ways to make the vision statement visible in the team's work area.

Don

TECHNICAL STRATEGY

Much of the discussion so far has been about business strategy.

It is quite common for Product Owners to stay with this line of thinking. However more and more, technical strategy is becoming a bigger part of the role (see Figure 2-10).

As mentioned in the previous chapter, there are two types of products: (1) the end business product that the customer is ultimately paying for and consuming; and (2) the software product, which is often the channel used to access the business product. An example would be a savings account (business product) that yields a certain interest rate and the mobile application (software product) that allows the customer to access the product.

These days it is the software product landscape where companies are increasingly competing. At a certain point, it isn't your interest rate that attracts customers to your financial product; it is whether you have a useable mobile app and website.

Strategic Alignment Index

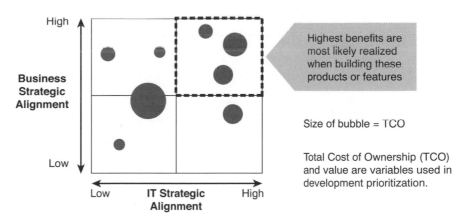

Figure 2-10 Strategic alignment (Source: "Measuring the Business Value of Information Technology," Intel Press.)

What does this have to do with you, the Product Owner? Well, it should be your responsibility to also understand and promote the technical direction of your product. If you come from a technical background, this may be easier. If not, leverage the knowledge on your Development Team and within your stakeholder community.

There is no need to be coding along with your team. In fact, getting too involved in solutions could be quite harmful to your role. A Product Owner needs to focus on the "what" (strategy), not the "how" (tactics).

Consider this quote from the *Forbes* article "Great CEOs Must be Either Technical or Financial":[10]

> Technology skills do not necessarily mean hands-on skills, though they can arise from hands-on experience. It means simply understanding the technical state of play in the environment in a way that you can make exceptional decisions.
>
> Technology changes suddenly expand the strategy canvas and offer new ways of doing old things, or entirely new things to do.

Some strategic questions a Product Owner should be considering are these:

- What are some of the latest technologies that we should be taking advantage of?
- Should we be in the cloud?
- Would wearable devices like watches add value?
- What about opening our API up to the public?
- Native iOS or HTML5?

These are all technical yet exceedingly strategic decisions that need to be made.

---

10. Venkatesh Rao, "Great CEOs Must be Either Technical or Financial," Forbes.com, March 9, 2012, https://www.forbes.com/sites/venkateshrao/2012/03/09/great-ceos-must-be-either-technical-or-financial/#479cf37a63c6.

It is important to understand that there is a timing aspect to consider. Features that align perfectly to your business strategy and IT strategy today may not align in the future. Priorities shift over time. Sometimes the most strategic move is to stop and to refocus your investment. Consider ramping down or even retiring products altogether.

Discontinuing a product can be a healthy business decision. Remember the following products from successful companies?

- Apple Newton
- Apple iPod classic
- Google Glass
- Google Wave
- iGoogle
- Google Reader
- Amazon Fire Phone

QUIZ REVIEW

Compare your answers from the beginning of the chapter to the ones below. Now that you have read the chapter, would you change any of your answers? Do you agree with the answers below?

Statement	Agree	Disagree
A product vision will emerge over time.	☐	✔
Every Scrum Team member should have a clear understanding of who the customers are and how the product generates revenue.	✔	☐
Most great products are created by happenstance.	☐	✔
A good vision should be free of emotion.	☐	✔
Agile is all about getting started; the right product will emerge eventually.	☐	✔
It is an advantage to have a technically minded Product Owner.	✔	☐

VALUE 3

The mind is the laboratory where products, both fake and genuine are manufactured. People grow wild weeds, others grow flourishing flowers!

—Israelmore Ayivor

QUIZ

To set the stage for this chapter, try answering each of the following statements with Agree or Disagree. Answers appear at the end of the chapter.

Statement	Agree	Disagree
There is no value until a product is released.	☐	☐
For for-profit organizations, value is ultimately represented in terms of money (revenue and cost).	☐	☐
Attaching incentives to value metrics improves performance and morale.	☐	☐
Metrics can help validate business hypotheses and the impact of releases.	☐	☐
Velocity is a good measure of value delivered.	☐	☐
A release can produce negative value.	☐	☐

VALUE DEFINED

When was the last time a new product or service brought a smile to your face? Would you consider that product or service to be valuable? Absolutely. But what exactly is value?

It depends on the context.

As people, anything we consider to be of value ultimately comes down to one elusive element: Happiness. Is money valuable? Only if it makes you happy. More time with your family? Only if that makes you happy (not all families are worth being around). Time, money, good job; these are only circumstantial evidence of value. We assume having more of them will make us happy.

Value is not just about people. Organizations strive for value too.

As companies, anything they consider to be of value ultimately comes down to one elusive element: money. Are happy customers valuable? Only if they pay for your product. Is a good culture valuable? Only if it reduces the cost of attracting and retaining employees. Happy customers, good culture, streamlined processes; these are only circumstantial evidence of value. We assume having more of them will make (and save) us more money.

An obvious exception is nonprofit organizations like charities and government where value is about improving society. For nonprofits, money is circumstantial. In fact, increasing revenue while not positively impacting society would be considered negative value.

Why are these definitions of value important for a Product Owner? Generating money (or improving society) is the reason you are in business and it maps to what this book refers to as the *producer benefit*. On the other hand, happiness is what your customers care about and is mapped to your value propositions.

Both are relevant and connected. You cannot make money without having a customer who appreciates your product or service.

As a Product Owner, you need to understand your business and your customers.

Stephen Denning describes this well with his "delighting clients" thinking.[1] The customer always comes first; money follows. In the end, it is about money, but do not let the money blind your actions. Do not let the money betray your customer loyalty or your desire to make a customer smile. In the 21st century, the customer is king.

DELIVERING VALUE

When can you actually deliver value?

Well, there is only one possible answer to that question. **Release!**

Each release is an opportunity to create value. Everything leading up to a release is an investment: inventory, bound capital, money you cannot use for other important initiatives.

How often does your company release? Many companies release about twice a year. That schedule represents a lot of investment before seeing a penny in return.

All of the earlier mentioned activities of product management lead to value only through a release, when you put your product into the hands of customers.

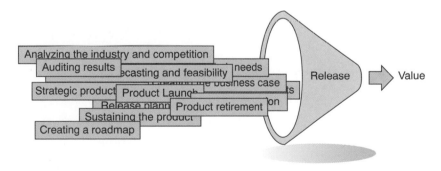

Figure 3-1 Release is the funnel toward value

1. Steve Denning, *The Leader's Guide to Radical Management: Reinventing the Workplace for the 21st Century* (Hoboken, NJ: Jossey Bass, 2010), 57.

Think about a release as a funnel through which you squeeze all your product development activities (see Figure 3-1). The time this release-funnel consumes is crucial: it's your lead time.

If you ever find yourself in a debate between waterfall and agile, there is only one point you need to make to upper management: When do you get value to your customer?

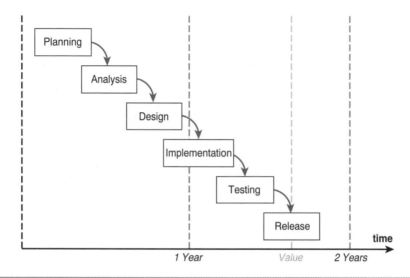

Figure 3-2 Traditional waterfall approach delays value.

Release equates to value. With the waterfall approach, when do you release? By definition, it is the last step (see Figure 3-2). Therefore, by design, *waterfall delays value*.

By contrast, a Scrum Team produces potentially releasable increments of the most valuable items every 30 days or less (see Figure 3-3).

Admittedly, releasing is easier said than done. Because of this, many organizations delay all the activities needed to release on a consistent basis. You should recognize that this investment in getting value out to your customer sooner is worthwhile. Using Scrum makes this more evident.

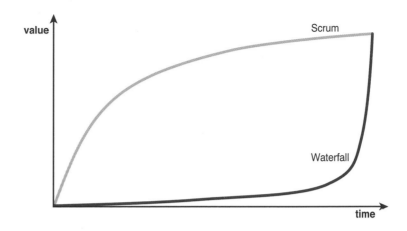

Figure 3-3 Delivering value: Scrum versus waterfall

Figure 3-4 shows the potential value accumulation in Scrum versus the waterfall approach. However, until you release, you are adding no value, only costs. This is often correlated with the financial term Cost of Delay, which demonstrates how value leaks away over time.

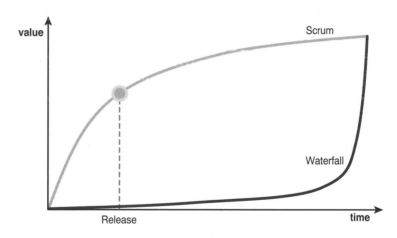

Figure 3-4 Accumulating value: Scrum versus waterfall

Each Sprint, you are spending tens of thousands of dollars. If you wait six months before releasing, you could be looking at hundreds of thousands (or even millions) without a single penny of return on that investment. Each release should be looked at as a return on investment. If that return is not

what was expected, or if better investment opportunities show up, pivot
(see Figure 3-5).

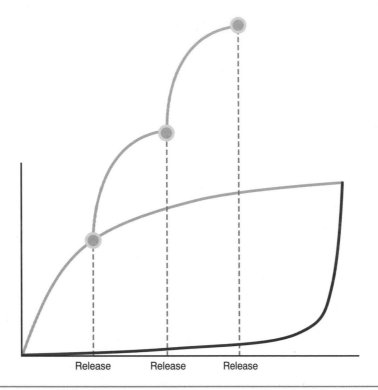

Figure 3-5 Learning from releases and pivoting

This is the true benefit of using a framework such as Scrum. It is not
a project management tool. Rather, it creates a competitive advantage for
organizations by providing them the ability to test out their hypotheses more
often. You will explore this concept further in the next chapter.

VALUE METRICS

How do you know you are creating value? For a Product Owner to properly
adapt a product, she needs some empirical evidence, something to inspect.
That is where the right metrics come in.

Let's talk pizza.

Imagine you work at a growing pizza chain. You are part of their delivery organization. You and your colleagues are responsible for getting pizzas out the door to hungry customers. You have managers, drivers, phone operators, vendors, and other necessary personnel.

How do you know whether you are being successful? What metrics will you measure your progress against?

Do they look something like these?

- Pizzas delivered per trip
- Time taking an order
- Time for delivery
- Distance per delivery
- Fuel costs
- Order accuracy
- Customer complaints
- Orders per driver
- Incidents (accidents, tickets)
- Route efficiency

A perfectly reasonable set of metrics, right? If you care about improving your department, you should definitely track them.

Now, switch roles. You are owner/partner of the pizza chain. Come up with another list of metrics that matter to you and your partners.

Do they look like these?

- Revenue
- Investment
- Operating costs
- Profit

- Customer satisfaction
- Employee satisfaction
- Repeat customers
- Time to market
- Growth
- Market share
- Market drivers (trends, ingredients, events)

Are your two lists very different? Yes, mostly they are, with a few exceptions (e.g., customer satisfaction, costs). Why is that?

Consider three things:

1. **Efficiency**

   The delivery organization now has a set of shiny metrics it can work toward. The practices and processes put in place will focus on moving these numbers. The assumption is that by improving these intermediate metrics, the business will benefit:

   "Hey look, we spent thousands implementing these new route efficiency algorithms so that we can save 60 seconds on each delivery." You may reasonably assume that this will be good for the business, but it's no guarantee and may even become more of a distraction than a benefit. Do you even know that customers want quicker pizza delivery? Is the ROI there? Popular practices are great, but they are not the end goal, and you cannot lose sight of the business's true needs. Otherwise you end up with a Cargo Cult mentality, which "slavishly imitates the working methods of more successful development organizations."[2]

2. **Vision**

   The more your people know and understand the true vision and goals of the organization and the product, the better decisions they will make. Like it or not, assumptions and decisions are often made independently of one

---

2. *New World Encyclopedia*, s.v. "cargo cult," accessed March 5, 2018, http://www.newworldencyclopedia.org/entry/Cargo_cult.

another. Wrong assumptions lead to bad decisions. You can minimize the negative impact of these decisions by educating your people on the true organizational drivers.

In 1993, Domino's Pizza replaced its 30-minute or free guarantee with a promise that their customers will be satisfied with their product, making it a quality guarantee rather than a time-dependent one. "If for any reason you are dissatisfied with your Domino's Pizza dining experience, we will remake your pizza or refund your money" is now the company's Satisfaction Guarantee.[3] This is an example of focusing instead on true valuable metrics (customer satisfaction) rather than delivery metrics (time for delivery), which empowers employees to make decisions based on the company vision.

3. **Incentive**

   Your pizza shop has quarterly bonuses to hand out. What would you base them on? The delivery metrics or the owner metrics? Which ones have a greater potential for corruption? Any metric can be gamed, but you will notice that the more intermediate circumstantial metrics in the delivery department have bigger opportunity for abuse. This doesn't just create unintended behaviors; it also reduces the transparency and therefore the usefulness of these metrics.

A few years ago, my wife and I went to dinner at a chain restaurant. Before finishing our mediocre meal, we were presented with a customer satisfaction survey and told that if we gave all "excellent" scores, we would receive a free appetizer for our next visit. This was obviously not the way the business intended to use these surveys. (Of course, we gave them all "excellents.")

Don

So, what does this all mean?

---

3. "History," Domino's Pizza, accessed February 17, 2018, https://biz.dominos.com/web/public/about-dominos/history

The delivery metrics aren't without worth. They are very helpful, even essential, for guiding the more operational practices. But you run into problems when they are used as false representations of value and set as achievement goals. If the business doesn't establish the goals along with more direct value metrics, then the delivery organization will have no choice but to offer up its own.

Let's get back to software.

Can you now correlate these metrics with ones used when developing software products? Which metrics are used by software delivery? Which ones by the business? Table 3-1 provides some examples.

Table 3-1 Comparison of Delivery and Owner Metrics

Delivery Metrics	Owner Metrics
Velocity	Revenue
Number of Tests	Costs
Code Coverage	Customer Satisfaction
Defects	Employee Satisfaction
Coupling and Cohesion	Lead & Cycle Time*
Code Complexity	Innovation Rate* (percentage of new vs. maintenance work)
Build Failures	Usage*
Process Adherence	
Lines of Code	

*This metric is defined later in the chapter.

So how does your organization measure value? Does it spend too much time on metrics in Table 3-1's left column? Is it missing opportunities to instead apply metrics that reflect true business outcomes?

Delivery metrics are still important, but they must be considered value-neutral. Otherwise they lose their importance as feedback mechanisms for the delivery organization. Compare them to an airplane cockpit, filled with dials and information radiators about altitude, engine temperature, oil levels, outside temperature, and so on. All that important information is for the pilots only so they can successfully complete their mission. This information, however, does not reflect the value delivered. Customers and the airline organization measure value by being on time, safety, and fuel costs. Pilots should be held accountable for those final outcome metrics, not the cockpit metrics. In the same way, software teams should be held accountable for business metrics, not circumstantial metrics like velocity, test coverage, and process adherence.

This disconnect between the delivery organization and the business (the Product Management Vacuum, discussed in Chapter 1) prevails in the software industry. Somewhere along the line, the true vision behind the products gets lost.

Challenging managers, Product Owners, and Development Teams to identify and promote metrics related to actual outcomes is key to bridging that gap. This can promote true agility beyond IT departments and give organizations a true competitive advantage.

This concept of using direct rather than circumstantial evidence is known as Evidence-Based Management (EBMgt). It is gaining traction in the technology field and has industry leaders like Ken Schwaber advocating for it. And it is the topic of our next section.

EVIDENCE-BASED MANAGEMENT

Humans have practiced medicine for about 2,900 years. For 2,800 of those years, snake oil and other nonsensical treatments predominated. People drank mercury because they thought it must have magical properties.

About a hundred years ago, the medical field started to require evidence that a medication or a procedure improves the outcome. Evidence-based medicine was born.

I once went to a dermatologist for a red mark on my cheek. After examining it, the doctor said she needed to order a biopsy. When I asked if she knew what the mark was, she replied with confidence, "Oh that's basal cell carcinoma. I've seen it hundreds of times." Confused, I asked why we couldn't just take it out. Why do a biopsy that would add recovery time and cost? She responded, "That's just not how it's done. We need the evidence first."

Since these principles have helped prove assumptions and therefore improved overall health, what if the same principles were applied to the domain of management?

What is Evidence-Based Management (EBMgt)?

Over the past two decades, most organizations have significantly increased the value gained from software by adopting the Scrum framework and agile principles. Evidence-Based Management practices promise to deliver even further gain.

But how can you, as an IT leader, make the biggest impact on your organization? You manage investments based on ROI and value. You know that frequent inspection of results will limit the risk of disruption. You influence the organization to create a culture that allows it to take advantage of opportunities before your competitors do. By following EBMgt practices, you can put the right measures in place to invest in the right places, make smarter decisions, and reduce risk.

Figure 3-6 shows a series of EBMgt metrics that act as evidence for the value produced from products. These value metrics are organized into three Key Value Areas (KVA): Current Value, Time to Market, and Ability to Innovate. Within each KVA are Key Value Measures (KVMs), also shown in Figure 3-6.

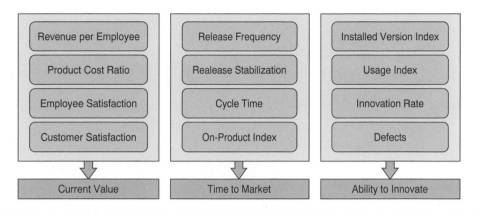

Figure 3-6 Value metrics based on EBMgt (Figure adapted from Evidence-Based Management for Software Organizations [EBMgt], http://www.ebmgt.org/)

Before getting into the descriptions of each metric, there is an important distinction to make between two types of metrics: leading and lagging indicators.

Lagging indicators are typically "output" oriented, easy to measure but hard to improve or influence. These are much more meaningful to the business because they represent the reason for having a product. Leading indicators are typically "input" oriented over which you have more influence because you understand the practices that drive them.

Another way to look at them is that leading indicators are pre-product and lagging indicators are post-product.

A common example used to illustrate this distinction is trying to lose weight. The ultimate goal is to lower the weight measurement. Weight is a lagging indicator, easy to measure—just step on a scale—but harder to directly influence (unless you cut off a limb). How much you eat and exercise are leading indicators. It certainly is not easy, but you have more influence over these leading indicators. The hope is that as you positively influence calories taken in and calories burned, eventually your lagging weight indicator is affected (hopefully in the right direction).

In product development, measuring both is just as important. As practitioners, you need to influence your current practices to eventually see changes in your business objectives.

CURRENT VALUE

From the *EBMgt Guide*

Current Value reveals the organization's actual value in the marketplace. Current Value establishes the organization's current context, but has no relevance on an organization's ability to sustain value in the future.[4]

Notice the emphasis on the organization. While measuring value at the product level is important, understanding how it compares to the overall organization's current value provides you with a more holistic view.

The following, mostly lagging, metrics represent the ultimate benefit for the producer of the product.

Revenue per Employee

Gross revenue divided by the number of employees

Revenue by itself is an important metric. It is the benchmark by which organizations are compared. Products are no different, and it should be measured unless your product vision is strictly about cost savings.

Measuring revenue by employee gives a little more context. This measure is interesting to observe when your product or organization is going through a growth phase. Often growth and revenue per employee do not increase linearly; once a company doubles in size, the revenue per employee usually drops. Normally this is attributed to more hierarchies and longer chains of command—the cost of scale.

---

4. Ken Schwaber and Patricia Kong, *Evidence-Based Management Guide* (2014), 4.

Product Cost Ratio

All expenses in the organization that develop, sustain, provide services, market, sell, and administer the product or system.

There are two ways to look at cost:

- The investment in product development—a *leading* metric that can be measured each Sprint. The biggest cost here is likely the salaries of the Development Team.

  The better you understand this metric, the easier it is to measure your return on investment.

- The cost of running the product in production—a *lagging* metric that can include everything from the cost of the production servers and training users to salaries of internal users and support staff.

  The better you understand this metric, the easier it is to measure your total cost of ownership.

I was working with an organization in the Minneapolis area to gather metrics around cost. When I asked about Development Team costs, the stakeholders in the room responded that they had no access to salary information. Rather than remove or delay that metric, we decided instead to just search the web for average IT salaries in the greater Twin Cities area. We multiplied that number by the number of team members, which led to an estimated cost-per-Sprint metric. The important point here is that we want people thinking about costs, even if the number is not 100 percent accurate. We also want to just get started (often the hardest part) so that we have some sort of a baseline. If anyone who has the real information sees our metric and raises an issue, then they can provide us with the more accurate data. As with many solutions in the agile world, get started with what you have and refine as you go. Nothing will be perfect at the beginning.

Don

Employee Satisfaction

Engaged employees that know how to maintain, sustain, and enhance the software systems and products are one of the most significant assets of an organization.

According to recent studies, more than 50 percent of the U.S. workforce are not engaged and close to 20 percent are actively disengaged.[5] Often, the only reason they hang in is for health insurance.

Moving away from extrinsic rewards (carrots and sticks) to more intrinsic rewards is key. Dan Pink describes intrinsic motivation in detail in his book *Drive: The Surprising Truth about What Motivates Us*.[6] He asserts that intrinsic motivation comes down to three elements:

- **Autonomy:** the desire to be self-directed
- **Mastery:** the itch to keep improving at something that's important to us
- **Purpose:** the sense that what we do produces something transcendent or serves something meaningful beyond ourselves

In Chapter 6, you will explore how Scrum injects all three of these motivating elements into its framework.

Jurgen Appelo also provides interesting thoughts and ideas about motivation with his Management 3.0 approach[7]—ideas and practices for fostering employee engagement. Going into the details here, however, are out of the context of this book.

---

5. Gallup, *State of the American Workplace: Employee Engagement Insights for U.S. Business Leaders* (2013).

6. Daniel H. Pink, *Drive: The Surprising Truth about What Motivates Us* (Edinburgh: Canongate, 2010).

7. Ralph is also a licensed Management 3.0 facilitator.

I find that the Sprint Retrospective is a great time to measure the employee satisfaction of the Development Team. A simple consistent question to conclude the Retrospective creates a useful "happiness metric" that will allow you to spot trends over time. Consider asking something like "On a scale from '5 - I am super happy!' to '1 - I never want to experience that again,' how did you feel about that last Sprint?"

— Don

I like to hand out feedback cards (see Figure 3-7) to developers at the end of each Sprint. In this questionnaire I ask the developers on the Development Team about their happiness in various areas. The "Product Owner" and "Scrum Master" happiness questions are set, while the other questions depend on the context. This enables me to discover trends and take action early on.

— Ralph

Happiness Index										
Poll		1			2			3	
Date		April 05			April 19			May 03	
Product Owner	4	◐		4	◯		4	◯	
Scrum Master	4	◐		4	◯		4	◯	
Influence Work	3	◯		4	◐		4	◯	
Easy to Release	3	◯		2	◯		2	●	
Process that Fits the Team's Mission	4	◯		3	◯		3	◯	
Org Support	3	◯		3	◯		3	◯	
Mission	4	◐		4	◐		3	◯	

Figure 3-7 Happiness index

Customer Satisfaction

Meeting or surpassing your customer's expectation

> *The purpose of business is to create and keep a customer.*
>
> —Peter Drucker

This is a lagging metric for how satisfied your customers are with your product and the services that support it.

There are many ways to measure customer satisfaction, and you may even be able to leverage existing measurements from your organization.

A common industry recognized way of measuring customer satisfaction is the Net Promoter Score (NPS). NPS measures customer experience and predicts business growth. This proven metric transformed the business world and now provides the core measurement for customer experience management programs around the world.[8]

Calculate your NPS using the answer to a key question: **"Using a 0–10 scale: How likely is it that you would recommend [product] to a friend or colleague?"**

Respondents are grouped as follows:

- *Promoters* (score 9–10) are loyal enthusiasts who will keep buying and refer others, fueling growth.
- *Passives* (score 7–8) are satisfied but unenthusiastic customers who are vulnerable to competitive offerings.
- *Detractors* (score 0–6) are unhappy customers who can damage your brand and impede growth through negative word of mouth.

Subtracting the percentage of Detractors from the percentage of Promoters yields the Net Promoter Score, which can range from a low of -100 (if every customer is a Detractor) to a high of 100 (if every customer is a Promoter).

Consider building a feedback mechanism for customer satisfaction right into your product. Microsoft Office made this a standard feature in its toolset in 2016 (see Figure 3-8).

---

8. "What Is Net Promoter?," NICE Satmetrix, accessed February 17, 2018, https://www.netpromoter.com/know/.

Figure 3-8 Direct feedback from a Microsoft Office product

TIME TO MARKET

From the *EBMgt Guide*

Time-to-Market evaluates the software organization's ability to actually deliver new features, functions, services, and products. Without actively managing Time-to-Market, the ability to sustainably deliver value in the future is unknown.[9]

Release Frequency

The time needed to satisfy the customer with new, competitive products

As it was already established, the only way to bring value to your customer is to release. But how often are you getting value out to your customer? Are you talking hours, weeks, months, or even years? Many of the larger companies choose to release around existing schedules, such as fiscal quarters, without much thought (or with complete ignorance) toward the marketplace and their customers' needs. A truly agile company should have the desire and the capability to release as frequently as necessary to stay relevant in an increasingly unpredictable marketplace. The right measurements here are crucial.

Consider using a rolling window time period to count how many production releases were made. Let's pretend that in the first three-month period, you made two releases. One year later, you steadily raised that releases-over-time number to 12 (see Figure 3-9).

---

9. Schwaber and Kong, *Evidence-Based Management Guide*, 4.

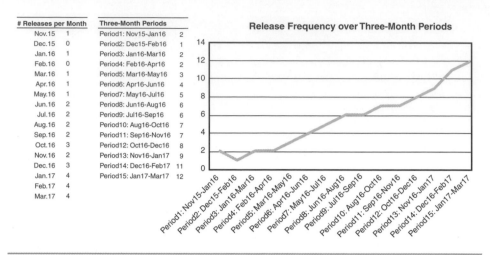

# Releases per Month		Three-Month Periods	
Nov.15	1	Period1: Nov15-Jan16	2
Dec.15	0	Period2: Dec15-Feb16	1
Jan.16	1	Period3: Jan16-Mar16	2
Feb.16	0	Period4: Feb16-Apr16	2
Mar.16	1	Period5: Mar16-May16	3
Apr.16	1	Period6: Apr16-Jun16	4
May.16	1	Period7: May16-Jul16	5
Jun.16	2	Period8: Jun16-Aug16	6
Jul.16	2	Period9: Jul16-Sep16	6
Aug.16	2	Period10: Aug16-Oct16	7
Sep.16	2	Period11: Sep16-Nov16	7
Oct.16	3	Period12: Oct16-Dec16	8
Nov.16	2	Period13: Nov16-Jan17	9
Dec.16	3	Period14: Dec16-Feb17	11
Jan.17	4	Period15: Jan17-Mar17	12
Feb.17	4		
Mar.17	4		

Figure 3-9 Release frequency chart

Tracking release frequency trends in this way demonstrates time-to-market agility in a much clearer way than velocity or scope ever could.

Release Stabilization

The impact of poor development practices and underlying design and code base. Stabilization is a drag on competition that grows with time.

After feature development stops, often called feature freeze, how long does it take to release the software? This period is called release stabilization, a time frame in which you prepare the Increment for release with activities such as regression testing, deployment, user acceptance, documentation, and bug fixing.

It is important to note that the idea of a "stabilization" period goes against the very foundation of continuous value delivery. Stabilizing is more about fixing something that is broken, more about stability—number of crashes, defects, data integrity—than about overall product quality and user experience. In Scrum, it is expected that the Increment is "stable" (Done) every Sprint.

Release frequency is directly affected by the time it takes to stabilize a release. In other words, the time between releases (lead time) is always constrained by the time required to stabilize a release (see Figure 3-10).

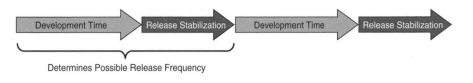

Determines Possible Release Frequency

Figure 3-10 Impact of long release stabilization

The closer to zero your release stabilization period is, the better.

Cycle Time

The time (including stabilization) to satisfy a key set of customers or to respond to a market opportunity competitively.

Cycle time for a feature starts when development on it begins. It ends when the feature is ready for production (see Figure 3-11).

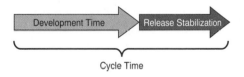

Cycle Time

Figure 3-11 Cycle time

Contrast this to lead time, which is the time from when a customer asks for a feature to when they actually receive it.

The more you consider cycle time to be synonymous with lead time, the more agile you will be. Whenever you are "Done" with the development of a feature, you should make a release. Any delay beyond that is considered waste.

On-Product Index

The time developers are allowed to work on exactly one initiative like a product. The more developers task-switch between competing work, the less they are committed and the more delays are introduced.

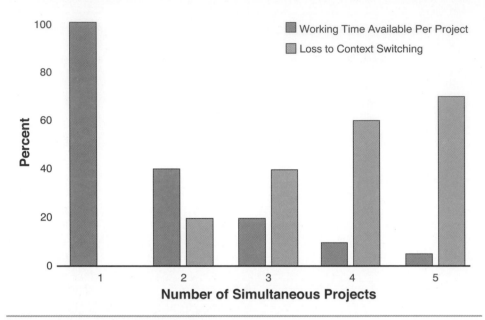

Figure 3-12 The price of task switching

Gerald Weinberg asserts that for each additional project someone undertakes, he lose up to 20 percent of his time to the act of context switching.[10] For example, as Figure 3-12 illustrates, working on four simultaneous projects could have you spending upwards of 60 percent of your time just juggling the different work (as opposed to doing it).

Assume you work on a major waterfall project to be released 15 months from now. Halfway through your design phase, an important initiative arises that, in your opinion, is urgent enough to be addressed right now.

10. Gerald Marvin Weinberg, *An Introduction to General Systems Thinking* (New York: Wiley, 1975).

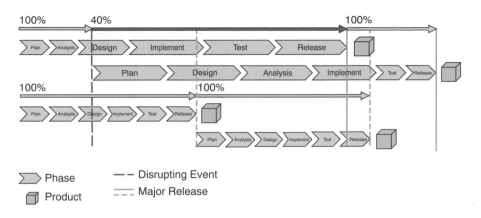

Figure 3-13 Parallel versus serial on-product index

Because there is no other team available, your team is tasked to work on both projects in parallel. However, because of the cost of task switching, a 20 percent loss decreases your capability to make progress. So, it is not 50 percent per project but only 40 percent (100% − 20% / 2 = 40%). Assuming the amount you plan is the same as in the first project, it would take more than twice as long to complete. Also, the remaining design effort will take 20 percent longer. This drags on until the first project releases a major release. After that release, the second project can speed up again if the on-product index is now back to 100 percent (see Figure 3-13).

The end result of all this context switching is that it directly affects time-to-market as well as employee satisfaction.

Today many companies consider their employees as resources, commodities like electricity and raw material. That thinking created the idea that humans are replaceable like batteries. "Let's replace a Duracell with an Energizer," or "Let's replace this programmer with that programmer. Both are programmers, what's the difference?" Plenty: experience from former projects, technologies used, tools used, social skills . . . the list is long.

> *Have you ever heard of the term "Full-Time-Equivalent (FTE)"? Two 50 percent resources make one FTE, something that is supposedly equivalent to one human being.*
>
> *I have seen up to four people adding up to one FTE. What nonsense!*
>
> *Frederick Brooks uses a good counterexample when describing his law (Brooks's Law): "While it takes one woman nine months to make one baby, nine women can't make a baby in one month."*
>
> **Ralph**

ABILITY TO INNOVATE

From the *EBMgt Guide*

The Ability to Innovate is necessary but often a luxury. Most software is overloaded by non-valuable features. As low-value features accumulate, more of the organization's budget and time is consumed maintaining the product, reducing its available capacity to innovate.[11]

Organizations without strength in all three KVAs may have short-term value but will not be able to sustain it. The Current Value of any organization must be accompanied by evidence of its ability to meet market demand with timely delivery (time-to-market) while being able to sustain itself over time (Ability to Innovate).

Below is a series of metrics that together provide a way to measure potential innovation.

Installed Version Index

The distribution of customers across the installed versions in production. The maintenance of the older versions has a negative impact on Ability to Innovate.

How many of your customers are using your latest product version? This percentage is a direct reflection of the value you are delivering each release. For example, if 70 percent of users are on the latest release, then only 70 percent of them are getting any value from your most recent features.

---

11. Schwaber and Kong, *Evidence-Based Management Guide*, 4.

A high absorption cost reduces the willingness of customers to upgrade. The absorption costs can be

- time of installation;
- new hardware;
- training;
- data migration; and
- pilots.

Tracking this metric can lead to more of an investment into reducing the absorption cost. Not having to support older versions of your product allows for more investment into new innovative features.

Usage Index

Determines how a product and its features are difficult to use and whether excess software is being sustained even though it is rarely used

How are your customers using your product? Do you know which features are used the most/least? Are they being used the way you predicted? All of this is important information when deciding what to build next.

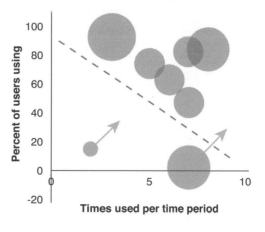

Size of bubble = Time spent using

Figure 3-14 Visualization of usage index

The feature at the bottom right of Figure 3-14 could be an admin feature that only a few dedicated personnel use. It might also be the new "killer" feature that you assume is going to have a huge positive impact. In either case, it warrants some attention. Its position on the graph could mean the feature is great but not easy to discover. This may be an opportunity to inspect and adapt your user interface or coordinate user training.

The Chaos Standish report, which is often cited, was revisited in 2014, and the findings were comparable to those in the original 2002 report. As Figure 3-15 shows, only 20 percent of product functionality is "often" used while 50 percent is "hardly ever" used.

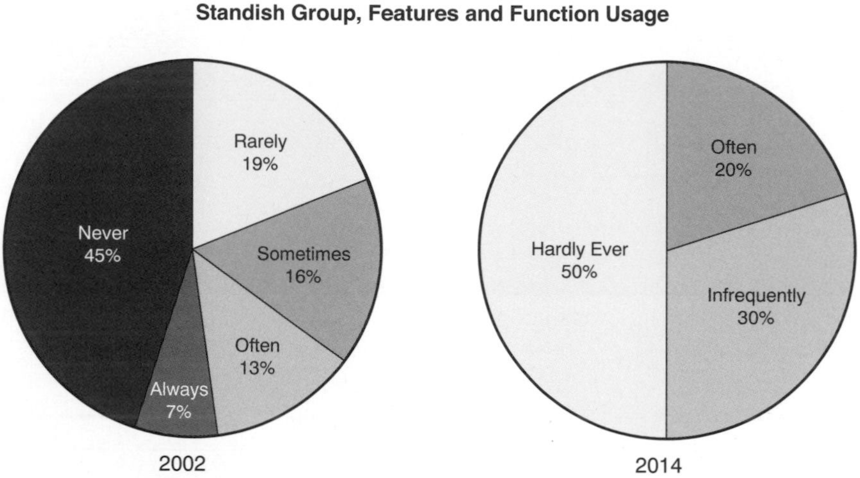

Standish Group, Features and Function Usage

Figure 3-15 shows two pie charts. The 2002 chart: Never 45%, Rarely 19%, Sometimes 16%, Often 13%, Always 7%. The 2014 chart: Often 20%, Infrequently 30%, Hardly Ever 50%.

2002

2014

Figure 3-15 Usage of features and function by Standish group

Innovation Rate

Growth of technical debt caused by poorly designed and developed software. Budget is progressively consumed as the old software is kept alive.

How costly is it to keep your product up and running? How much of your development budget is spent on maintenance and support? The healthier your code base is, the more test automation you have, the more capacity you have for innovative features. This extra bandwidth gives you more ability to respond to the market trends and outpace your competition.

This is essentially the definition of technical debt. If you fail to address it now, you will end up paying more interest in the future. You eventually might find yourself in technical bankruptcy, resulting in a complete system rewrite: "Let's just file Chapter 11 and start over."

Netscape's project to improve HTML layout in Navigator 4 has been cited as an example of a failed rewrite.[12] The consensus was that the old Netscape code base was so bad, that the developers simply couldn't work in it anymore; hence Navigator itself was rewritten around a new engine, breaking many existing features and delaying release by several months. Meanwhile, Microsoft focused on incremental improvements to Internet Explorer and did not face the same obstacles.[13]

Some examples of technical debt include the following:

- Lack of automated
  - Build
  - Unit tests
  - Acceptance tests
  - Regression tests
  - Deployment
- Code quality
  - Highly coupled code
  - High code complexity
  - Business Logic in the wrong places
  - High cyclomatic complexity (McCabe-Metric)
  - Duplicated code or modules
  - Unreadable names or algorithms

---

12. See Joel Spolsky, "Things You Should Never Do," *Joel on Software* (blog), April 6, 2000, https://www.joelonsoftware.com/2000/04/06/things-you-should-never-do-part-i/.
13. Jamie Zawinski, "Resignation and Postmortem," March 31, 1999.

A Forrester research[14] study showed that in 2010, less than 30 percent of IT budgets were spent on new features versus maintenance and expansion (see Figure 3-16).

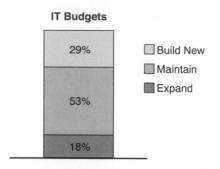

Figure 3-16 Industry average distribution of IT budgets

Having a similar metric for your product or organization can be an important way to create transparency around innovation. This can justify investment into quality and automation practices.

Here are three ways to measure innovation rate:

1. Count the number of Product Backlog items that are new features versus the planned maintenance items that are about technical debt, bugs, and upgrades.

2. Some organizations have dedicated maintenance teams or individuals. Measure the ratio of maintenance people versus new product development people.

3. When the maintenance work is unpredictable, measure the time spent on unplanned maintenance items each Sprint.

Any of these will give you an innovation ratio that can be monitored over time.

---

14. Forrester, "IT Budget Planning Guide for CIOs," October 2010.

I have worked with multiple organizations whose existing accounting structures made it impossible to correlate the long-term maintenance costs to new product development. This caused a huge deficiency in transparency as it was not an accurate measure of the total product costs. The consequence was a lack of quality, which left little room for innovation.

Defects

Measures increasingly poor-quality software, leading to greater resources and budget to maintain it and potential loss of customers

This is likely the most common metric used in software development. Although not the best indication of value, it is still a good practice to create a cadence of tracking the number of defects. The importance of this metric is more about the trend over time rather than the actual number. Not all defects are worth fixing. However, noticing that the number of defects is increasing over time can be an indication that the quality of the system is decreasing, and therefore you may have less time to devote to innovation.

TRACKING METRICS

An important aspect of putting value metrics in place is establishing the discipline to remeasure over time. The trends that emerge are as important as the data itself. These trends provide you with the information necessary to adapt your products and processes in a timely manner.

Radar graphs like the one in Figure 3-17 provide an interesting way of visualizing progress over time.

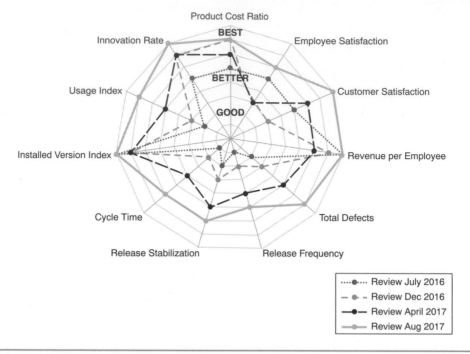

Figure 3-17 Spider graph showing metric changes over time

A more detailed way to organize your metrics uses a "scoreboard" style spreadsheet such as the one in Figure 3-18. This approach draws clear separation between the more circumstantial progress metrics (top), the leading value metrics (left), and the lagging metrics (right).

I like to make a scoreboard like this visible in a common area. Such a placement keeps the vision and the value of the product front and center with Development Teams and stakeholders.

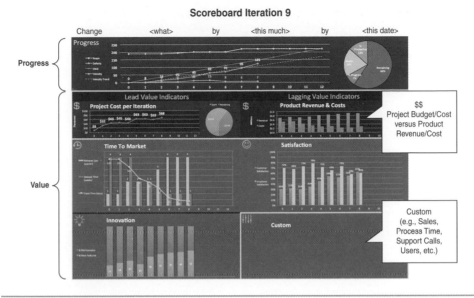

Figure 3-18 Representation of metrics in a scoreboard-style spreadsheet (done with Microsoft Excel)

WHERE YOUR MONEY GOES

Combining the four KVMs is a powerful way to visualize where your money is not going. The example shown in Figure 3-19 is a visualization using industry averages.

Investing $1 leads to only $0.06 in ROI.

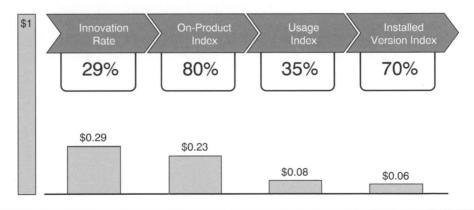

Figure 3-19 How much of your money goes toward value

- **Innovation Rate** of 29 percent, reflecting the Forrester study where 53 percent is spent on maintenance and support on top of 18 percent for expanding capacity
- **On-Product Index** of 80 percent, showing a situation where a team is working on two initiatives in parallel, causing a 20 percent task-switching loss
- **Usage Index,** reflecting the Standish Chaos study where 35 percent of the features are used often or frequently
- **Installed Version Index,** showing a situation where 70 percent of the users are on the latest release

Keeping track of where your money is going in a format similar to this provides great insight that can justify an investment in more strategic initiatives around innovation, maintenance, team structure, automation, and user guidance.

NEGATIVE VALUE

It is often assumed that value is always positive, but value can also be negative. Perceived negative value has a far stronger impact than positive value. According to several studies, people are between three to seven times more likely to share negative experiences than positive ones.

> *I have a nice diesel Volkswagen. I've always bought Volkswagens; my mother worked at a Volkswagen dealer. After Dieselgate[15] I'm done. No more Volkswagens—ever!*
>
> *Ralph*

Negative value can be either visible or invisible.

---

15. Karthick Arvinth, "VW Scandal: Carmaker Was Warned by Bosch about Test-Rigging Software in 2007," *International Business Times*, September 28, 2015.

VISIBLE

Negative value can be in the form of new bugs, rendering an important feature no longer usable; too much system down time, decreasing performance; or clunkier user interface. These all create negative value, which the customer directly experiences.

Sometimes the cost of a bug-free release outweighs its value. Consider the cost of user training, environment validation (like a forensic lab), and regulatory audits.

I worked with a company that designed systems for manufacturing plants across the United States. Its users were not computer proficient and needed training across the country every time they updated the software. In this case, the absorption costs outweighed the value of the release, so the company instead decided to make monthly releases to a single manufacturing plant (beta) where they could collect feedback to inspect and adapt the direction of the product. They released nationwide every six months.

INVISIBLE

The other form of negative value is internal—not visible to the customer. One example is a new feature that nobody uses. It was implemented, tested, documented without generating any value. Even worse, from now on you must maintain this feature. This uses money you no longer have for innovation. Rushing a Development Team forces them to cut corners and sacrifice technical quality—and thus to fall short of the high standards you expect. The fix is quick and dirty, and the result is technical debt. You know the saying about quick and dirty? The dirty stays, while the quick is long gone.

The 2×2 matrix in Table 3-2 adapted from Philippe Kruchten[16] is a good way to look at it.

---

16. Philippe Kruchten, "The (Missing) Value of Software Architecture," Kruchten Engineering Services, Ltd. (blog), December 11, 2013, https://philippe.kruchten.com/2013/12/11/the-missing-value-of-software-architecture/.

Table 3-2 Value 2×2

	Visible	Invisible
Positive Value	New features	Architecture
	Added functionality	Infrastructure
		Design
		Automation (CI, CD) (Technical debt only temporary)
Negative Value	Defects/bugs	Technical debt
	System down times	Not used features
	Performance	Cost of deployment
	User experience	
	Cost of training	

Consider the following statement:

Technical debt is not, not "Done."

What does this mean exactly? In some occasions it could be the right business decision to create technical debt—for example, being first to market, creating a quick prototype, or reacting to an unexpected event.

You might be "Done" yet still have accumulated technical debt.

If you do not address technical debt right away, just understand that you will have to pay it back eventually—with interest. It may not be as visible as the interest rate on your credit card account, but you pay for it nevertheless. Think back to the innovation rate: Bad technical software quality will slow you down as simple changes take longer and require more effort than they should.

Having a solid definition of "Done" can help minimize the amount of technical debt produced. For any existing technical debt, ensure that you have a plan to repay it before the interest payments get out of control. Keep in mind that the time needed to pay off the debt will result in less visible value delivered each Sprint. Just like with financial debt, you will have less to spend on other things until your debt is paid off.

VALUE NEUTRALITY

This chapter has introduced you to a lot of interesting metrics. Their number one purpose is to provide data to generate information, so that you can make better decisions in the uncertain world of product development. Keeping these metrics free from influence and judgment is key. There is no bad or good information; there is only the current reality. This is what is meant by value neutrality.

Not having truly value-neutral metrics can cause unintended consequences and mask transparency. This is known as the Perversion of Metrics.

PERVERSION OF METRICS

I was taught that you cannot manage what you cannot measure. I still believe that this is right. On the other hand, I also strongly believe that what you measure drives the behavior of the people involved.

Ralph

In the 1990s in Europe, far too much milk was produced because it was highly subsidized. The commonly used terms in the news were "milk sea" and "mountain of butter." This drove the price so far down that milk was transformed into a more storable form like butter and milk powder. But even those actions eventually reached their limit. Finally, the European Union decided that the number of milk-producing cows needed to be reduced. As proof that they were following through on this plan, farmers were asked to mail in an ear of each slaughtered cow. Once the ear was received, a financial money reward was sent to the farmer. The first mistake was that the EU did not ask for a specific ear, left or right. The second mistake was that cows are able to live without ears. At some point, reporters discovered whole fields with earless cows.[17]

The cobra effect[18] occurs when an attempted solution makes a problem worse—an instance of unintended consequences. The term stems from an anecdote set at the time of British rule of colonial India. The British government was concerned about the number of venomous cobra snakes in Delhi. The government therefore offered a bounty for every dead cobra. Initially this was a successful strategy as large numbers of snakes were killed for the reward. Eventually, however, enterprising people began to breed cobras for the income. When the government became aware of this, the reward program was scrapped, causing the cobra breeders to set the now-worthless snakes free. As a result, the wild cobra population further increased. The apparent solution for the problem made the situation even worse.

There is neither good nor bad news; there is only data. If you punish bad news, you will only get good news—or, more accurately, camouflaged bad news made to look good. Goodhart's law expresses the same idea: "When a measure becomes a target, it ceases to be a good measure." (See Figure 3-20.)

A good (or bad) example of something that is easy to count, easy to fake, and meaningless (perhaps even dangerous) to measure is productivity of a single developer by number of lines of code written in a given time frame. By doing this, you substitute growing functionality with lines of code, leading to one of the worst practices in software development called "copy paste programming."

---

17. David Medhurst, *A Brief and Practical Guide to EU Law* (Hoboken, NJ: Wiley, 2008), 203.
18. Patrick Walker, "Self-Defeating Regulation," *International Zeitschrift* 9, no. 1 (2013): 31.

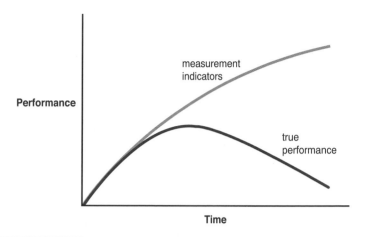

Figure 3-20 Goodhart's law visualized

Whatever you start to measure, play devil's advocate and have a creative brainstorming session about how the metric can be gamed. Try it with a couple of colleagues to increase your chances of surfacing the ingenuity of the people being measured.

I worked with a large organization whose well-intentioned Project Management Organization truly wanted to help the teams undertaking a Scrum adoption. The PMO put in place a rule that any team that varied its Sprint velocity by plus or minus 20 percent would need to meet with a PMO representative, who would see how he could help. Guess what started happening to the velocity metric? The teams did not see this as an act of goodwill but as punishment, and velocity was no longer a value-neutral metric.

Don

QUIZ REVIEW

Compare your answers from the beginning of the chapter to the ones below. Now that you have read the chapter, would you change any of your answers? Do you agree with the answers below?

Statement	Agree	Disagree
There is no value until a product is released.	✔	☐
For for-profit organizations, value is ultimately represented in terms of money (revenue and cost).	✔	☐
Attaching incentives to value metrics improves performance and morale.	☐	✔
Metrics can help validate business hypotheses and the impact of releases.	✔	☐
Velocity is a good measure of value delivered.	☐	✔
A release can produce negative value.	✔	☐

VALIDATION

QUIZ

To set the stage for this chapter, try answering each of the following statements with *Agree* or *Disagree*. Answers appear at the end of the chapter.

Statement	Agree	Disagree
Validation is the act of making sure a project stays within scope, budget, and schedule.	☐	☐
Creating a simple online survey that collects data about your potential users is a valid release that provides value.	☐	☐
Everything is just a hypothesis until it is tested against the marketplace.	☐	☐
The more stakeholders provide feedback, the more they become accountable for the direction of the product.	☐	☐
Being compliant with all the internal governance rules provides all the validation needed to be successful.	☐	☐

Validation is all about closing the feedback loop to collect and measure data. By analyzing the data, you get information that turns into knowledge that can be leveraged for future benefit.

Since value is about delighting the customers who consume and buy your products, it raises this question: When do you actually deliver value?

Does a grand plan have value? Maybe indirectly to internal people who are creating the product. But does it have any value to customers? A plan is just an assumption that the prescribed path will lead to value.

Two famous military leaders and one boxer sum this idea up nicely:

> *Plans are useless but planning is indispensable.*
>
> —Dwight D. Eisenhower

> *No plan survives contact with the enemy.*
>
> —Helmuth von Moltke

> *Everyone has a plan until they get punched in the face.*
>
> —Mike Tyson

Eisenhower's distinction between planning and plans is even more important in today's globalized economy where everything moves faster and faster. To be successful, you need to validate your business assumption as quickly as possible. Eric Ries calls this the *value hypothesis*.[1] All ideas are nothing but hypotheses until customers validate them by paying for and using the resulting products or services. This is called validated learning. When you think along these lines, every new product feature becomes an experiment.

"Eighty percent of the time you/we are wrong about what a customer wants" is the realization from Microsoft.[2] The company that can fail and learn the fastest on an ongoing basis will be the most successful and sustainable.

---

1. Eric Ries, *The Lean Startup* (New York: Random House, 2011), 61.
2. Ronny Kohavi et al., "Online Experimentation at Microsoft" (ThinkWeek paper, Microsoft Corp., Seattle, WA, 2009), http://ai.stanford.edu/~ronnyk/ExPThinkWeek2009Public.pdf.

As an entrepreneur you need to develop the capability to deliver value quickly and learn from your mistakes (or false hypotheses) as quickly as possible.

Former Cisco CEO John Chambers described this in his last public speech as CEO: "Forty percent of businesses in this room, unfortunately, will not exist in a meaningful way in 10 years. 70% of companies will attempt to go digital but only 30% of those will succeed. If I'm not making you sweat, I should be."[3]

STAKEHOLDER FEEDBACK

A Scrum product development effort succeeds or fails through the Product Owner. However, the Product Owner is rarely the one and only customer. Typically, the Product Owner represents other stakeholders or even whole market segments.

It is critical to identify and communicate with all stakeholders from the beginning to ensure that you build the best possible product.

Scrum provides an excellent opportunity for stakeholder feedback with the Sprint Review, which creates transparency around the Increment. Stakeholders are the key audience for this event, where you incorporate their feedback into the Product Backlog. Putting your product in front of your stakeholders at least once a Sprint provides these opportunities:

1. *Engaging stakeholders.* Implementing stakeholder feedback each Sprint helps stakeholders feel listened to and will have them coming back for more.
2. *Correcting course.* The more often stakeholders see the product, the less you risk going in the wrong direction for too long.
3. *Creating accountability.* The more transparency you create, the harder it is for stakeholders to hide behind ignorance.

---

3. Julie Bort, "Retiring Cisco CEO Delivers Dire Prediction: 40% of Companies Will Be Dead in 10 Years," *Business Insider*, June 8, 2015, http://uk.businessinsider.com/chambers-40-of-companies-are-dying-2015-6.

A good example of stakeholder validation is a Subway sandwich shop. Subway creates transparency between the sandwich creation and the customer (see Figure 4-1):

1. *Engaging stakeholders*. At Subway, you build the sandwich together. The sandwich maker does not go for too long without direction from the customer.

2. *Correcting course*. Change your mind on sandwich ingredients along the way. "Oooh, those peppers look good, can I have more of those?"

3. *Creating accountability*. If a customer ends up with a sandwich that doesn't have the mushrooms they want, whose fault is it? The customer should have said something along the way.

Figure 4-1 Transparent sneeze guard at a sandwich bar

MARKETPLACE FEEDBACK

You can run your product by all the smartest people in the world, but there is only one true way to ultimately validate your idea: get it into the marketplace.

As Product Owner, your focus must always be on getting the product to its next shippable state—a Minimum Viable Product (MVP).

MINIMUM VIABLE PRODUCT

MVPs are about the validation of your hypotheses. You need to validate two kinds of hypotheses: technical and market.

Technical

If you cannot do something from a technical point of view, then there is no product. Therefore, you need to address these risks as early as possible to validate that what you want to do is technically feasible.

Market

The other hypothesis is market acceptance: Do people want to buy the product? You need to get to market as soon as possible or at least as close to the actual marketplace as possible to validate your ideas.

If your hypotheses prove to be wrong, you have not lost too much money and can still investigate other options—or *pivot* as Eric Ries calls it. This also helps to avoid the "trap of sunk costs,"[4] the tendency to irrationally follow through on an activity that is not meeting expectations just because of the time and/or money already spent on it. Poker players call this "pot committed."

---

4. "Definition of 'Sunk Cost Trap,'" *Investopedia*, accessed February 22, 2018, http://www.investopedia.com/terms/s/sunk-cost-trap.asp.

I worked on a year-long initiative to create a first-of-its-kind online document printing product. Five months in, we had the ability to upload a file and set some minimal printing options, without the ability to pay or add more complex finishing options (tabs, inserts, bindings, etc.) At the time, management did not want to hear about going to production early as we were not yet "finished." Seven months later, after going to production, we realized that few customers actually used all the extra finishing options we painfully added to the product. Through a Special Instructions text area, we found out what customers really wanted: oddly sized posters and banners. Looking back, the ideal MVP would have been a simple upload with minimal printing options and an instructions text field. We could have then guided product development based on what our actual retail users were asking for—speeding up the feedback loop and generating true value more often.

Hypothesis validation should be a part of your Product Backlog and can be considered active risk management. The higher the impact, the higher the priority order should be and the earlier you get to inspect at a Sprint Review and Retrospective.

To properly validate the hypothesis, of course, you need to put the right measurements in place. As discussed in the preceding chapter, there are many metrics from which to choose. Avoid using the more circumstantial vanity metrics.[5] Keep your metrics value neutral—objective/free from opinion—so that they tell you the real story. Face your challenges and work through them one after the other.

MINIMUM VIABLE PRODUCT THROUGH KANO

The model described by Kano[6] is simple yet powerful. It plots two types of features on a two-dimensional graph: what a customer needs and their satisfaction level (see Figure 4-2).

---

5. Ibid.
6. Noriaki Kano, Nobuhiku Seraku, Fumio Takahashi, and Shinichi Tsuji, "Attractive Quality and Must-Be Quality," *Hinshitsu* 14, no. 2 (1984): 147–56.

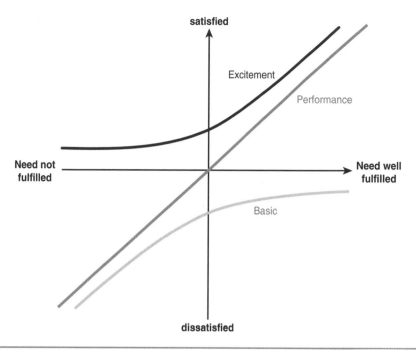

Figure 4-2 Kano model

These features are grouped into three categories:

- *Basic:* Essential features that customers assume are included with the product. A product without these basic features would come as an unpleasant surprise to customers and likely not sell, resulting in negative value. A car's basic features, for example, include the engine, seat belts, steering wheel—everything you'd expect to see in a car.

- *Performance:* Features that customers ask for as they are not always assumed to be included. They carry your customers over the satisfaction threshold from "good enough" toward "very satisfied." The more *performance* features you can offer, the better. A car's performance features are air conditioning, stereo system, navigation system, and some of the more gimmicky things that make driving fun.

- *Excitement:* Features that your customers have likely not even thought about, but are thrilled once they discover them. Excitement features get people talking about your product. A car's excitement features include seamless smartphone integration, massage seats, self-parking, or even a bird's-eye view when parking (see Figure 4-3).

Figure 4-3 Jaguar's bird's-eye car view

Once you cover the basic features, enough performance features, and a few exciters, you have an MVP (see Figure 4-4).

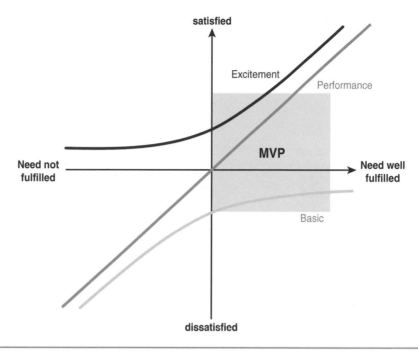

Figure 4-4 Kano model overlaid with MVP

Because no product is ever "done," you create a series of MVPs, one after the other. Once the MVP is on the market, you collect your key value metrics, create the next Product Backlog for the next MVP, and so on.

Over time, exciters turn into performance features and eventually into basic features (see Figure 4-5). Anti-lock braking systems (ABS) were once features found only in high-end cars. Now they are considered basic in all cars.

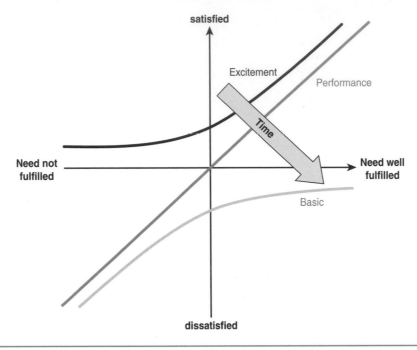

Figure 4-5 Excitement turning into performance and eventually into basic features

MVP PATTERNS

It takes a lot of courage to release something to production before it is "complete." However, as was already described, market validation is crucial when building something unique and uncertain. Rethinking what could possibly constitute a releasable product can help. Below are some MVP patterns that can serve as early milestones for your product. MVPs are too often associated with externally facing products looking for potential markets. However, each of these patterns can and should be considered with internal products, which arguably make up the majority of software development efforts.

PROMOTIONAL MVP

Promotional MVPs include videos, UI mockups, viral campaigns, or anything that gets people talking about your product and to maybe even raise capital. Setting up a crowdfunding campaign (like Kickstarter) could be considered an MVP. For products internal to larger organizations, a promotional MVP could be about promoting a future set of features to stakeholders to build buy-in and a business case.

MINING MVP

Mining MVPs include surveys, proofs of concept, or anything else that collects data about your potential market and therefore validates your business model. A mining MVP is likely disposable after you mine the data.

For example, before investing months of time and lots of dollars into Bitcoin integration for an e-commerce application, in the very first Sprint you could add a Bitcoin payment option for your users that instead leads to a simple survey. Then you could count how many people actually click on the option and gauge their interest further by asking targeted questions like "Do you have a Bitcoin account?" and "Given the chance, would you pay for these purchases with Bitcoin?" Data like this provides valuable information to determine the validity of your product direction without investing in a complete development effort.

LANDING PAGE MVP

Release a single page that explains the value of your product (performers and exciters) and provides a foundation from which all other features can emerge. A landing page MVP provides stakeholders a place to go to see progress.

You can also leverage the landing page to gather data about traffic or create a call to action.

Landing pages are typically easy to do build in early Sprints and get the Development Team in the habit of releasing something right off the bat.

WIZARD OF OZ MVP

A "Wizard of Oz" MVP[7] looks complete from the customer's standpoint, but behind the scenes, humans are doing all the work. The idea here is to avoid investing in a complete automated backend when you are not even sure customers will buy your services.

---

7. Ries, *Lean Startup.*

The classic example of this is Zappos. The founder posted photographs of shoes found in local stores, putting them on a blog page where people could order them. As orders came in through e-mail, he ran down to the shoe stores to buy them and shipped them off himself. Only after he saw that there was demand did he invest in building out a backend system, inventory, fulfillment, and the other elements of his business.

Single-Feature MVP

Once you have a product in the market, you can start to use this foundation as a basis for experimentation. Release a function, even as small as a single Product Backlog item, and then measure and compare with the expected outcome.

Pivot or Persevere

Scientific method is a recognized research practice that builds continuously on past experience. Future experiments are based on empirical evidence from previous experiments (see Figure 4-6).

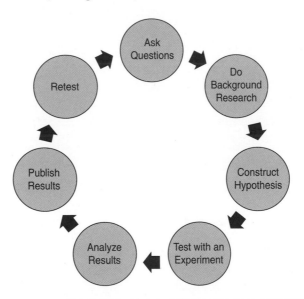

Figure 4-6 Steps of the scientific method

The step "Publish Results" is where fellow scientists are asked for feedback. That part could take a long time, making the whole feedback loop long.

In *Lean Startup*, Eric Ries introduces a simplified product-centric version of the scientific method steps with the intent of speeding up the feedback cycle. Ries describes this as the Build-Measure-Learn principle (see Figure 4-7).

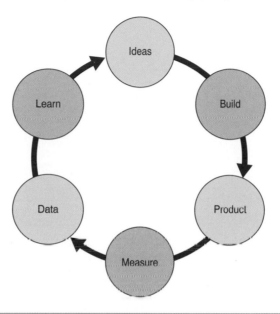

Figure 4-7 Build-Measure-Learn feedback loop

As described in Chapter 6, the three pillars of the empirical process control theory fit nicely into this picture: Measure is **transparency**, learn is **inspection**, and build is **adaptation**. This also aligns nicely with the three Vs: ideas as **vision**, product as (potential) **value**, and data as **validation**.

With every product, initiative, or feature there should always be the question, "Have we created enough value?" Empirical process control allows you to inspect and adapt along the way.

At the core of Lean Startup thinking are two activities:

1. **Persevere**
2. **Pivot**

When the data validates assumptions or is inconclusive, then you continue to persevere, gathering more data along the way.

When the data reveals that you are not gaining the value originally hoped for, then it is time to cut bait, pivot, and avoid the trap of complacency. Even if the expected value is there, the data could unveil a new, more prosperous path that you must have the courage to pivot toward.

Figure 4-8 summarizes these concepts.

> *The problem is that we do not understand the problem.*
> —Paul MacCready

A pivot is about adjusting your path toward your vision or even establishing a whole new vision. Having data available—direct evidence—is helpful, but intuition also plays an important role in coming up with new ideas. Shorter feedback cycles give you courage to follow intuition more often as your ideas will eventually be substantiated through constant validation.

> *Customer Feedback is the basis for ideas, customer data is the basis for decisions.*
> —Roman Pichler

Pivoting is not an easy thing to do. It requires that you accept you have been wrong and that you must adapt. Too often the acceptance of failure is masked by vanity metrics or false loyalty to your product.

Once you accept that you are here to learn as quickly as you can and reduce the time spent between learnings, you will have more opportunities to pivot and hence improve your chances of success.

In 1959 Henry Kremer offered, in today's value, a prize of $2 million USD for the first person to cross the English Channel by a human powered aircraft. This was achieved 20 years later in 1979 by Paul MacCready. Why so long? It certainly wasn't a lack of interest. The many previous attempts by competitors spent months and years designing and building their crafts just to see them shatter after seconds into their flight. This fear of failure would weigh heavily on most and result in even longer, "better" plans.

> *For MacCready, he had no such fear. . . . He did, however, set himself up to fail time and time again as he knew that in order to succeed he needed to be able to iterate and test hundreds of times. Is this failure or is it the courage to fail?*[8]

Paul MacCready realized that it was not about the plane itself but about the possibility to build a plane that could be tested and retested within hours. He achieved about four attempts per day, and with his 223rd try, he was successful. The speed of learning was essential to his success.

Ensure that the Vision, Value, Validation feedback loop is closed as often as possible. The higher the frequency, the more often you can pivot and the better your chances of success.

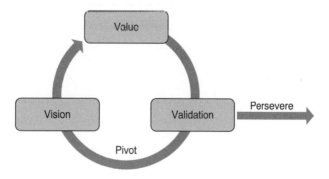

Figure 4-8 Three Vs leading to persevere or pivot decision

8. Anthony Morris, "A Willingness to Fail Solved the Problem of Human-Powered Flight," *Financial Review*, October 16, 2015.

Your limited resources provide you with only so much runway (time and budget). By the time you reach the end of your runway, you must have enough speed to take flight. The length of the runway is set, so your ability to pivot is the determining factor for success, or you find yourself crashed at the end of that runway.

QUIZ REVIEW

Compare your answers from the beginning of the chapter to the ones below. Now that you have read the chapter, would you change any of your answers? Do you agree with the answers below?

Statement	Agree	Disagree
Validation is the act of making sure a project stays within scope, budget, and schedule.	☐	☑
Creating a simple online survey that collects data about your potential users is a valid release that provides value.	☑	☐
Everything is just a hypothesis until it is tested against the marketplace.	☑	☐
The more stakeholders provide feedback, the more they become accountable for the direction of the product.	☑	☐
Being compliant with all the internal governance rules provides all the validation needed to be successful.	☐	☑

II

SCRUM

EMPIRICISM

QUIZ

To set the stage for this chapter, try answering each of the following statements with Agree or Disagree. Answers appear at the end of the chapter.

Statement	Agree	Disagree
Agile practices are best suited for simpler products such as websites.	☐	☐
If you have the right people and they take enough time to analyze a complex problem, they can accurately predict all the variables.	☐	☐
The most efficient way to approach a simple problem is to continuously inspect and adapt.	☐	☐
Taking risks is a good thing when working on complex problems.	☐	☐
Each time a working Increment is developed and inspected, the complexity is reduced.	☐	☐

IT'S A COMPLEX PROBLEM

Assume you are responsible for keeping a conference room at a constant
70°F/21°C from 9 a.m. to 5 p.m. There is no thermostat in the room and no

way for you to read and adjust the temperature throughout the day. The building manager insists that you provide all the variables that could possibly affect the temperature each morning by 9 a.m. These variables will then be entered into a master heating/cooling system to control the room's temperature throughout the day.

It should be straightforward to calculate at which points throughout the day you need to heat or cool, right? Which information do you need? If you think about it for a little bit, you will likely come up with a list similar to this:

1. Number of people in the room: a human body when sitting is roughly a 100-watt heat source

2. Level of activity of the people in the room: the more active they are, the more heat they generate

3. Volume of the room: Length × Width × Height

4. Capacity of the HVAC: how fast the system can cool/heat a certain amount of volume

5. Start temperature at 8 a.m.: the starting point

6. Other heat sources: laptop, projector, food, etc.

7. Weather forecast: change in outside temperature during the day; clouds vs. sun

8. Insulation of the room: how the outside temperature changes affect the temperature in the room

9. Time of year: the position of the sun throughout the day

10. Windows and doors opened and closed: expected lost or gained temperature

11. Orientation of the room: north, south, penthouse, basement, etc.

Which of these remain constant throughout the day?

~~1. Number of people in the room~~
~~2. Level of activity of the people~~
3. **Volume of the room**
4. **Capacity of the HVAC**

5. Start temperature at 8 a.m.

~~6. Other heat sources~~

~~7. Weather forecast~~

8. Insulation of the room

9. Time of year

~~10. Windows and doors opened and closed~~

11. Orientation of the room

Quite a few are predictable, so you should be okay creating the plan for the day.

What happens if only half the people show up because of a traffic problem? What if the projector malfunctions and you work with flip charts? What if everyone uses a personal laptop? What if the weather forecast changes and the current heat wave is disrupted by a severe storm? What if someone opened the window for some fresh air?

Even if most parameters are predictable, the few unpredictable ones have the power to ruin the best plan. A minor change can have a huge impact on the final outcome. In fact, you may even find yourself trying to control the environment and people whenever they seem to veer from the initial plan: "You can't open the door to go to the bathroom yet. A break isn't scheduled for another 22 minutes." Sound like any projects you've been on?

This obviously isn't the way you keep rooms at a comfortable temperature. There is a simpler solution: **a thermostat.**

The thermostat compares current temperature with the target temperature. Every couple of minutes the thermostat calculates the delta and reacts accordingly. This feedback allows you to ignore all those unruly variables. It doesn't matter if only half the people show up, the weather forecast is wrong, more heat sources are introduced. The thermostat just copes with the variability.

The thermostat is a beautiful metaphor. It decouples you from all the unknowns and instead introduces a feedback loop. It takes a transparent reading, inspects, then adapts. The shorter this loop, the more accurate the temperature.

Let's bring this back to product development.

What variables do you need to consider now?

1. Number of people
2. Scope
3. Budget
4. Schedule
5. Technology
6. Infrastructure
7. Skills of the people working in the project
8. Dependencies to other systems or components
9. Quality
10. Vacations/sick days
11. Attrition
12. Marketplace changes
13. Regulations
14. Access to the right people

Which of these are constant or predictable?

Compare this list to the temperature variables. Which are more predictable? You have hopefully determined how difficult it would be to predict the variables for the temperature problem. So why do people continue to try in the world of product development?

You may already have a team, but people may quit, get sick, or take leave. The budget and schedule may be fixed at first, but both can certainly change over the course of the effort. Some core infrastructure and technology decisions are made early on, but how they are implemented varies quite a bit. And let's not even waste any paper on whether scope is predictable.

Very quickly, you see how the world of product development is even more complex than the temperature problem. And just like the temperature

problem, you need a simpler approach that introduces **transparency →
inspection → adaptation** feedback loops. So, what is the product development
industry's version of a thermostat?

Scrum.

The more detailed mechanics of Scrum are addressed in Chapter 6. For now,
let's look at the theory behind Scrum and much of the agile movement.

CERTAINTY QUIZ

To measure the uncertainty of your environment, take the following quiz.

Our team . . .

is very senior	1 ——— 5	is very junior
is stable, changing about once a year	1 ——— 5	is constantly changing or is part time
considers one another true friends	1 ——— 5	"just" works together
has the necessary technical skills to deliver successfully	1 ——— 5	needs to acquire new technical skills to deliver successfully
has complete control over infrastructure and tooling solutions	1 ——— 5	has no control over tooling and infrastructure needs
has built the same technical solution before	1 ——— 5	is building a solution that nobody in the world has built before
has access to industry leaders in our business domain	1 ——— 5	is brand new to the domain and must come up with functionality on its own
is working in an established domain that rarely changes	1 ——— 5	is working in a volatile and emerging domain that changes constantly
has a customer who knows exactly what she wants	1 ——— 5	has a customer whose real needs become clearer as he sees the product progress

Answer: 9-13   → Obvious

14-23   → Complicated

24-35   → Complex

36-45   → Chaos

Most product development initiatives fall into the complex domain. So what does "complex" mean?

Ralph Douglas Stacey created the Stacey Matrix in 2001 to visualize the complex reality of product development.[1]

VISUALIZING COMPLEXITY

In the modified Stacey graph (see Figure 5-1),[2] the x-axis displays the certainty about the technology you are planning to use. How certain are you that it will work as planned? Toward the left side, you are very certain, probably based on past experience. The more you move to the right, the less certain you become. The extreme right side could indicate that you need to develop new technology with many challenges along the way. It took Edison 3,000 different designs and two years to finally produce an incandescent light bulb.[3] This invention had a tremendous degree of complexity.

The y-axis displays the degree to which the requirements are agreed upon. Close to the origin there is agreement with exactly what is needed: no changes are expected. The further you move away from the origin, the less agreement there is. At the extreme, nobody agrees; they may not even agree on some high-level goals.

---

1. "The Stacey Matrix," gp-training.net, accessed February 23, 2018, http://www.gp-training.net/training/communication_skills/consultation/equipoise/complexity/stacey.htm.

2. Ken Schwaber and Mike Beedle, *Agile Software Development with Scrum* (Upper Saddle River, NJ: Prentice Hall, 2002), 93.

3. Elizabeth Palermo, "Who Invented the Light Bulb?," *Live Science*, August 16, 2017, http://www.livescience.com/43424-who-invented-the-light-bulb.html.

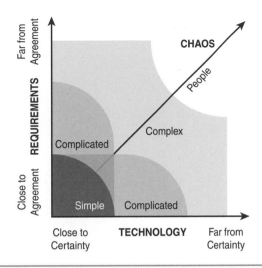

Figure 5-1 Modified Stacey graph

The third axis, added by Ken Schwaber, introduces the team dimension. How well are all the people working together? Does the Development Team have all the skills needed to deliver a "Done" (releasable) product Increment at the end of the Sprint? Do you even have a complete team yet? Has the team gone through the Forming-Storming-Norming-Performing[4] phases? Does trust exist? One of the most important ingredients for high-performing teams is trust—without it, no effective team behavior will emerge.[5]

Considering the three axes, think about your current development effort (or just pick one from your past) and try to place it on the below graph. Are you in the simple, complicated, complex, or even chaos domain?

Usually, you will observe that technology and requirements are in the complicated area, and if you plot that point, the intersection is in the complex domain (see Figure 5-2), which completely changes the game.

4. Bruce W. Tuckman, "Developmental Sequence in Small Groups," *Psychological Bulletin* 63, no. 6 (1965): 384–99.

5. Patrick Lencioni, *The Five Dysfunctions of a Team* (San Francisco: Jossey-Bass, 2002).

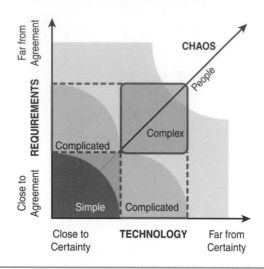

Figure 5-2 The intersection of complicated dimensions is complex

CYNEFIN

Dave Snowden, a researcher on complexity theory and knowledge management, created the Cynefin[6] framework in 1999 while working for IBM. Cynefin has five domains: *obvious*[7] and *complicated* on the right-hand side, *complex* and *chaos* on the left-hand side. A fifth domain—disorder—is reserved for when the domain is unclear.

Figure 5-3 shows the basic structure.

Cynefin is often considered as a categorization framework, whereas Snowden is adamant that it is a "sense-making" framework, constructed from people's pasts, anticipating future experiences. Table 5-1 outlines the difference.

---

6. David J. Snowden and Mary E. Boone, Mary E., "A Leader's Framework for Decision Making," *Harvard Business Review*, November 2007, 69–76.

7. It was called *simple* until January 2015.

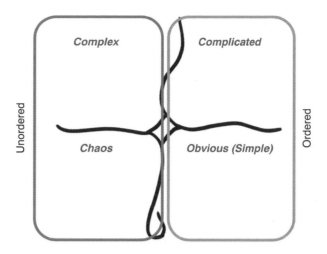

Figure 5-3 Cynefin basic structure: ordered vs. unordered domains

Table 5-1 Comparison of Categorization and Sense-Making Models

Categorization Model	Sense-Making Model
Framework precedes data.	*Data precedes framework.*
You need to find the fit for the data and therefore categorize into an existing framework.	You collect data and learn whether you are operating in an *ordered* domain or in an *unordered* domain. In the unordered domain you need to identify the agents influencing the system so that you can steer.

The goal of Cynefin is to answer this question: How do you approach problems differently, depending on the domain they belong to?

OBVIOUS

Cooking is a perfect example for simple work. You decide what you would like to eat, and you shop, slice, dice, fry, and stir as described by the instructions. As long as you are capable of following the given set of instructions, you will be successful. Usually, the recipe tells you the preparation and cooking time upfront. You operate with *known-knowns*. The approach is *sense-categorize-respond*, which is repeatable for anyone who can follow the instructions. Therefore, in the obvious domain are *best practices* (see Figure 5-4).

COMPLICATED

Now let's build a house, a two-story one-family home. You know how to do it; there are professions for this type of work: architects, structural engineers, civil engineers, to name a few.

Depending on where the home is being built, you need to consider certain general conditions.

 *Where I live in Switzerland, many houses are built on steep hillsides, requiring reinforced and anchored foundations. Before moving to Switzerland, I lived in Silicon Valley, where each of my rented houses was built for earthquakes.*

Ralph

Certain problems need to be analyzed correctly. If not, bad things might happen. You operate with *known-unknowns*, and the approach is to *sense-analyze-respond*.

For an expert, the complicated domain repeats itself from project to project, therefore *good practices* are established over time. This is unlike the obvious domain where the same steps (best practices) are always applicable.

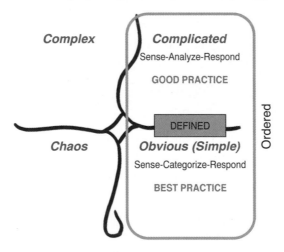

Figure 5-4 With Cynefin, simple and complicated are ordered domains.

These two domains are *ordered*; there is a clear relationship between cause and effect. Because of this repeatability, a defined linear approach can be used.

COMPLEX

If building a house is complicated, what about building an airport? There are many airports in the world, but because of their magnitude and inconceivable number of dependencies, it is unrealistic to plan everything upfront in detail. Many situations unfold as progress is made, requiring changes to the plan as you go. A contracted company goes bankrupt, poured concrete has the wrong chemical composition requiring additional metal reinforcement which then blocks a chute. These changes often have a tremendous impact, requiring adaptation of the plan as you execute it. Complexity is best described as the domain with the *unknown-unknowns*, which calls for a *probe-sense-respond* approach (see Figure 5-5).

To be successful, it is essential that the applied process makes the unknown-unknowns visible. By making them visible, you can address them accordingly. You get a chance to analyze them.

In the *obvious* domain, you have *tight* constraints because you can rely on the established best practices. You know how long a certain job will take and how much it will cost. In the *complicated* domain, you work with *governing* constraints. You review certain calculations and have an agency oversee your work to make sure you do not deviate and that you analyze correctly. However, in the *complex* domain, you need *enabling* constraints that will help you understand the problem at hand so that you can tackle it. Has a team ever told you they cannot estimate a certain feature because they have absolutely no idea what technology to use or how to design it?

You have likely already used enabling constraints like proof of concepts, prototypes, or technical "spikes" that allow you to understand the problem you're facing. This knowledge allows you to inspect and adapt the plan as you go with *emerging practices* along the way.

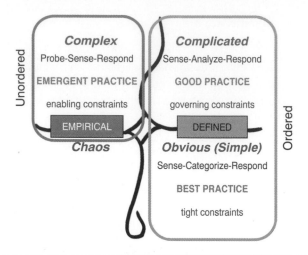

Figure 5-5 With Cynefin, complex is an unordered domain.

I like to arrange four tables for the four domains and then have my team place each high-level requirement (often use cases) in each of those domains. I learned this exercise from Dave Snowden himself. Not everything we have to do will be complex. There will be simple, complicated, and complex items. The simple ones only mean work, nothing to worry about. The complicated ones, we need to make sure that we analyze them correctly. We could use pair work, reviews, or other practices. For all the complex ones, we need to figure out what to do first to gather enough information so that we can plan to do it.

Now the problem you often face, is that companies expect a date and cost estimate before you start the project as it needs to be budgeted well ahead. Later in the release planning chapter (Chapter 8), you will be provided with ways around this, such as two-phased budgeting.

Scrum is an empirical management framework for complex initiatives. It appreciates the uncertainty and complexity with the resulting inability to plan everything upfront in product development.

CHAOS

In *chaos*, the behavior is *act-sense-respond* without any relationship between cause and effect as there are no constraints. It is the *unknowable-unknowables*. Imagine a group of strangers thrown into a situation where they had no experience or skill to cope, like a natural disaster. Whatever they decide to do would be done once and likely never repeated. These are referred to as *novel practices*.

PUTTING IT ALL TOGETHER

There are essentially two approaches to "manage" a product. The approach you choose depends on the predictive nature of what you are producing. On one end of the spectrum is *ordered* (obvious and complicated) and on the other is *unordered* (complex and chaos).

Ordered

Imagine that you are an experienced contractor who has built hundreds of single-family homes.

- Would you prefer your team to be made up of cross-functional individuals or specialists?
- Would you like to increase opportunities for communication and learning or limit them?
- Would you want the team to self-organize or have a manager assign their tasks?
- Who should make the decisions? The team members or their manager?
- What kind of activities would you like a job site manager to do?

A good contractor will put together an upfront plan based on industry best practices and on what he learned from previous projects. He will bring in specialists like carpenters, plumbers, and masons who focus only on their own jobs with no obligation to understand the overarching vision. Learning on the job is likely not an option. Communication should mostly happen through the plan or the site manager.

Unordered

Imagine you are organizing a team of doctors in an emergency room.

- Would you prefer your team to be made up of cross-functional individuals or specialists?
- Would you like to increase opportunities for communication and learning or limit them?
- Would you want the team to self-organize or have a manager assign their tasks?
- Who should make the decisions? The team members or their manager?
- What kind of activities would you like an ER manager to do?

Your answers are likely quite different from the home construction scenario. A team of doctors in an emergency room need to be cross-functional rather than specialists as they cannot predict what's coming through the door next. They need to keep communication at a high level and allow extra slack time to help and learn from each other. They need a manager who essentially gets out of their way so that they can do their jobs. An ideal manager would act as a servant leader and help wherever she can by removing obstacles and setting up a cadence of inspection and adaptation of their processes. She would ask questions like "How did that day go? How can we improve tomorrow? How can I help?"

Both examples are of well-established industries and are perfectly reasonable strategies. It comes down to the predictive nature of what they are building that changes the way the teams are put together and managed. When there is a mismatch between management style and the type of complexity of the product, you will see problems.

With product development, most of what you build resides in the *complex* domain. These products are typically far too difficult to analyze upfront, often leading to "analysis paralysis."[8]

---

8. *Oxford Dictionaries* (American English), s.v. "analysis paralysis," accessed March 5, 2018 ("Inability to respond effectively to a situation due to an over-analytical approach or to an excess of available information.").

By breaking out a piece of the *complex* pie, Scrum allows you to analyze just that piece for the upcoming Sprint and make it plannable. This is done through continuous refinement, preparing just enough of the Product Backlog for Sprint Planning. In Sprint Planning, a plan for the next Sprint is created— the Sprint Backlog, which the Development Team tracks closely throughout the Sprint.

By doing this, you establish a circular current between the *complex* and *complicated* domains. The product is *complex*, the plan for the Sprint is *complicated*. At the end of the Sprint, the Scrum Team and stakeholders reflect by reviewing the new product Increment in the context of the whole and update the *complex* Product Backlog accordingly. However, the product will always remain *complex*; you are never completely safe from the unknown-unknowns. Strange things can and will happen along the way, possibly causing short interludes with *chaos* (see Figure 5-6).

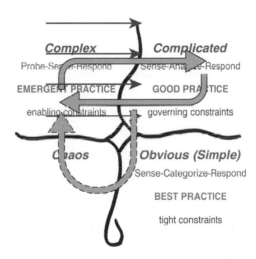

Figure 5-6 *Complex* to complicated and back, creating a continuous learning flow with an interlude with *chaos*

Scrum helps you cope with *complex* problems by implementing empirical process control.

TYPES OF COMPLEXITY

Complexity is your reality. Consider two types: *essential complexity* and *accidental complexity*.[9]

- **Essential complexity** is complexity inherent to the problem and cannot be removed.
- **Accidental complexity** is the entanglement of components/ideas that is not necessary for solving the problem. This complexity is accidental because it emerges based on our own decisions.

> ### From the *Scrum Guide*
> Scrum is a framework for developing, delivering, and sustaining complex products.[10]

Doing Scrum well means that you can sustain the product by being "Done" at the end of each Sprint, which requires sound engineering. When problems arise over time, making your product harder to release, think about these obstacles as accidental complexities. Scrum addresses essential complexity (the product) by minimizing accidental complexity (the process)—and therefore minimizes risks.

MANAGING RISK

No product development endeavor will ever be without risks. Risks are interesting as they can be both good and bad.

I like to show a short TED talk by Tim Harford, "Trial, Error and the God Complex," in my Management 3.0 classes. Tim explains the importance of taking risks and subsequent learning—what he calls making "good mistakes."

Ralph

---

9. Ben Moseley and Peter Marks, "Out of the Tar Pit" (Feb. 6, 2006), https://github.com/papers-we-love/papers-we-love/blob/master/design/out-of-the-tar-pit.pdf (referencing Frederick P. Brooks, Jr., "No Silver Bullet—Essence and Accident in Software Engineering" [1986], http://worrydream.com/refs/Brooks-NoSilverBullet.pdf).

10. Ken Schwaber and Jeff Sutherland, *The Scrum Guide* (Nov. 2017), 3.

What is a good mistake? A good mistake is when you try to solve a problem that belongs in the realm of essential complexity. If you tackle a specific feature or technological challenge first, then you gain an advantage over your competition. You may fail, but you will also learn and possibly come up with another potential solution. Therefore, you have made a good mistake. Without mistakes, you do not take enough good risks and will disappear into the sea of mediocrity.

In Lewis Carroll's *Through the Looking-Glass*, the Red Queen and Alice are constantly running but not making any progress.

"Well, in our country," said Alice, still panting a little, "you'd generally get to somewhere else—if you run very fast for a long time, as we've been doing."

"A slow sort of country!" said the Queen. "Now, here, you see, it takes all the running you can do, to keep in the same place. If you want to get somewhere else, you must run at least twice as fast as that!"

Figure 5-7 Alice in Wonderland learning about pace

As the allegory in Figure 5-7 suggests, to stay relevant in business, you must outcompete and outpace the competition by tackling essential risks faster than they do. These risks could be feature or technical risks that you address as part of the Product Backlog. In general, it is a good practice to have high-risk Product Backlog items higher up in the Product Backlog to enable quick learning and allow enough time to find an alternative solution or even to cancel the product without having lost too much money. Other ongoing, product-specific essential risks can be addressed through the definition of "Done."

> *If there's no risk on your next project, do not do it.*
>
> —Tom de Marco

You need to take risks and keep them in your sights until they are handled. Eessential risks emerging from essential complexity are good and can lead to a competitive advantage.

What about accidental complexity and accidental risks?

Tharwon Arnuphaptrairog's meta study on software project risks defines "risk" several ways:

> PM-BOK (Project Management Body of Knowledge) defines risk as: "an uncertain event or condition that, if it occurs, has a positive or negative effect on a project's objectives." . . . PRINCE2, the UK government sponsored project management standard[,] defines risk as: "uncertainty of outcome."[11]

The PRINCE2 definition is more suitable here as it closely relates to the complexity of product development.

---

11. Tharwon Arnuphaptrairong, "Top Ten Lists of Software Project Risks: Evidence from the Literature Survey," in *Proceedings of the International MultiConference of Engineers and Computer Scientists* (Hong Kong: IAENG, 2011).

Arnuphaptrairog's work analyzed 12 studies to identify similarities. Important categories were "risk frequency by dimension" (see Table 5-2) and "risk items by frequency" (see Table 5-3).

Table 5-2 Software Risk Frequency by Dimension

Dimension	Total Frequency
User	14
Requirements	17
Complexity	4
Planning and Control	27
Team	9
Organizational Environment	9
Total	80

- User

  User dimension included points such as lack of adequate user involvement, failure to gain user commitment, lack of cooperation from users, failure to manage end user expectations.

- Requirements

  Requirements dimension included misunderstanding of the requirements, continuous requirements changes, unclear system requirements, too narrow a focus on the IT project issues, and overlooking the impact on the business in general.

- Complexity

  Complexity dimension included inadequate security features built into the system, use of new technology, performance shortfalls, strained science capabilities.

- Planning and Control

  Planning and control dimension included unrealistic time and cost esti-mates, gold plating, change not managed properly, unclear/misunderstood scope/objectives, changing scope, artificial deadlines, project ambiguity, lack of effective project management methodology, inadequate estimation of required resources, project progress not monitored closely enough.

- Team

  Team dimension included personnel shortfalls, lack of required knowledge/skill in the project personnel, lack of people skill in project leadership, changes to membership on the project team

- Organizational Environment

  Organizational Environment dimension included lack of top management commitment to the project and lack of support, corporate politics with negative effect on project.

Table 5-3 Software Risk Item by Frequency

Risk Item	Frequency
1. Misunderstanding of requirements (*Requirements*)	5
2. Lack of top management commitment and support (*Organizational Environment*)	5
3. Lack of adequate user involvement (*User*)	4
4. Failure to gain user commitment (*User*)	3
5. Failure to manage end user expectations (*User*)	3
6. Changes to requirements (*Requirements*)	3
7. Lack of an effective project management methodology (*Planning and Control*)	3

Let's look at how the empiricism of Scrum helps address each of these points:

1. Misunderstanding of requirements

The ongoing refinement done by the Scrum Team, fostering crucial conversations between the Product Owner and the Development Team, helps to paint a cohesive picture and understanding of the product under development. Only "Ready" Product Backlog items are being brought into a Sprint. The resulting review of the "Done" Increment closes the feedback loop of the product. You see a working product, not only documentation.

2. **Lack of top management commitment and support**

   The key to getting support from management is building trust. In many ways, Scrum becomes a trust generation framework by delivering results each Sprint and by providing transparency.

3. **Lack of adequate user involvement**

   Change is good, the more the better. The more the users get a chance to influence the product under development, the better the product and the higher the resulting value will be. Providing users with the chance to inspect a working product is crucial.

   A late change in requirements is a competitive advantage.

   —Mary Poppendieck

4. **Failure to gain user commitment**

   See point 3 above. Allowing a user to see and understand that the product under development can be molded, even while it is being developed, creates more engagement and confidence.

5. **Failure to manage end user expectations**

   See points 3 and 4 above. When end users see working software every Sprint and can provide valuable feedback, they will not be disappointed.

6. **Changes to requirements**

   See points 3, 4, and 5 above. Change is good; embrace it.

7. Lack of an effective project management methodology

> Scrum is not a methodology by design. Scrum helps teams create their own adaptable process for navigating the rough waters of complexity in an empirical way where a linear and defined methodology is bound to fail. We discuss this in more detail in the next chapter.

The good news is that Scrum allows you to address most of the essential and accidental risks directly. The remaining ones can be put into a classic risk matrix (Table 5-4) and addressed at least once a Sprint.

Table 5-4 Example of a Risk Matrix

Risk	Status	Notes	Probability	Impact	Contingency	Mitigation
High Risk	Red	Description	High	High	Workaround plan	How to make risk go away or bearable
Medium Risk	Amber	...	High	Middle	...	...
Medium Risk	Amber	...	Middle	High	...	...
Low Risk	Green	...	Low	High	...	...
Low Risk	Green	...	High	Low	...	...

$$\text{Overall Risk} = \text{Probability} \times \text{Impact}$$

The overall risk is the combination of probability and impact. You must either make sure the risk cannot happen or is of no consequence if it does happen. Either option is described in the contingency and mitigation column. Once you can set probability or impact to zero, the risk is managed.

QUIZ REVIEW

Compare your answers from the beginning of the chapter to the ones below. Now that you have read the chapter, would you change any of your answers? Do you agree with the answers below?

Statement	Agree	Disagree
Agile practices are best suited for simpler products such as websites.	☐	✔
If you have the right people and they take enough time to analyze a complex problem, they can accurately predict all the variables.	☐	✔
The most efficient way to approach a simple problem is to continuously inspect and adapt.	☐	✔
Taking risks is a good thing when working on complex problems.	✔	☐
Each time a working Increment is developed and inspected, the complexity is reduced.	✔	☐

SCRUM

QUIZ

To set the stage for this chapter, try answering each of the following statements with Agree or Disagree. Answers appear at the end of the chapter.

Statement	Agree	Disagree
Scrum is an agile process.	☐	☐
Scrum Teams do very little planning.	☐	☐
If a Scrum Team changes the Scrum framework, they are no longer doing Scrum.	☐	☐
If a Scrum Team adds to the Scrum framework, they are no longer doing Scrum.	☐	☐
Every Scrum event is time-boxed.	☐	☐
The development process is owned by the Development Team. The Product Owner does not have a say.	☐	☐

From the *Scrum Guide*

Scrum is a *framework* for developing, delivering, and sustaining complex products.[1]

WHY A FRAMEWORK?

Scrum is a framework (see Figure 6-1). But what does that mean? Why not call it a process?

Scrum carefully avoids referring to itself as a process. Why?

In a court of law, you would likely lose the argument that Scrum isn't a process. It has ordered events, roles, and artifacts. Sounds like a process.

The key element here is ownership. Who should truly "own" the process? Management? Your organization's Project Management Office (PMO)? Some book or guide? Schwaber and Sutherland?

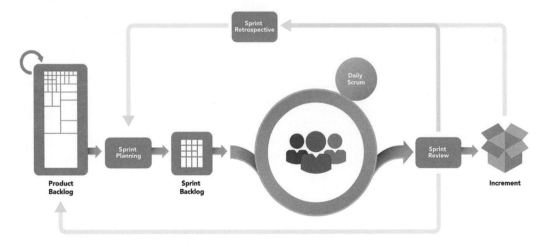

Figure 6-1 The Scrum Framework

---

1. Ken Schwaber and Jeff Sutherland, *The Scrum Guide* (November 2017), 3.

Of course not. If you have been following along so far, the answer here should be obvious. The Scrum Team needs to own the process. Each team, each product, each company is different, and each process must emerge to support their unique needs. However, it would be helpful if teams could start with something to build upon, a minimal set of rules: a framework.

A metaphor that works here is renting versus owning a house. If you rent a house and something goes wrong, what do you do? You pick up the phone and complain to the landlord. Then you complain about how things are always breaking and you deserve better support from the landlord. You feel victimized.

However, if you own a house and something goes wrong, what do you do? Nowhere to turn, right? You need to suck it up and deal with the problem yourself. You make decisions based on return (value) and investment (cost, time). Sometimes you fix it on your own, sometimes you call an expert, and in some cases, you just live with it. In the end, it's all about finding a workable solution for which you are accountable.

The same happens with processes. If the process is defined and installed from outside of the team and "forced" upon them, when something goes wrong they call their management/PMO. They assign blame to the process and complain about it over lunch with their colleagues and online with angry posts. It becomes all about finger pointing.

Now when a team sees Scrum as a starting point, a true *framework* with built-in opportunities to change and improve, they take ownership. They have nowhere to point to but themselves if (when) things do not work out. This is the essential ingredient for accountability and self-organization.

As the previous chapter explains, complexity requires emergent practices. Team ownership over a flexible (empirical) process is key to this.

If organizations are not careful, Scrum can also be viewed as a *rented process*.

I have worked with companies that started with a pilot team to test Scrum. Since Scrum is just a framework, described in a 17-page document,[2] there is no step-by-step installation guide. So the Scrum Team needs to figure it out for themselves. They read books and blogs, they experiment, they fail, and eventually they land on something that works for them—a true process, owned by the Scrum Team.

Seeing the ultimate success of the pilot, management then asks the team to list out everything they did so that they can have all other teams do the same. What title did your Scrum Master have? What about the Product Owner? What tools did you use? How long were your Sprints? What time of day did you hold your Daily Scrums? What color stickies did you use?

Unfortunately, by having the subsequent teams copy the pilot team's Scrum-based process instead of the Scrum framework, we are back to renting a process. The subsequent teams will not have the same sense of ownership and will fall back into blaming the Scrum process, the managers, and maybe even the pilot team.

You can see this reflected within almost any anti-Scrum rhetoric online.

Do a little digging and you will see the complaints are not about framework elements but instead about practices that were instituted on top of Scrum (often sizing mechanics, requirements capture, Sprint *commitment*, task management, etc.) by people outside the team (managers, PMOs, agile "coaches," tools, etc.).

With help from the *Scrum Guide* itself, let's look at the core elements of the Scrum framework.

---

2. Schwaber and Sutherland, Scrum Guide.

THE PILLARS OF SCRUM

From the *Scrum Guide*

Scrum is founded on empirical process control theory, or empiricism. Empiricism asserts that knowledge comes from experience *and* making decisions based on what is known. Scrum employs an iterative, incremental approach to optimize predictability and control risk.

Three pillars uphold every implementation of empirical process control: transparency, inspection, and adaptation.[3]

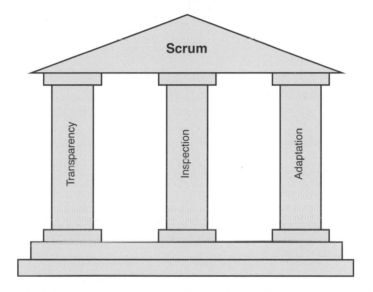

Figure 6-2 Empirical pillars of Scrum: transparency, inspection, and adaption

Figure 6-2 symbolizes the three pillars of Scrum. Without all three in place, the whole construct collapses.

---

3. Ibid., 4.

TRANSPARENCY

> ### From the *Scrum Guide*
>
> Significant aspects of the process must be visible to those responsible for the outcome. Transparency requires those aspects be defined by a common standard so observers share a common understanding of what is being seen.
>
> For example:
>
> - A common language referring to the process must be shared by all participants; and,
> - Those performing the work and those inspecting the resulting increment must share a common definition of "Done."[4]

Imagine an organization that has all the data (inspection) and the ability to change (adaptation), but no transparency. The data may not reflect the true reality and may not be visible to the right people. Therefore, what they inspect will be incorrect and how they adapt will be wasteful. Having a culture that promotes openness and communication is essential for any empirical process to work effectively.

A lack of transparency is like putting a wet washcloth over a thermostat. The thermostat will inspect inaccurate data and adapt in the wrong way.

INSPECTION

> ### From the *Scrum Guide*
>
> Scrum users must frequently inspect Scrum artifacts and progress toward a Sprint Goal to detect undesirable variances. Their inspection should not be so frequent that inspection gets in the way of the work. Inspections are most beneficial when diligently performed by skilled inspectors at the point of work.[5]

Imagine an organization that has nothing to hide and has solid communication (transparency) as well as the ability to change (adaptation). However,

---

4. Ibid., 5.

5. Ibid.

they have not taken the time to gather and analyze the data in any consistent way. You will end up with people *feeling* like they should adapt a certain way; but with no hard evidence to back it up, real change becomes more difficult. Having consistent and short feedback loops as well as clear information radiators is essential for any empirical process to work effectively.

ADAPTATION

From the *Scrum Guide*

If an inspector determines that one or more aspects of a process deviate outside acceptable limits, and that the resulting product will be unacceptable, the process or the material being processed must be adjusted. An adjustment must be made as soon as possible to minimize further deviation.

Scrum prescribes four formal events for inspection and adaptation . . . :

- Sprint Planning
- Daily Scrum
- Sprint Review
- Sprint Retrospective[6]

Imagine an organization that has all the accurate data (transparency and inspection) necessary to change in a meaningful way. However, nobody is empowered or willing to do anything about it (adaptation). The ability to execute is essential for any empirical process to work effectively.

> *Vision without execution is hallucination.*
>
> —Thomas Edison

SCRUM ROLES

The three defined Scrum roles are Product Owner, Development Team, and Scrum Master. While there are many other roles within organizations that are

---

6. Ibid.

vital to the success of the product, these three must be in place for the Scrum framework.

PRODUCT OWNER

From the *Scrum Guide*

The Product Owner is responsible for maximizing the value of the product resulting from the work of the Development Team. How this is done may vary widely across organizations, Scrum Teams, and individuals.

The Product Owner is the sole person responsible for managing the Product Backlog. Product Backlog management includes:

- Clearly expressing Product Backlog items;
- Ordering the items in the Product Backlog to best achieve goals and missions;
- Optimizing the value of the work the Development Team performs;
- Ensuring that the Product Backlog is visible, transparent, and clear to all, and shows what the Scrum Team will work on next; and,
- Ensuring the Development Team understands items in the Product Backlog to the level needed.

The Product Owner may do the above work, or have the Development Team do it. However, the Product Owner remains accountable.

The Product Owner is one person, not a committee. The Product Owner may represent the desires of a committee in the Product Backlog, but those wanting to change a Product Backlog item's priority must address the Product Owner.

For the Product Owner to succeed, the entire organization must respect his or her decisions. The Product Owner's decisions are visible in the content and ordering of the Product Backlog. No one can force the Development Team to work from a different set of requirements.[7]

---

7. Ibid., 6.

A single person who truly owns the product and has the last say is crucial for product success.

What good is it to have the best Development Team if the wrong product is being built? The Product Owner is the keystone on which the right product—the overall product quality—depends.

Figure 6-3 shows how Scrum uses a built-in flow of service. Ultimately, the Development Team is there to serve the Product Owner, and the Scrum Master serves the Development Team. You could also say that the Product Owner serves the customer and other stakeholders.

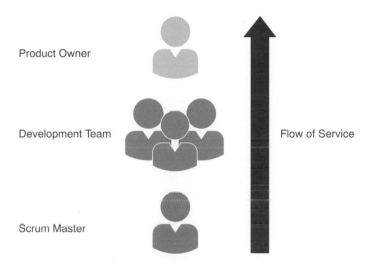

Figure 6-3 The service model of Scrum

Building on top of what is covered in "The Product Owner" section in the first chapter, let's look at how the Product Owner works on a day-to-day basis.

I often draw the Product Owner with a crown (see Figure 6-4). As queen or king, you have the right to make all decisions regarding your kingdom. As long as you do a good job, your stakeholders will respect and even love you. If things go south for too long, you might face a revolution with dire consequences.

Figure 6-4 Product Owner shown with crown

As the Product Owner, you have the absolute right to make all product deci-sions. This is in contrast to a traditional project manager who is responsible for making sure that the project stays within scope, schedule, and budget. Whether the product is the right product and whether the product creates value for the users and customers are likely not a project manager's top con-cerns. As a Product Owner, this is your purpose. You are the value maximizer for the product.

Domain Expert and Relationship to Stakeholders

As the value maximizer, it is mandatory to understand the domain of the product and to identify and work closely with all stakeholders such as customers, users, and executives.

I was once coaching and overseeing a large program to replace the existing scanner at Swiss Postal Services. Since more than 20,000 personnel used the device, we invited postal workers on a regular basis. They took part in the Product Backlog refinement when chal-lenging processes were being refined, in user-interface workshops, and every two weeks for the Sprint Review. Our goal was not to just replace the old system, but to create value to thousands of people as they deliver millions of letters and boxes every day.

It should be obvious that being appointed as Product Owner for a product in a domain you do not actually understand is a questionable decision. Most likely this Product Owner will become a proxy (as described in Chapter 1), which will result in delays and information loss every single day. A good Product Owner is a domain expert who knows the business from many angles. This allows the Product Owner to quickly navigate and adjust as new information emerges in synchronization with the stakeholders. A Product Owner who is a proxy only collects stakeholder requests and orders them in a way that pleases their loudest stakeholders (squeaky wheels). A Product Owner who steps up and owns the product plays an important role toward creating an agile business.

Realistically, demanding a Product Owner to know everything about the domain is an almost impossible request. While still maintaining the vision and ownership, an effective Product Owner should be able to leverage other Subject Matter Experts (SMEs) to help guide the product. The Product Owner could even create direct communication lines between Development Teams and the stakeholders. This is even more true in a scaled environment where the Product Owner's capacity is strained.

I have had a Product Owner who brought an SME from the legal department to Sprint Planning and announced that she honestly did not know much about the legal details for the features we were focusing on that Sprint. She made it clear that we could go directly to the SME for the specifics and that she trusted any decisions made by him. It was obvious that this did not relieve the Product Owner of accountability. She was doing what was right to create an excellent product Increment that Sprint.

DEVELOPMENT TEAM

From the *Scrum Guide*

The Development Team consists of professionals who do the work of delivering a potentially releasable Increment of "Done" product at the end of each Sprint. A "Done" increment is required at the Sprint Review. Only members of the Development Team create the Increment.

Development Teams are structured and empowered by the organization to organize and manage their own work. The resulting synergy optimizes the Development Team's overall efficiency and effectiveness.

Development Teams have the following characteristics:

- They are self-organizing. No one (not even the Scrum Master) tells the Development Team how to turn Product Backlog into Increments of potentially releasable functionality;

- Development Teams are cross-functional, with all of the skills as a team necessary to create a product Increment;

- Scrum recognizes no titles for Development Team members, regardless of the work being performed by the person;

- Scrum recognizes no sub-teams in the Development Team, regardless of domains that need to be addressed like testing, architecture, operations, or business analysis; and,

- Individual Development Team members may have specialized skills and areas of focus, but accountability belongs to the Development Team as a whole.[8]

Product Owner and Development Team

Apart from working closely with all stakeholders, a good Product Owner also works closely with the Development Team. Actually, the Product Owner should include the Development Team in quite a bit of tactical work on the Product Backlog, refinement, acceptance criteria, and other areas. Figure 6-5 shows that while some areas are squarely the responsibility of either the Product Owner or the Development Team, the Scrum framework also builds in plenty of opportunities for both parties to collaborate and share responsibility.

---

8. Ibid., 7.

Figure 6-5 Overlapping and distinct responsibilities of Product Owner and Development Team

What you really need to avoid is a requirements hand-off from the Product Owner to the Development Team. The more closely the Development Team is engaged with the features and their refinement, the more the Product Backlog items become theirs. This leads to more ownership, stronger engagement, and pride, which are key steps toward achieving excellence.

On a day-to-day basis, this means that you, as Product Owner, spend less time specifying requirements and more time educating the Development Team about the value of the requirements. Give them the support they need and then trust them to come up with a solution.

When refining the Product Backlog for upcoming Sprints, do not just hand over and explain. Use the refinement to provide understanding, answer initial questions, and then let the Development Team do their work. During the Sprint, support the Development Team wherever needed and provide feedback on Product Backlog items. The benefit here is not only that the Development Team gains better understanding and ownership of the Product Backlog, but this approach also frees you up to do the more strategic Product Owner work, like analyzing the market, observing the competition, talking to sales and marketing, aligning with other Product Owners, talking to stakeholders, and so on.

You will want to keep an eye on overall progress of the Product Backlog as you still have overall accountability. However, the plan for the Sprint belongs to the Development Team, so dictating what they work on and when is not your call.

Remember, the Development Team's accountability is to produce a "Done" working Increment of the product every single Sprint. Accomplishing this requires the Development Team to have all the skills necessary to reach "no work remaining," as in "yes, we can ship."

Development Team = Product

What's in the Development Team can be in the product; what is not cannot.

Imagine you and your cooking friends are asked to cater a big event. All of you have spent quite some time in the kitchen cooking together. You know each other, you have established a routine for communication and moving around so as not to impede others. This, in combination with a stocked pantry, sets you up to amaze some palates.

But let's assume not everything is perfect. Maybe two of your friends cannot make it, or the pantry is missing some key ingredients, or your team really does not have the skills needed to pull off the requested menu. You could certainly improvise, but that choice carries risks. The likelihood of having a successful outcome is greatly reduced.

Taking this analogy into the world of a software product development, it becomes obvious that what is in the Development Team can be in the product, but what is not most likely cannot. You can improvise, depend on external people, or come up with other creative workarounds. But in doing so you create significant risk for the feature quality, the technical quality, and progress.

As Product Owner, you never start with a perfect Development Team. It emerges over time. So give them the time, focus, and resources they need to become a professional team. Making use of Sprint Retrospectives and measuring key indicators like on-product index, innovation rate, and employee satisfaction (as described in Chapter 3) can help.

---

9. Sandy Mamoli and David Mole, *Creating Great Teams* (Raleigh, NC: Pragmatic Bookshelf, 2015), 4–5.

According to Sandy Mamoli and David Mole, 60 percent of success depends on the people doing the work.[9] Companies that realize this do not fund projects. They fund teams that build and maintain a product, as shown in Figure 6-6.

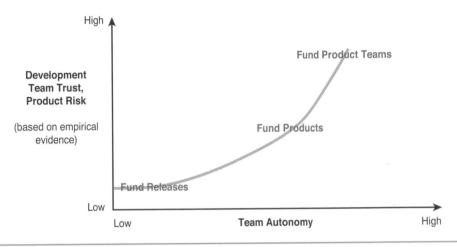

Figure 6-6 Emergence of funding from project releases over products to product teams

SCRUM MASTER

From the *Scrum Guide*

The Scrum Master is responsible for promoting and supporting Scrum as defined in the Scrum Guide. Scrum Masters do this by helping everyone understand Scrum theory, practices, rules, and values.

The Scrum Master is a servant-leader for the Scrum Team. The Scrum Master helps those outside the Scrum Team understand which of their interactions with the Scrum Team are helpful and which aren't. The Scrum Master helps everyone change these interactions to maximize the value created by the Scrum Team.

Scrum Master Service to the Product Owner

The Scrum Master serves the Product Owner in several ways, including:

• Ensuring that goals, scope, and product domain are understood by everyone on the Scrum Team as well as possible;

- Finding techniques for effective Product Backlog management;
- Helping the Scrum Team understand the need for clear and concise Product Backlog items;
- Understanding product planning in an empirical environment;
- Ensuring the Product Owner knows how to arrange the Product Backlog to maximize value;
- Understanding and practicing agility; and,
- Facilitating Scrum events as requested or needed.

Scrum Master Service to the Development Team

The Scrum Master serves the Development Team in several ways, including:

- Coaching the Development Team in self-organization and cross-functionality;
- Helping the Development Team to create high-value products;
- Removing impediments to the Development Team's progress;
- Facilitating Scrum events as requested or needed; and,
- Coaching the Development Team in organizational environments in which Scrum is not yet fully adopted and understood.

Scrum Master Service to the Organization

The Scrum Master serves the organization in several ways, including:

- Leading and coaching the organization in its Scrum adoption;
- Planning Scrum implementations within the organization;
- Helping employees and stakeholders understand and enact Scrum and empirical product development;
- Causing change that increases the productivity of the Scrum Team; and,
- Working with other Scrum Masters to increase the effectiveness of the application of Scrum in the organization.[10]

---

10. Schwaber and Sutherland, *Scrum Guide*, 7–8.

Product Owner and Scrum Master

The Scrum Master is there to help you, the Product Owner, to maximize value. This is mostly done with the Scrum Master coaching the Development Team. While doing this, the Scrum Master brings focus to all kinds of impediments that have an impact on the Development Team. As the Product Owner, you need information about the product quality, the progress, the status of the risks, and more, depending on the product you develop. These are all things you can and should expect from your Scrum Master and Development Team as this information is vital to making sound decisions. Ensuring that the proper mechanisms are in place for transparency, inspection, and adaptation is a big part of the Scrum Master role and allows the Product Owner and Development Team to do their jobs more effectively.

Should the Scrum Master be knowledgeable about the business domain? There clearly is no harm; however, it is not a necessity. This is the beauty of the separation of roles within Scrum. The product quality, building the right product with value for the users, is with the Product Owner. The technical quality of the product lies with the Development Team. The Scrum Master facilitates all these responsibilities. In fact, a lack of knowledge of the domain could even be considered a benefit, freeing the Scrum Master to focus on facilitation, coaching, team dynamics, and to ensure that a process, based on the Scrum Framework, is emerging.

Ralph   Don

As consultants, we spend a lot of time facilitating Scrum Teams from all sorts of industries. In many cases, they seem to be speaking a completely different language. However, as facilitators, our focus is not on the solution but on the process. Not getting too entangled in their domain actually makes us more effective at reading the room, keeping things on track, and looking for process gaps.

OTHERS

Other roles relevant to Scrum include the Scrum Team and stakeholders.

Scrum Team

From the *Scrum Guide*

The Scrum Team consists of a Product Owner, the Development Team, and a Scrum Master. Scrum Teams are self-organizing and cross-functional. Self-organizing teams choose how best to accomplish their work, rather than being directed by others outside the team. Cross-functional teams have all competencies needed to accomplish the work without depending on others not part of the team. The team model in Scrum is designed to optimize flexibility, creativity, and productivity. The Scrum Team has proven itself to be increasingly effective for all the earlier stated uses, and any complex work.

Scrum Teams deliver products iteratively and incrementally, maximizing opportunities for feedback. Incremental deliveries of "Done" product ensure a potentially useful version of working product is always available.[11]

Too often, the terms "Development Team" and "Scrum Team" are used interchangeably. They are not the same: The Development Team is part of the Scrum Team. Often this subtle difference can have a big impact when generically talking about the "Team" and understanding where the responsibilities belong.

Stakeholders

Although not an official Scrum role, stakeholders are key to the success of any Scrum development effort. These are the users, customers, investors, executives, compliance officers, and anybody whose lives are affected by the product under development.

As Product Owner, it is your responsibility to identify the stakeholders who have a say in the direction of the Product and to ensure they are included.

---

11. Ibid., 6.

Scrum provides many built-in opportunities to engage with your stakeholders. The obvious one is the Sprint Review, where stakeholders can provide feedback on the Increment that subsequently affects the Product Backlog.

However, including stakeholders in Sprint Planning and Product Backlog refinement can also be beneficial and should be done at the discretion of the Product Owner.

A good brainstorming activity to identify your stakeholders is to work through a mind map such as the one in Figure 6-7.

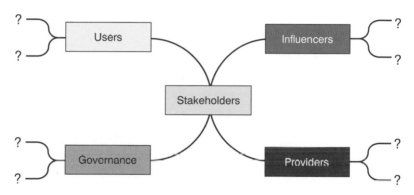

Figure 6-7 Mind map showing various stakeholders

For each category shown in Figure 6-7 (consider adding new categories that are specific to your product), name organizational roles and even the people in those roles. Doing so will likely result in an extensive list of stakeholders, each with unique needs and expectations about the direction of the product and how they would like to be included.

Another helpful technique is to place your stakeholders on an "influence 2×2" such as the one in Figure 6-8.[12]

---

12. Rachel Thompson, "Winning Supportyou're your Projects," MindTools, accessed February 28, 2018, https://www.mindtools.com/pages/article/newPPM_07.htm.

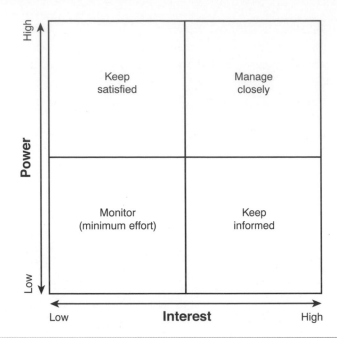

Figure 6-8 Influence 2×2

This tool gives you a better idea of how to involve your stakeholders. Consider involving your interested parties more often, even during the Sprint where they can help with details. You may be able to accommodate the less interested parties in other ways that are less time consuming but still keeps them happy. Active stakeholder management builds trust, especially once they see the impact they can have on the product. It also shifts accountability to stakeholders: The more they are involved during development, the less they can complain once the product is released.

For stakeholders who have high interest yet low power (bottom right of Figure 6-8), consider putting them to work. As Product Owner, there is a lot to do. Maybe these stakeholders are willing to help with the more tactical items while you focus more on strategy.

Scrum Artifacts

There are just three mandatory artifacts in Scrum: the Product Backlog, the Sprint Backlog, and the Increment.

The three artifacts are linked: The Increment is generated from the Sprint Backlog, and the Sprint Backlog is generated from the Product Backlog. The Product Backlog is then refined based on feedback from the Increment (see Figure 6-9).

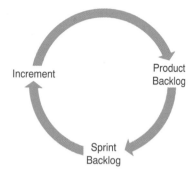

Figure 6-9 Interconnected Scrum artifacts

PRODUCT BACKLOG

From the *Scrum Guide*

The Product Backlog is an ordered list of everything that is known to be needed in the product. It is the single source of requirements for any changes to be made to the product. The Product Owner is responsible for the Product Backlog, including its content, availability, and ordering.

A Product Backlog is never complete. The earliest development of it lays out the initially known and best-understood requirements. The Product Backlog evolves as the product and the environment in which it will be used evolves. The Product Backlog is dynamic; it constantly changes to identify what the product needs to be appropriate, competitive, and useful. If a product exists, its Product Backlog also exists.

The Product Backlog lists all features, functions, requirements, enhancements, and fixes that constitute the changes to be made to the product in future releases. Product Backlog items have the attributes of a description, order, estimate, and value. Product Backlog items often include test descriptions that will prove its completeness when "done."

As a product is used and gains value, and the marketplace provides feedback, the Product Backlog becomes a larger and more exhaustive list. Requirements never stop changing, so a Product Backlog is a living artifact. Changes in business requirements, market conditions, or technology may cause changes in the Product Backlog.

Multiple Scrum Teams often work together on the same product. One Product Backlog is used to describe the upcoming work on the product. A Product Backlog attribute that groups items may then be employed. . . .

Higher ordered Product Backlog items are usually clearer and more detailed than lower ordered ones. More precise estimates are made based on the greater clarity and increased detail; the lower the order, the less detail. Product Backlog items that will occupy the Development Team for the upcoming Sprint are refined so that any one item can reasonably be "Done" within the Sprint time-box. Product Backlog items that can be "Done" by the Development Team within one Sprint are deemed "Ready" for selection in a Sprint Planning. Product Backlog items usually acquire this degree of transparency through the above described refining activities.

The Development Team is responsible for all estimates. The Product Owner may influence the Development Team by helping it understand and select trade-offs, but the people who will perform the work make the final estimate.[13]

In the next chapter, we will get into more details about how to create and maintain a Product Backlog.

Product Owner and the Product Backlog

As Product Owner, consider the Product Backlog as your current path. This path represents a snapshot of your best understanding on how to get to your final destination. No matter how good your velocity is, the wrong path will not get you to your goal; you will simply end up at the wrong destination faster.

A well-refined, ordered, and estimated Product Backlog provides you with direction and with all the information necessary for reporting and planning. However, for this to work, you need to make sure that the Product Backlog is your only—as in one—source of work for the Development Team. Assume that you have a Product Backlog for the features, a bug backlog for the issues,

---

13. Schwaber and Sutherland, *Scrum Guide*, 15.

a technical backlog for infrastructure and architectural work, and you have unplanned work injected during the Sprint. In that suboptimal (yet common) situation, there is no true transparency regarding your direction. It is hard or even impossible to measure your bearings.

At the risk of repeating ourselves, the following rule always applies:

One Product → One Product Owner → One Product Backlog

And this Product Backlog contains all the work for the Development Team.

SPRINT BACKLOG

From the *Scrum Guide*

The Sprint Backlog is the set of Product Backlog items selected for the Sprint, plus a plan for delivering the product Increment and realizing the Sprint Goal. The Sprint Backlog is a forecast by the Development Team about what functionality will be in the next Increment and the work needed to deliver that functionality into a "Done" Increment.

The Sprint Backlog makes visible all of the work that the Development Team identifies as necessary to meet the Sprint Goal. To ensure continuous improvement, it includes at least one high priority process improvement identified in the previous Retrospective meeting.

The Sprint Backlog is a plan with enough detail that changes in progress can be understood in the Daily Scrum. The Development Team modifies the Sprint Backlog throughout the Sprint, and the Sprint Backlog emerges during the Sprint. This emergence occurs as the Development Team works through the plan and learns more about the work needed to achieve the Sprint Goal.

As new work is required, the Development Team adds it to the Sprint Backlog. As work is performed or completed, the estimated remaining work is updated. When elements of the plan are deemed unnecessary, they are removed. Only the Development Team can change its Sprint Backlog during a Sprint. The Sprint Backlog is a highly visible, real-time picture of the work that the Development Team plans to accomplish during the Sprint, and it belongs solely to the Development Team.[14]

---

14. Ibid., 16.

Product Owner and the Sprint Backlog

The Sprint Backlog belongs to the Development Team. It is their plan on how best to meet the Sprint Goal. As the Product Owner, you can determine the most important Product Backlog items for the Development Team to consider in their Sprint plan, but you cannot dictate how much they take on or how they will break down their work.

This is an essential part in building a mutually respectful relationship between these two roles. A Development Team that truly owns the plan for the Sprint will demonstrate much more accountability and ownership over the work of the Sprint.

Together with the Development Team, you define the Sprint Goal in Sprint Planning and then trust them to create the Sprint Backlog and maintain it throughout the Sprint.

Sprint Goal → Sprint Backlog = Forecasted Product Backlog items (what) + Plan to deliver them (how)

INCREMENT

If Scrum was reduced to one and only one sentence, it would be to have "releasable working product every 30 days or less." That releasable working product is the Increment.

> ### From the *Scrum Guide*
>
> The Increment is the sum of all the Product Backlog items completed during a Sprint and the value of the increments of all previous Sprints. At the end of a Sprint, the new Increment must be "Done," which means it must be in useable condition and meet the Scrum Team's definition of "Done." An increment is a body of inspectable, done work that supports empiricism at the end of the Sprint. The increment is a step toward a vision or goal. The Increment must be in useable condition regardless of whether the Product Owner decides to actually release it.[15]

---

15. Ibid., 17.

Product Owner and the Increment

As Product Owner, a valuable Increment at the end of each Sprint is the goal you share with the Development Team. Although you do not have much say in how the Development Team plans their work in a Sprint, you should still expect a working "Done" Increment each time. Product Owners do have the right to challenge their Development Teams to create an Increment of value and not settle for just plans, designs, mock-ups, and similar outputs.

If the Product Backlog represents the direction of your current path, then the Increment is your GPS device that determines your current position. The Increment provides transparency for you and your stakeholders. In that sense, it is the most important element in the Sprint Review and fuels the most important feedback loop in an empirical process control. A working Increment allows you to inspect and adapt together and to determine the next steps, thereby updating your path—the Product Backlog.

For this to work, your Increment needs to be truly "Done." How could you find your position with an inaccurate GPS reading? You can't; and this lack of transparency is detrimental or even catastrophic. In the long run, you will lose your way.

OTHERS

Although not official Scrum artifacts, other generally accepted Scrum practices that should be strongly considered are burn-down/burn-up charts and a definition of "Done".

"Done"

> ### From the *Scrum Guide*
>
> When a Product Backlog item or an Increment is described as "Done," everyone must understand what "Done" means. Although this may vary significantly per Scrum Team, members must have a shared understanding of what it means for work to be complete, to ensure transparency. This is the definition of "Done" for the Scrum Team and is used to assess when work is complete on the product Increment.

The same definition guides the Development Team in knowing how many Product Backlog items it can select during a Sprint Planning. The purpose of each Sprint is to deliver Increments of potentially releasable functionality that adhere to the Scrum Team's current definition of "Done."

Development Teams deliver an Increment of product functionality every Sprint. This Increment is useable, so a Product Owner may choose to immediately release it. If the definition of "Done" for an increment is part of the conventions, standards or guidelines of the development organization, all Scrum Teams must follow it as a minimum.

If "Done" for an increment is not a convention of the development organization, the Development Team of the Scrum Team must define a definition of "Done" appropriate for the product. If there are multiple Scrum Teams working on the system or product release, the Development Teams on all the Scrum Teams must mutually define the definition of "Done."

Each Increment is additive to all prior Increments and thoroughly tested, ensuring that all Increments work together.

As Scrum Teams mature, it is expected that their definitions of "Done" will expand to include more stringent criteria for higher quality. New definitions, as used, may uncover work to be done in previously "Done" increments. Any one product or system should have a definition of "Done" that is a standard for any work done on it.[16]

Product Owner and "Done"

If the Product Backlog is your path and the Increment is your compass, then "Done" is the magnetic field that points the needle. No needle, no location, no path-calibration.

At least once a Sprint, your Increment (your product) must be "Done": "Done" as in no work remaining, as in it can be released. Whatever "Done" means in your context is something you as the Product Owner (representing the stakeholders) and the Development Team must work out. All needs regarding "Done" have to be addressed accordingly. "Done" reaches from the end user all the way to operations.

Not "Done" → no Increment → nothing to show in the Sprint Review

---

16. Ibid., 18.

If you ignore "Done," at best, you are just making progress. The question is toward what?

Read more about "Done" in the next chapter on Product Backlog management.

Burn-down/Burn-up Charts

Continuing with the path metaphor, during your journey in creating an awesome product, it is helpful to have a map with you. Two popular tools in the Scrum community are burn-down and burn-up charts. They can bring visibility to your journey's progress so that you can better inspect and adapt your path.

Sprint Burn-down   The Sprint burn-down provides transparency—location—for the Development Team. It allows them to inspect and adapt their plan during the Sprint and to gauge their progress toward the Sprint Goal.

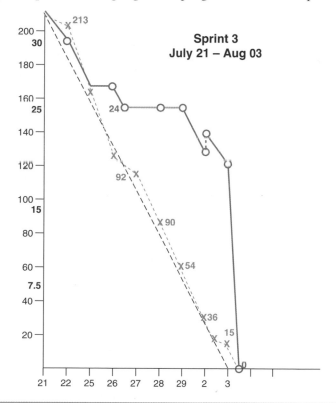

Figure 6-10 Example Sprint burn-down

Figure 6-10 shows a Sprint burn-down chart. The dashed line (with x's) represents the hours remaining from the Sprint Backlog. The solid line represents the story points remaining from the forecast.

Although the Sprint burn-down chart is not meant for you, the Product Owner, you should be able to see it to get a gauge on how the Sprint is going. But it is not your responsibility to act on it.

A Product Owner and their stakeholders are likely more interested in progress across Sprints. For that, you have release burn-downs or burn-ups.

Release Burn-down

From the *Scrum Guide*

At any point in time, the total work remaining to reach a goal can be summed. The Product Owner tracks this total work remaining at least every Sprint Review. The Product Owner compares this amount with work remaining at previous Sprint Reviews to assess progress toward completing projected work by the desired time for the goal. This information is made transparent to all stakeholders.

Various projective practices upon trending have been used to forecast progress, like burn-downs, burn-ups, or cumulative flows. These have proven useful. However, these do not replace the importance of empiricism. In complex environments, what will happen is unknown. Only what has already happened may be used for forward-looking decision making.[17]

The important words here are "work remaining." How much the team has worked is irrelevant; you should care only about how much work is remaining so that you can plan better. Your Development Team can work for 10 hours and discover 20 extra hours of work, or complete three Product Backlog items and discover five more, increasing the amount of work remaining. Regardless of what they did in the past, it does not change the fact that this new work still needs to get done. So you adapt the plan going forward.

---

17. Ibid., 16.

Burn-down charts are a great way to visualize work remaining. But feel free to use other charts as long as they provide visibility to the work remaining.

Building release burn-downs/burn-ups (see Figures 6-11 and 6-12) as a way to represent release plans will be covered in more detail in Chapter 8.

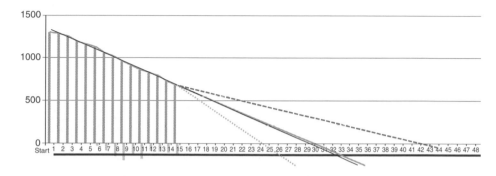

Figure 6-11 Release burn-down

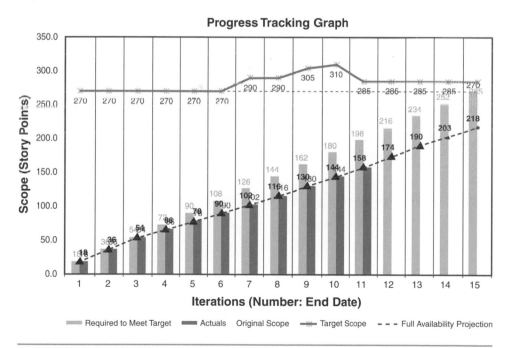

Figure 6-12 Release burn-up

SCRUM EVENTS

There are five mandatory events in Scrum: the Sprint, the Sprint Planning, the Daily Scrum, the Sprint Review, and the Sprint Retrospective.

In Scrum, each time-boxed event is designed to provide a specific inspect and adapt opportunity. In other words, there is always tangible input and always an explicit output for each event.

SPRINT

The Sprint is the container for all the other Scrum events. It is like a mini-project after which you have a working product—the Increment. The worst-case scenario is that you waste one Sprint. The shorter the Sprint, the smaller the risk.

From the *Scrum Guide*

The heart of Scrum is a Sprint, a time-box of one month or less during which a "Done," useable, and potentially releasable product Increment is created. Sprints have consistent durations throughout a development effort. A new Sprint starts immediately after the conclusion of the previous Sprint.

Sprints contain and consist of the Sprint Planning, Daily Scrums, the development work, the Sprint Review, and the Sprint Retrospective.

During the Sprint:

- No changes are made that would endanger the Sprint Goal;
- Quality goals do not decrease; and,
- Scope may be clarified and re-negotiated between the Product Owner and Development Team as more is learned.

Each Sprint may be considered a project with no more than a one-month horizon. Like projects, Sprints are used to accomplish something. Each Sprint has a goal of what is to be built, a design and flexible plan that will guide building it, the work, and the resultant product increment.

Sprints are limited to one calendar month. When a Sprint's horizon is too long the definition of what is being built may change, complexity may rise, and risk may increase. Sprints enable predictability by ensuring inspection and adaptation of progress toward a Sprint Goal at least every calendar month. Sprints also limit risk to one calendar month of cost.[18]

Product Owner and the Sprint

As Product Owner, the Sprint is the feedback loop with which you can inspect and adapt the direction of your product. Each Sprint must end with a working Increment that you can test with a sampling of stakeholders or, better yet, against the marketplace. Based on that feedback, you can have the Development Team work on anything you deem most valuable in the next Sprints. This provides you with the utmost flexibility.

Keep in mind, although you have the flexibility to change direction from Sprint to Sprint, you must avoid changing the scope of a current Sprint as much as possible. If the need for changing the Sprint scope is a recurring problem, consider shorter Sprints.

A Sprint provides stability in a world of unpredictability. The Scrum Team makes hard choices about requirements, infrastructure, and people. It tries to stick with those choices for at least one Sprint and then inspects and adapts for the next Sprint. Sprints that are too long could set you too far off course, increasing the cost of getting back on track.

The length of the Sprint should be determined by how much of this stable work a Scrum Team can (should) take on. This is the Product Owner's planning horizon.

---

18. Ibid., 9.

Realistically, there will be exceptions to keeping a Sprint stable. Consider the following scenario:

As Product Owner, an exciting new feature comes across your desk. Arguably, it is more valuable than any of the Product Backlog items that the Development Team is working on in the current Sprint. What do you do? You have three options.

1. The best response is to place the new feature on the top of your Product Backlog and not disrupt the current Sprint. If what is already in the Sprint still has value, then let the Development Team finish. Too often, they are interrupted with new work and do not get to finish what they have started. There are few things more inefficient than constant starting and stopping. Help your team to "stop starting and start finishing."

When I was a programmer on a Development Team, I used to get constant interruptions by managers and business people about new requests. My first question was always, "Is this more important than this thing I am currently working on?" The honest answer was often "Yes!" But this often meant that my work was consistently getting trumped by something else, which resulted in plenty of wasted effort and stress with no value to show for it. Today, I spend a lot of time coaching Product Owners and always make a point of telling them about my experience as a Development Team member so that they realize the overall impact of disrupting the Sprint.

I teach my Development Team to answer the following way every time someone outside of the Scrum Team approaches them with a small, but very important favor: "It sure is important, but this is not my decision to make. Please go and talk to my Product Owner." If the Product Owner does not handle the situation correctly, then it is up to the Scrum Master to protect the Development Team.

2. When the new feature request nullifies some of the Product Backlog items being worked on in the current Sprint, then the situation is different. There is no point in working on items that have no value. The obvious thing to do here is to go ahead and adjust the scope of the Sprint, without endangering the Sprint Goal. This will likely mean swapping out Product Backlog items.

3. The third option is that if you determine that the new feature replaces the need for *everything* in the current Sprint and voids the Sprint Goal, then this is where the Product Owner can consider canceling the entire Sprint. Since there is no point to continuing, stop the Sprint and immediately start planning a new Sprint. Given all the previous options, this should certainly not be a common activity.

From the *Scrum Guide*

A Sprint would be cancelled if the Sprint Goal becomes obsolete. This might occur if the company changes direction or if market or technology conditions change. In general, a Sprint should be cancelled if it no longer makes sense given the circumstances. But, due to the short duration of Sprints, cancellation rarely makes sense.[19]

SPRINT PLANNING

From the *Scrum Guide*

The work to be performed in the Sprint is planned at the Sprint Planning. This plan is created by the collaborative work of the entire Scrum Team.

Sprint Planning is time-boxed to a maximum of eight hours for a one-month Sprint. For shorter Sprints, the event is usually shorter. The Scrum Master ensures that the event takes place and that attendants understand its purpose. The Scrum Master teaches the Scrum Team to keep it within the time-box.

Sprint Planning answers the following:

• What can be delivered in the Increment resulting from the upcoming Sprint?

• How will the work needed to deliver the Increment be achieved?[20]

---

19. Ibid., 10.
20. Ibid.

Topic One: What Can Be Done This Sprint?

The Development Team works to forecast the functionality that will be developed during the Sprint. The Product Owner discusses the objective that the Sprint should achieve and the Product Backlog items that, if completed in the Sprint, would achieve the Sprint Goal. The entire Scrum Team collaborates on understanding the work of the Sprint.

The input to this meeting is the Product Backlog, the latest product Increment, projected capacity of the Development Team during the Sprint, and past performance of the Development Team. The number of items selected from the Product Backlog for the Sprint is solely up to the Development Team. Only the Development Team can assess what it can accomplish over the upcoming Sprint.

During Sprint Planning the Scrum Team also crafts a Sprint Goal. The Sprint Goal is an objective that will be met within the Sprint through the implementation of the Product Backlog, and it provides guidance to the Development Team on why it is building the Increment.

Topic Two: How Will the Chosen Work Get Done?

Having set the Sprint Goal and selected the Product Backlog items for the Sprint, the Development Team decides how it will build this functionality into a "Done" product Increment during the Sprint. The Product Backlog items selected for this Sprint plus the plan for delivering them is called the Sprint Backlog.

The Development Team usually starts by designing the system and the work needed to convert the Product Backlog into a working product Increment. Work may be of varying size, or estimated effort. However, enough work is planned during Sprint Planning for the Development Team to forecast what it believes it can do in the upcoming Sprint. Work planned for the first days of the Sprint by the Development Team is decomposed by the end of this meeting, often to units of one day or less. The Development Team self-organizes to undertake the work in the Sprint Backlog, both during Sprint Planning and as needed throughout the Sprint.

The Product Owner can help to clarify the selected Product Backlog items and make trade-offs. If the Development Team determines it has too much or too little work, it may renegotiate the selected Product Backlog items with the Product Owner. The Development Team may also invite other people to attend to provide technical or domain advice.

By the end of the Sprint Planning, the Development Team should be able to explain to the Product Owner and Scrum Master how it intends to work as a self-organizing team to accomplish the Sprint Goal and create the anticipated Increment.

Sprint Goal

The Sprint Goal is an objective set for the Sprint that can be met through the implementation of Product Backlog. It provides guidance to the Development Team on why it is building the Increment. It is created during the Sprint Planning meeting. The Sprint Goal gives the Development Team some flexibility regarding the functionality implemented within the Sprint. The selected Product Backlog items deliver one coherent function, which can be the Sprint Goal. The Sprint Goal can be any other coherence that causes the Development Team to work together rather than on separate initiatives.

As the Development Team works, it keeps the Sprint Goal in mind. In order to satisfy the Sprint Goal, it implements functionality and technology. If the work turns out to be different than the Development Team expected, they collaborate with the Product Owner to negotiate the scope of Sprint Backlog within the Sprint.[21]

Figure 6-13 outlines the flow of Sprint Planning.

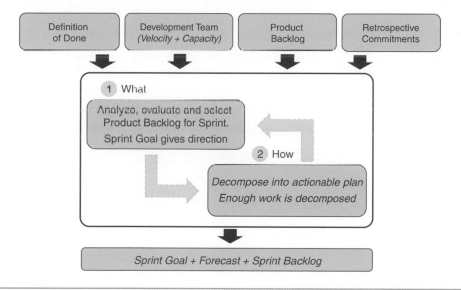

Figure 6-13 Flow of Sprint Planning

21. Ibid., 10–11.

Product Owner and Sprint Planning

In Sprint Planning, the Scrum Team comes up with a Sprint Goal, the supporting items out of the Product Backlog: the forecast (1. What), and the resulting work to be done for each of those items (2. How). All of this together is referred to as the Sprint Backlog: the plan for the current Sprint.

Let's look at two possible scenarios of Sprint Planning.

Scenario 1   You, as Product Owner, have created all the Product Backlog items for this Sprint. You spent a fair amount of time writing the Product Backlog items as user stories, coming up with acceptance criteria and even a few UI sketches. At Sprint Planning, the Development Team is pointed to this Product Backlog and asked to plan the Sprint.

Scenario 2   Before the upcoming Sprint, you as Product Owner—potentially during prior Product Backlog refinement—explain to the Development Team your next highest level goals. When you take a more narrative approach, the Development Teams gets a clearer understanding of what needs to be done. They get a chance to ask questions and solidify their understanding. Once they understand, they can help to create or refine the Product Backlog items (even on their own) until they feel the items are ready for the next Sprint. During the next Sprint Planning, you go through the top of the Product Backlog together and make any last-minute changes and answer any other questions.

Which scenario has a higher likelihood of being successful?

The first scenario is a handoff, with all its associated risks.

The good news is that you are only handing over a smaller portion of the product. But it is still a handoff. And like any handoff, it can cause ambiguity as the written word is never the best way to communicate complexity.

I once heard this great example: A mother leaves a note for her son: "We are running low on milk, could you go to the store around the corner and buy a gallon of milk and if they have eggs, get six." The son runs off to the store and when he returns, he puts six gallons of milk on the table and tells his mom, "Yes, they had eggs."

Ralph

Agile blends the business with engineering, which avoids the classic handoff problem in a phased linear development approach. As the first scenario above showed, even Scrum is not immune to this handoff problem. It is likely that some items turn out slightly different than anticipated, and often the answer from the Development Team is, "OK, but we did what was specified here, it is not our fault!" Back to finger pointing, blaming, and requesting more detailed requirements (CYA).[22]

The second scenario engages the Development Team from the beginning. They understand the purpose of why they are doing this. They take owner-ship of the functionality; it becomes theirs. If something is yours, you watch out for it, you take care of it, you want to make it a success.

As described previously, you as the Product Owner are motivating the Development Team by leveraging what is described in Dan Pink's book *Drive*:

$$\text{Autonomy} \rightarrow \text{Mastery} \rightarrow \text{Purpose}$$

Sprint Goal

Each Sprint Planning event must capture a shared Sprint Goal. A good Product Owner should enter Sprint Planning with a goal in mind. However, this should be open for negotiation with the Development Team based on their input, ability, and capacity. The resulting Sprint Goal is owned by the whole Scrum Team.

Your Sprint Goal should be considered as the elevator pitch for the Sprint. Imagine a stakeholder passes you in the hallway one day and says, "Looking

---

22. Cover Your @$$.

forward to the Sprint Review next week! What will I get to see?" How will you respond? Would you rattle off the nine Product Backlog items being worked on? Or would you give her a more concise summary of the most important element? If you find it hard to give an overall summary, it is likely a sign that there isn't much cohesion in your Sprint. In other words, the harder it is to come up with a good concise Sprint Goal, the more you probably need one.

This does not mean that you cannot have Product Backlog items in a Sprint that are unrelated to the Sprint Goal. Certainly, they could also work on an extra feature, report, or bug that a stakeholder has asked for. However, they should be in the minority and would likely be the items dropped from the Sprint when the Sprint Goal is at risk of not being met.

Think about the Sprint Goals as a linked list of objectives that are guiding you toward your overall product vision one step at time. Having homed in on your vision, you identify upcoming goals toward the grand goal (see Figure 6-14). The Sprint goals are not afterthoughts, but honing beacons. Figure 6-15 shows some examples of Sprint Goals.

I have seen great results using what I call the "Sprint Goal Driven Development" approach. Instead of "feeding" the Development Team with requirements for an upcoming Sprint, provide them with a Sprint Goal ahead of time and let them drive out the details, let them create the Product Backlog items, let them take ownership. You as Product Owner provide feedback and guidance during the refinement.

Ralph

Your Sprint Goal should never be a comma list of user stories (Product Backlog items) to be completed by the end of the Sprint.

I once saw the following Sprint Goal: "Our Sprint Goal is to reach the Sprint Goal." Please put in a better effort than this.

Ralph

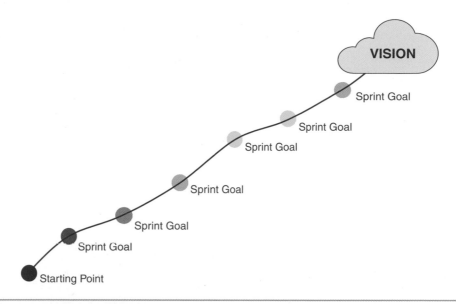

Figure 6-14 Sprint Goals lead to the Vision

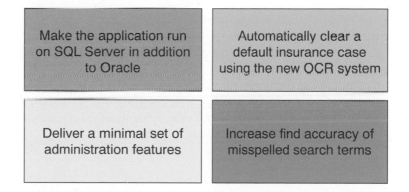

Figure 6-15 Example Sprint Goals

DAILY SCRUM

From the *Scrum Guide*

The Daily Scrum is a 15-minute time-boxed event for the Development Team. The Daily Scrum is held every day of the Sprint. At it, the Development Team plans work for the next 24 hours. This optimizes team collaboration and performance by inspecting the work since the last Daily Scrum and forecasting upcoming Sprint work. The Daily Scrum is held at the same time and place each day to reduce complexity.

The Development Team uses the Daily Scrum to inspect progress toward the Sprint Goal and to inspect how progress is trending toward completing the work in the Sprint Backlog. The Daily Scrum optimizes the probability that the Development Team will meet the Sprint Goal. Every day, the Development Team should understand how it intends to work together as a self-organizing team to accomplish the Sprint Goal and create the anticipated Increment by the end of the Sprint.

The structure of the meeting is set by the Development Team and can be conducted in different ways if it focuses on progress toward the Sprint Goal. Some Development Teams will use questions, some will be more discussion based. Here is an example of what might be used:

- What did I do yesterday that helped the Development Team meet the Sprint Goal?

- What will I do today to help the Development Team meet the Sprint Goal?

- Do I see any impediment that prevents me or the Development Team from meeting the Sprint Goal?

The Development Team or team members often meet immediately after the Daily Scrum for detailed discussions, or to adapt, or replan, the rest of the Sprint's work.

The Scrum Master ensures that the Development Team has the meeting, but the Development Team is responsible for conducting the Daily Scrum. The Scrum Master teaches the Development Team to keep the Daily Scrum within the 15-minute time-box.

> The Daily Scrum is an internal meeting for the Development Team. If others are present, the Scrum Master ensures that they do not disrupt the meeting.

Daily Scrums improve communications, eliminate other meetings, identify impediments to development for removal, highlight and promote quick decision making, and improve the Development Team's level of knowledge. This is a key inspect and adapt meeting.[23]

---

23. Schwaber and Sutherland, *Scrum Guide*, 12.

Product Owner and the Daily Scrum

The Daily Scrum is about the Development Team inspecting and adapting their Sprint Plan on a daily basis. As the Sprint Plan is owned by the Development Team, the Daily Scrum is not for you, the Product Owner. Therefore, this is not your opportunity to ask for a status update or to inform the Development Team on recent events. You are welcome to attend to show your engagement and to make yourself available afterward, but you do not participate during the Daily Scrum.

Having regular communication with the Development Team is still a great idea. Just do not hijack the Daily Scrum for this. Set something else up that works best for your particular situation.

I worked with a team that was complaining about the availability of their Product Owner, Irene. Irene was a VP who was committed to the product, but if we did not reserve her time weeks ahead, others filled up her calendar. Not knowing exactly how much time we would need from her each day made it hard to schedule anything. When this was brought up in a Sprint Retrospective, a team member came up with a great solution. Like in college, what if we scheduled "professor office hours" with the Product Owner? Irene could block one hour each day during which we could ask her questions and show her completed work. She responded with great enthusiasm to the idea and happily used any leftover minutes to catch up on e-mail and other tasks. This is a great example of process ownership and adaptation.

I once worked on internal software for researchers at a pharmaceutical company. Very interesting product in a very complex domain. Our Product Owner set aside two hours every week to provide us with a 101 into pharmaceutical research.

SPRINT REVIEW

From the *Scrum Guide*

A Sprint Review is held at the end of the Sprint to inspect the Increment and adapt the Product Backlog if needed. During the Sprint Review, the Scrum Team and stakeholders collaborate about what was done in the Sprint. Based on that and any changes to the Product Backlog during the Sprint, attendees collaborate on the next things that could be done to optimize value. This is an informal meeting, not a status meeting, and the presentation of the Increment is intended to elicit feedback and foster collaboration.

This is at most a four-hour meeting for one-month Sprints. For shorter Sprints, the event is usually shorter. The Scrum Master ensures that the event takes place and that attendees understand its purpose. The Scrum Master teaches everyone involved to keep it within the time-box.

The Sprint Review includes the following elements:

- Attendees include the Scrum Team and key stakeholders invited by the Product Owner;

- The Product Owner explains what Product Backlog items have been "Done" and what has not been "Done";

- The Development Team discusses what went well during the Sprint, what problems it ran into, and how those problems were solved;

- The Development Team demonstrates the work that it has "Done" and answers questions about the Increment;

- The Product Owner discusses the Product Backlog as it stands. He or she projects likely target and delivery dates based on progress to date (if needed);

- The entire group collaborates on what to do next, so that the Sprint Review provides valuable input to subsequent Sprint Planning;

- Review of how the marketplace or potential use of the product might have changed what is the most valuable thing to do next; and,

- Review of the timeline, budget, potential capabilities, and marketplace for the next anticipated releases of functionality or capability of the product.

The result of the Sprint Review is a revised Product Backlog that defines the probable Product Backlog items for the next Sprint. The Product Backlog may also be adjusted overall to meet new opportunities.[24]

---

24. Ibid., 13.

Product Owner and the Sprint Review

In many ways, the Sprint Review is the Product Owner's most valuable event. This is your opportunity to recalibrate your compass and adjust your path. This is not your opportunity to provide feedback and accept or reject the work done in the Sprint (although many suboptimal Sprint Reviews violate this guideline). You should be doing that during a Sprint and not even demonstrating any of the work you did not approve. The core objective of the Sprint Review is to get feedback from your stakeholders and, based on that feedback, update the Product Backlog (your future path).

I have a simple rule for the Sprint Review: No PowerPoint! So, what to show? How about real, working "Done" software?

Ralph

The stance you should take in the Sprint Review is more like a representative of the Scrum Team and host. You should kick it off by revisiting the product vision with everyone and sharing the Sprint Goal. Then let the audience know how the Sprint went with regards to the Sprint Goal. A common and useful next step is to invite members from the Development Team to demonstrate the "Done" work. This is a great opportunity to give stakeholders facetime with the Development Team, which builds trust, motivation, and ownership. While the Increment is being inspected, encourage feedback from stakeholders and make sure to capture it—hopefully directly in the Product Backlog. A good way to conclude the Sprint Review is to review the release plan with everyone. Given that a Sprint was just completed, this will provide new data from which to inspect and adapt the future path of the Product Backlog. Figure 6-16 shows an example agenda for a Sprint Review.

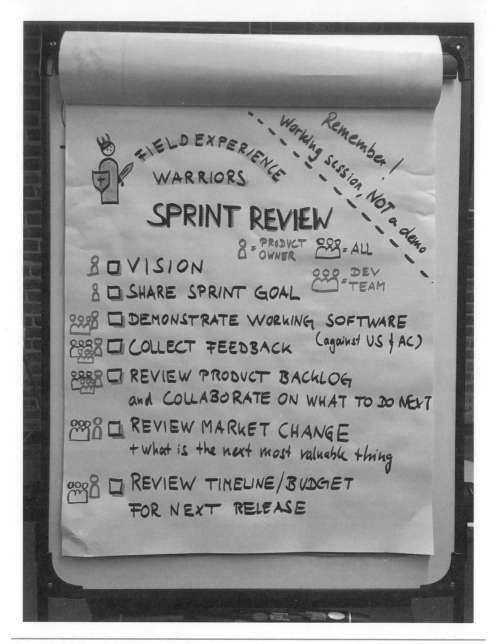

Figure 6-16 Sprint Review agenda[25]

---

25. Thanks to Ty Crockett.

SPRINT RETROSPECTIVE

From the *Scrum Guide*

The Sprint Retrospective is an opportunity for the Scrum Team to inspect itself and create a plan for improvements to be enacted during the next Sprint.

The Sprint Retrospective occurs after the Sprint Review and prior to the next Sprint Planning. This is at most a three-hour meeting for one-month Sprints. For shorter Sprints, the event is usually shorter. The Scrum Master ensures that the event takes place and that attendants understand its purpose.

The Scrum Master ensures that the meeting is positive and productive. The Scrum Master teaches all to keep it within the time-box. The Scrum Master participates as a peer team member in the meeting from the accountability over the Scrum process.

The purpose of the Sprint Retrospective is to:

- Inspect how the last Sprint went with regards to people, relationships, process, and tools;

- Identify and order the major items that went well and potential improvements; and,

- Create a plan for implementing improvements to the way the Scrum Team does its work.

The Scrum Master encourages the Scrum Team to improve, within the Scrum process framework, its development process and practices to make it more effective and enjoyable for the next Sprint. During each Sprint Retrospective, the Scrum Team plans ways to increase product quality by improving work processes or adapting the definition of "Done," if appropriate and not in conflict with product or organizational standards.

By the end of the Sprint Retrospective, the Scrum Team should have identified improvements that it will implement in the next Sprint. Implementing these improvements in the next Sprint is the adaptation to the inspection of the Scrum Team itself. Although improvements may be implemented at any time, the Sprint Retrospective provides a formal opportunity to focus on inspection and adaptation.[26]

---

26. Schwaber and Sutherland, *Scrum Guide*, 14.

Product Owner and the Sprint Retrospective

Notice that the *Scrum Guide* identifies the Sprint Retrospective as an opportunity for the "Scrum Team" to inspect and adapt themselves and their processes. That means you, the Product Owner, are also expected to participate and have input to the development process. Product Owners are too often left out of these crucial meetings, likely because they are not always seen as part of the team. If this sounds familiar, then you should set out to rectify it. Show that you are a team player by participating like an equal and being honest, open, and receptive.

Product Owners often find themselves in a position of authority. This could shut a Development Team down during a Retrospective. In other words, they may not be as outspoken with you around, which could reduce transparency. As Product Owner, make it your mission to bridge that gap. Participate in team-building activities, invite team members to stop by your office, ask them to text or call you about anything. Be a team player.

 Suboptimal Scrum implementations drop the Sprint Retrospective more often than any other Scrum event. However, I often refer to the Sprint Retrospective as the most important event. Imagine a team that had no process at all except for a weekly meeting to discuss how the week went and what they will do the following week to improve. Done correctly, the result of this will ultimately be an ideal set of practices, customized for that team. In other words, a process—fully owned by the team. So, the idea of dropping this event is somewhat absurd.

OTHER

Although not an official time-boxed event, another important activity in Scrum is Product Backlog refinement.

Product Backlog Refinement

After "Done," "Ready" is the next best thing. If you do not know what "Done" means, you will have a hard time finishing anything. If you are not "Ready," you will have a hard time starting anything. Refinement is about getting your Product Backlog "Ready" for upcoming Sprints. Refinement prepares the starting block for the Sprint, while "Done" sets the finish line.

> **Note**
>
> In 2013, the Scrum Guide renamed Product Backlog grooming to Product Backlog refinement. In certain parts of the world, the word "grooming" has a negative connotation.

Figure 6-17 is taken from "The New New Product Development Game," a popular *Harvard Business Review* article from 1986 by Hirotaka Takeuchi and Ikujiro Nonaka.[27]

> **Note**
>
> "The New New Product Development Game" is the paper that inspired Ken Schwaber and Jeff Sutherland to create Scrum. Takeuchi and Nonaka referred to this approach for developing new products as a "Rugby approach," which is constantly "moving the Scrum down the field."

EXHIBIT 1
Sequential (A) vs. overlapping (B and C) phases of development

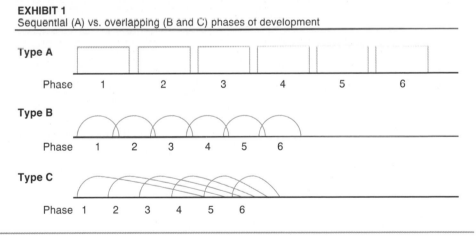

Figure 6-17 Sequential versus overlapping phases of development

---

27. Hirotaka Takeuchi and Ikujiro Nonaka, "The New New Product Development Game," 1986, *Harvard Business Review*, January 1986, https://hbr.org/1986/01/the-new-new-product-development-game.

In Figure 6-17, Type B describes how the phases overlap. If you replace classical project management phases with Scrum Sprints, the figure describes refinement. Type B shows refinement for one Sprint ahead.

The overlap from Sprint 1 to Sprint 2 and so on is the time in the current Sprint you invest to make the subsequent Sprint "Ready."

From the *Scrum Guide*

The *Scrum Guide* describes it in the following way:

> Product Backlog refinement is the act of adding detail, estimates, and order to items in the Product Backlog. This is an ongoing process in which the Product Owner and the Development Team collaborate on the details of Product Backlog items. During Product Backlog refinement, items are reviewed and revised. The Scrum Team decides how and when refinement is done. Refinement usually consumes no more than 10% of the capacity of the Development Team. However, Product Backlog items can be updated at any time by the Product Owner or at the Product Owner's discretion.[28]

What about Type C? Assume you have some future Product Backlog items that need more forethought before they are ready. Or maybe you need deeper User Experience design that could take some time before it is ready to be consumed by a Sprint. In these cases, you must look further ahead than just one Sprint. Type C shows refinement for multiple Sprints ahead.

I like to do one refinement per Sprint week. If you have a Sprint of two weeks, you would have two refinements. As scheduled time, I start with two hours at the end of the workday, usually from 3:00 p.m. to 5 p.m. That is 5 percent of the described 10 percent. Then I inspect and adapt if needed. Sometimes an ad hoc additional refinement is all that is needed, sometimes I extend the refinements or add another one. I've realized the required time for refinement does not jump a lot, but might change depending where you are within your release, especially if you have major releases.

Ralph

---

28. Schwaber and Sutherland, *Scrum Guide*, 15.

Done right, refinement provides you with a nice rolling Product Backlog (see Figure 6-18).

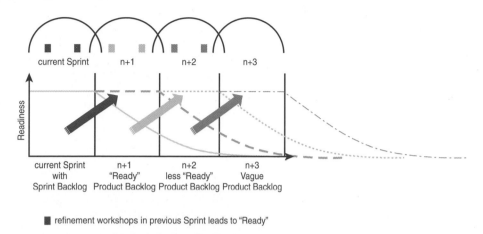

Figure 6-18 Conceptual refinement in a Sprint of two weeks in length

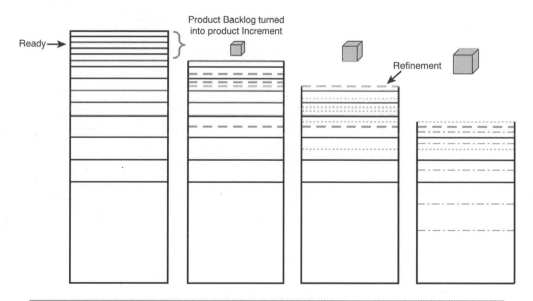

Figure 6-19 Emergent refinement of the Product Backlog

Velocity is the Development Team's capability to turn "Ready" Product Backlog into a "Done" product Increment and simultaneously refine the upcoming Product Backlog to be "Ready" for the subsequent Sprint (see Figure 6-19).

ITERATIVE AND INCREMENTAL

Incremental development is like playing with Legos. You build your product one brick at a time (see Figure 6-20). This approach makes a lot of sense if you know everything upfront—like all the APIs, each step of the flow, the screens, and so on. This is attainable when you are in a predictable and defined domain with a clear correlation between cause and effect. Since software product development resides in the complex domain, it usually doesn't work out exactly as planned.

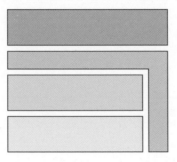

Figure 6-20 Incremental product development

Often an Increment is understood as just the addition to the existing product.

Merriam Webster's defines "increment" as "the action or process of increasing especially in quantity or value : enlargement." The word's origin is "from Latin, *incrementum*, from the stem of *increscere* 'grow.'"[29]

The Increment is the whole growing product, not just that little bit that was added since the last Sprint. The *Scrum Guide* also tells us that the Increment needs to be "Done" with no work remaining: that is, potentially releasable.

---

29. *Meriam Webster's*, s.v. "increment," accessed February 28, 2018, https://www.merriam-webster.com/dictionary/increment.

That also means that the former Increment still needs to be "Done" even though it might have been changed in the current Sprint. Maybe the Development Team had to extend an API with an additional field, to swap a library with a thread-safe one, to change some aspects of the architecture to accommodate the new features. Those changes are not a bad thing or a sign of being a bad engineer, but rather acknowledge the emergent complex nature of product development.

In the agile community, it is understood that quality is not something you can test into the product after you have completed implementation; it must be built into the product from day one. This raises a question: How can you ensure that existing quality is not disappearing? This is one of the fundamental challenges in iterative and incremental development.

It boils down to good engineering practices and a sound setup of continuous integration/delivery with strong test automation.

This gives you a product that is capable of self-testing, providing you with an "I am OK and fully functional" feedback after every single build. That way, the Increment can grow (see Figure 6-21) and increase value without degrading over time.

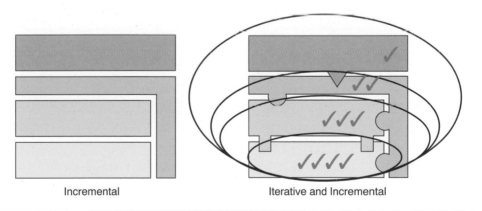

Incremental   Iterative and Incremental

Figure 6-21 Incremental versus iterative and incremental

I once worked with a team that developed a new service for a telecommunication company. I was fortunate that the developers on the Development Team were top notch and highly motivated. After the first major release, they had more than 10,000 unit tests and well above 600 integration tests. Their test coverage was around 95 percent. This coverage helped the future releases to go faster as the Scrum Team grew more confident in making changes to the code. They relied a lot more on machine feedback rather than error-prone human cycles.

Do not cut corners and sacrifice quality for speed. This only increases your technical debt, for which you have to pay dearly in the future. Your initial gain and more will be lost in the future when you struggle with existing implementation. Steve McConnell gets it right: "The problem with quick and dirty . . . is that dirty remains long after quick has been forgotten."[30]

AGILE MANIFESTO FOR SOFTWARE DEVELOPMENT

We are uncovering better ways of developing software
by doing it and helping others do it.
Through this work we have come to value:

Individuals and interactions over *processes and tools*
Working software over *comprehensive documentation*
Customer collaboration over *contract negotiation*
Responding to change over *following a plan*

That is, while there is value in the items on the right [in *italics*],
we value the items on the left [in **bold**] more.[31]

---

30. Steve C. McConnell, *Software Project Survival Guide* (Redmond, WA: Microsoft Press, 1998).

31. Kent Beck, Mike Beedle, Arie van Bennekum, Alistair Cockburn, Ward Cunningham, Martin Fowler, James Grenning, Jim Highsmith, Andrew Hunt, Ron Jeffries, Jon Kern, Brian Marick, Robert C. Martin, Steve Mellor, Ken Schwaber, Jeff Sutherland, and Dave Thomas, "Manifesto for Agile Software Development" (2001), http://agilemanifesto.org/.

The Agile Manifesto for Software Development was created in early 2001 and has been revisited multiple times since, without any resulting changes as it was still considered relevant. It was created by 17 leaders from the software industry, including the creators of Scrum, Ken Schwaber and Jeff Sutherland. It represents the underlying values and principles of good software development. Until the Agile Manifesto, agile software development was not called "agile." Until then it was usually referred to as light-weight.

At Agile 2008 in Toronto, Uncle Bob (Robert Martin) suggested in his keynote the addition of a fifth value:

Craftsmanship over *crap*

However, he realized that it doesn't fit the pattern of preferring the left-hand side over the right-hand side:

> The problem with my proposal is that it is not a balanced value statement. In the other four statements we value the second item. We just value the first item more. But in my proposed addition, we simply do not value crap at all.
>
> So I hereby change my original proposal, which was made for dramatic effect, to:
>
> **Craftsmanship** over *execution*
>
> Most software development teams execute, but they do not take care.
>
> We value execution, but we value craftsmanship more.[32]

In the end, it is all about creating the right product with the right quality.

---

32. Mike Bria, "Craftsmanship—The Fifth Agile Manifesto Value?," *InfoQ*, August 20, 2008, https://www.infoq.com/news/2008/08/manifesto-fifth-craftsmanship.

QUIZ REVIEW

Compare your answers from the beginning of the chapter to the ones below. Now that you have read the chapter, would you change any of your answers? Do you agree with the answers below?

Statement	Agree	Disagree
Scrum is an agile process.	☐	✔
Scrum Teams do very little planning.	☐	✔
If a Scrum Team changes the Scrum framework, they are no longer doing Scrum.	✔	☐
If a Scrum Team adds to the Scrum framework, they are no longer doing Scrum.	☐	✔
Every Scrum event is time-boxed.	✔	☐
The development process is owned by the Development Team. The Product Owner does not have a say.	☐	✔

III

TACTICS

7

PRODUCT BACKLOG MANAGEMENT

QUIZ

To set the stage for this chapter, try answering each of the following statements with Agree or Disagree. Answers appear at the end of the chapter.

Statement	Agree	Disagree
The Product Backlog replaces the need for any other requirement documents.	☐	☐
Agile requirements must be no more than a few sentences.	☐	☐
User story is synonymous with Product Backlog item.	☐	☐
Defects should not be in the Product Backlog because they are triaged by the Development Team.	☐	☐
The Development Team should not allow any Product Backlog items into the Sprint unless they meet a definition of "Ready."	☐	☐
A Product Backlog can be made up of tests.	☐	☐

WHAT IS A REQUIREMENT?

According to *Merriam-Webster*, a requirement is:

> a : something wanted or needed : NECESSITY
>
> b : something essential to the existence or occurrence of something else : CONDITION.[1]

A requirement is not a document. It exists whether it has been captured or not. It may not even be known yet. This adds to the complexity of developing a software product. The best you can do is to keep inspecting and adapting in an empirical way.

All requirements fall into one of these categories:

1. How/why someone uses the system = Functional
2. How the system should behave = Nonfunctional (stability, usability, performance, etc.)
3. The rules that surround the existing business domain (e.g., formulas, processes, laws, etc.)

The level of detail needed depends on your goal (see Figure 7-1). Is there value in the requirement itself? Or are you simply concerned with not forgetting something?

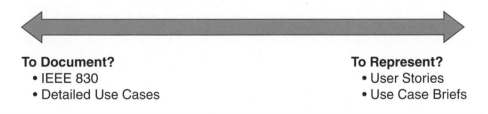

To Document?
- IEEE 830
- Detailed Use Cases

To Represent?
- User Stories
- Use Case Briefs

Figure 7-1 What is your goal for documenting requirements?

---

1. *Merriam-Webster Collegiate Dictionary*, 10th edition.

In some situations, the requirement document may have value to the business. If lives are on the line, you may need to specify more detail. Fixed price vendor contracts may need more documentation.

However, the reality of the vast majority of product development work today is that more value comes in *representing* stakeholder needs (or what they think they need) than in capturing detail.

Rather than worrying about requirements ambiguity and documentation, which in itself could be quite wasteful, strive to represent, or tag, the functionality.

Instead, consider creating a big *to-do list* for the product where the intent is not to capture detail; the intent is to not forget to ask all the right questions, either upfront or somewhere down the road.

Think about it: How much detail do you put into your personal to-do lists? Each to-do list item is nothing more than a reminder to get something done.

The details will be captured along the way, while you strive to better understand the underlying customer need, as acceptance criteria, tests, diagrams, conversations, and so on.

In Scrum, the Product Owner's "to-do list" is the Product Backlog.

PRODUCT BACKLOG

From the *Scrum Guide*

The Product Backlog is an ordered list of everything that is known to be needed in the product. It is the single source of requirements for any changes to be made to the product. The Product Owner is responsible for the Product Backlog, including its content, availability, and ordering.[2]

So what exactly do you put into a Product Backlog?

---

2. Ken Schwaber and Jeff Sutherland, *The Scrum Guide* (November 2017), 15.

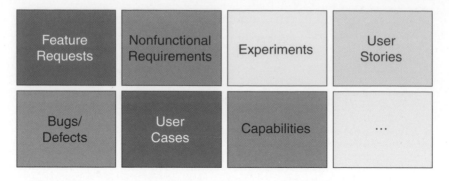

Figure 7-2 Valid Product Backlog items

As Figure 7-2 shows, the Product Backlog is open to all types of work:

- **Feature Requests:** Any request from a stakeholder (e.g., "I want admin access." "I want to be able to sort this list.")
- **Nonfunctional Requirements:** Qualities of the system (e.g., Performance, Scalable to 2,000 concurrent users, Legal Terms & Conditions)
- **Experiments:** Functionality that is released to production to test the marketplace (e.g., New UI, User Survey, Analytics); also, experiments can be "enabling constraints," as described in Chapter 5
- **User Stories:** Placeholders for conversations; popular in the agile community
- **Bugs/Defects:** Problems that have arisen from a previous release
- **Use Cases:** List of actions between an actor and a system (not as common these days)
- **Capabilities:** Different ways or channels to access existing functionality (e.g., mobile, web, cloud services, public API)

As a framework, Scrum does not prescribe any real method or template for Product Backlog items. However, the vast majority of Scrum Teams populate their Product Backlogs with user stories.

USER STORIES

Before user stories, requirement-capturing techniques were seen as a communication channel with the intent to gather as much information as possible.

A common approach to capturing requirements was use cases. Use cases were originally developed and used by Ivar Jacobson in 1986. They became popular in the 1990s by practitioners of the Unified Process (UP) and Unified Modelling Language (UML). Use cases break requirements into more manageable pieces (scenarios) and describe a specific behavior from the context of an actor working with a system. They also provide a mechanism to get into a lot of detail, which if you aren't careful can generate unnecessary documentation and actually reduce communication. The creation of a single use case could occupy a team for months before it is handed over for development.

Admittedly, use cases were never meant to be exhaustive documents. They were meant to be built iteratively as development was happening. However, too many organizations were writing tedious use cases that added little or no value and resulted in a lot of rework.

In an effort to fight back against the amount of unnecessary detail in use cases, user stories were introduced by the Extreme Programming community in the 1990s, with the intent to "force" brevity and create purposeful ambiguity. The idea is that this ambiguity would result in more face-to-face communication.

I often get asked what the difference is between a use case and a user story? The way I see it, a user story describes one flow through a use case. A use case often has a happy path, a couple of alternative or error paths, and a few exceptional paths. Often I see value in implementing the happy path first to validate the underlying assumption. Once we implement the first complete scenario and have received feedback that we are on the right track, we can then go ahead and implement the other paths.

Ralph

User stories are best explained with the Three Cs:[3]

- **Card:** Legend has it that when approached by eager entrepreneurs looking for an investor, Andrew Carnegie's standard response was to ask them to write their ideas on the back of their business cards. If he liked it, he would call them back. Given this opportunity, what do you suppose they would focus on?

  One would imagine they would be desperately trying to communicate value and make it interesting enough for a follow-up conversation.

  This same principle applies to user stories, which are commonly captured using a 3" × 5" card and a felt-tip marker. They are not the requirements. They are instead a tag that represents value to the business and a promise of a future conversation, the second C.

- **Conversation:** Teams often say that the area that needs the most improvement is communication. By being purposefully ambiguous and intriguing, user stories are designed to increase conversations. This can be tremendously freeing when creating Product Backlogs and when new requirements arise. It allows you to not stress about the details right away and instead quickly jot something down as a placeholder for a future conversation, at which point you will fill in the details. The details are captured as the final C.

- **Confirmation:** Rather than endlessly repeating the same conversations, agile teams capture details of a user story just in time. This detail is typically captured as acceptance criteria before a team takes on the story. Acceptance criteria is what the Product Owner, representing the stakeholders, deems as necessary to consider the story accepted.

  A good rule is to limit the acceptance criteria to the back of the user story card. If more room is needed, the story may need to be broken into smaller stories.

A popular and simple template for user stories, first used by Connextra and popularized by Mike Cohn in *User Stories Applied*,[4] is shown in Figure 7-3.

---

3. Ron Jeffries, "Essential XP: Card, Conversation, Confirmation," RonJeffries.com, August 30, 2001, http://ronjeffries.com/xprog/articles/expcardconversationconfirmation/.

4. Mike Cohn, *User Stories Applied* (Boston: Addison-Wesley, 2004), 135.

As a	<role/persona>
I want	<behavior>
so that	<the value>

Figure 7-3 Popular user story template

- **As a** *<role/persona> (who?)*: The focus is on a stakeholder, not just a user. Keep in mind that not all value is directed at a user of the system. For example, a company's lawyer would see the value in a "terms and conditions" user story, whereas it could be a distraction for an actual user. Try to identify specific roles from the business domain and avoid using generic roles like "user" or technical roles like "Product Owner," "Scrum Master," or "Developer."

I once saw a t-shirt at a conference that read something like this: "There are only two kinds of businesses on earth who call their users "user": software and illegal drugs."

- **I want** *<behavior> (what?)*: This is a business-oriented workflow or action that describes the requested feature. You should avoid technical actions, such as "I want to create a database" or "I want to refactor that nasty piece of code." These technical actions are solution oriented and should be done instead as part of a separate, more business-oriented user story.
- **So that** *<the value>) (why?)*: This is a crucial, yet often forgotten, part of a user story. The better you can communicate the reason for the requested functionality, the better decisions and assumptions will be made by all involved. If this seems challenging to create, then it may be telling you something about the validity of the user story.

Figure 7-4 provides an example.

As a	blog reader
I want	to comment on a blog entry
so that	I can contribute to the conversation

Figure 7-4 Example user story

INVEST is a useful mnemonic established by Bill Wake in *Extreme Programming Explored*.[5] It can be used to inspect the quality of your user story by validating it against each of the following (in Bill Wake's words):

- Independent

  Independent stories are the easiest to work with. That is, we'd like them to not overlap in concept, and we'd like to be able to schedule and implement them in any order.

  You can't always achieve this; once in a while we may say things like "3 points for the first report, then 1 point for each of the others."

- Negotiable . . . and Negotiated

  A good story is negotiable. It is not an explicit contract for features; rather, details will be co-created by the customer and programmer during development. A good story captures the essence, not the details. Over time, the card may acquire notes, test ideas, and so on, but we do not need these to prioritize or schedule stories.

- Valuable

  A story needs to be valuable. We do not care about value to just anybody; it needs to be valuable to the customer. Developers may have (legitimate) concerns, but these should be framed in a way that makes the customer perceive them as important.

- Estimable

  A good story can be estimated. We do not need an exact estimate, but just enough to help the customer rank and schedule the story's implementation. Being estimable is partly a function of being negotiated, as it's hard to

---

5. William C. Wake, *Extreme Programming Explored* (Boston: Addison-Wesley, 2002).

estimate a story we do not understand. It is also a function of size: Bigger stories are harder to estimate. Finally, it's a function of the team: what's easy to estimate will vary depending on the team's experience.

- Small

  Good stories tend to be small. Stories typically represent at most a few person-weeks' worth of work. (Some teams restrict them to a few person-days of work.) Above this size, it seems to be too hard to know what's in the story's scope. Saying, "it would take me more than month" often implicitly adds, "as I do not understand what-all it would entail." Smaller stories tend to get more accurate estimates.

- Testable

  A good story is testable. Writing a story card carries an implicit promise: "I understand what I want well enough that I could write a test for it." Several teams have reported that by requiring customer tests before implementing a story, the team is more productive. "Testability" has always been a characteristic of good requirements; actually writing the tests early helps us know whether this goal is met.

Another well-known acronym is DEEP[6]:

- **Detailed Enough**—acceptance criteria to get started
- **Emergent**—The Product Backlog is never "complete", it is refined over time
- **Estimated Relatively**—sized in terms of effort
- **Prioritized Ordered**—by value, risk, cost, dependencies, etc.

NONFUNCTIONAL REQUIREMENTS

Requirements that fall into any of the following categories are considered nonfunctional:

- Usability
- Scalability

---

6. Mike Cohn, "Make the Product Backlog DEEP," *Mountain Goat Software* (blog), December 14, 2009, https://www.mountaingoatsoftware.com/blog/make-the-product-backlog-deep

- Portability
- Maintainability
- Availability
- Accessibility
- Supportability
- Security
- Performance
- Cost
- Legal and Compliance
- Cultural

That is, they exist because of the fact that a system exists, as opposed to functional requirements, which may exist whether or not you have a system. For example, the need for depositing money into a bank account exists in the client banking business domain whether or not an ATM exists. But having an ATM introduces new nonfunctional requirements around security, accessibility, and usability.

In other words, functional requirements describe what the system should *do*, whereas nonfunctional requirements describe what the system should *be*.

Highlighting these nonfunctional concerns is important as they drive many key architectural decisions.

How do you capture nonfunctional requirements?

Capture your nonfunctional requirements in one of the following three ways:

1. **As a Product Backlog item**

   As nonfunctional requirements do have direct value to the business, it is perfectly acceptable to capture them on the Product Backlog, possibly even as user stories as represented in Figure 7-5.

```
As a                          blind person

I want                        audible prompts

so that   I can use the ATM by myself
```

Figure 7-5 Nonfunctional requirement as user story

2. **As acceptance criteria**

   Another option for nonfunctional requirements is to capture them as acceptance criteria for a particular Product Backlog item. That way, the nonfunctional requirement is completed as part of a larger functional item and may affect the effort needed to complete it.

   For example, a functional "Login" Product Backlog item, could have the following nonfunctional acceptance criteria:

   - *Login happens within two seconds.*
   - *Password is masked.*

3. **As part of the definition of "Done"**

   If the same nonfunctional acceptance criteria seem to apply across most of your Product Backlog items then consider anchoring it in the definition of "Done" as they are omnipresent.

   For example:

   - *All pages must load within three seconds.*
   - *Content must appear in both English and German.*

I like to put the nonfunctional requirements (listed as NFR) on a separate document or, even better, on the wall to be present and visible at all times. We label each NFR with a letter of the alphabet. Then as we refine and have conversations about the Product Backlog items, we can refer to the list of NFRs and include the labels as acceptance criteria (see Figure 7-6). When estimating each Product Backlog item, we can consider the additional NFR effort in our estimate. If any NFRs are added or removed, we would likely need to reestimate the item.

Ralph

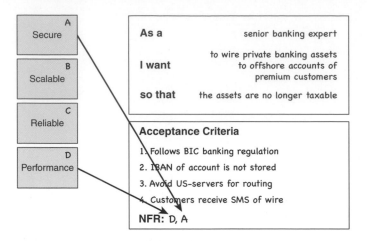

A Secure	**As a** senior banking expert
B Scalable	**I want** to wire private banking assets to offshore accounts of premium customers
C Reliable	**so that** the assets are no longer taxable
D Performance	

Acceptance Criteria

1. Follows BIC banking regulation
2. IBAN of account is not stored
3. Avoid US-servers for routing
4. Customers receive SMS of wire

NFR: D, A

Figure 7-6 Example of tying nonfunctional requirements to Product Backlog items

EPICS

Stories that are too large to implement in one Sprint are commonly referred to as epics (long stories). Having epics in your Product Backlog is not necessarily a bad thing. In fact, epics are often a crucial building block in a wide-reaching Product Backlog. However, at some point, you need to split the epic into more manageable stories.

> *I personally do not care whether you call them epics, stories, or doohickeys. I just see them as Product Backlog items of various sizes. If a Product Backlog item cannot be turned into "Done" by the end of the Sprint, it is too large. Refine it, until it is the right size.*

How large is too large?

One fairly widespread rule in the agile community is that if a story—a Product Backlog item—cannot be completed within one Sprint, then it is an epic. However, having just one big story in a Sprint is problematic: The success of the Sprint now hinges on the completion of that single story, so you put a lot more at risk. The other inevitable result is that all the testing for the story (and for the whole Sprint) will happen at the end of the Sprint. This unbalance of focus areas can create a lot of churn within the Development Team, making it more impossible to produce a bug-free "Done" increment within the Sprint.

So what can you do?

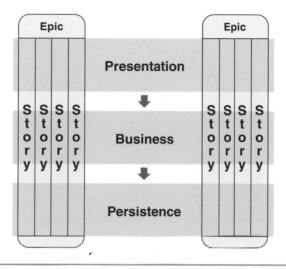

Figure 7-7 Epics broken down by story across architectural layers

Well, you break it down some more. A good number is to have between 6 and 12 Product Backlog items in the forecast for the Sprint. This also means that shorter Sprints will have smaller Product Backlog items. For a two-week Sprint, this means that every couple of days a Product Backlog item should be "Done," which helps spread testing throughout the Sprint. Development Teams that can achieve this will realize that they should actually release within the Sprint instead of delaying value until the end.

How do you split a story?

This can be a challenge for many teams. Remember, Product Backlog items should be valuable to the customer, which means each story slice has to still demonstrate some value, however small. For this reason, stories that are broken down by technology component (UI, Database, etc.) are considered invalid (see Figure 7-7).

The best place to start is with the acceptance criteria. You will learn more about how to write acceptance criteria later, but for now all you need to know is that they are the conditions of satisfaction for the stakeholders, not just the user.

A Development Team along with the Product Owner should ask: "What are we going to demonstrate to prove this story is complete?"

The resulting answer should be a concrete list of items that the stakeholders deem valuable (see Figure 7-8). Therefore, each and every one can then be translated into its own separate story.

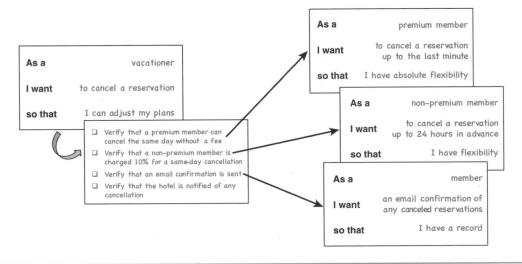

Figure 7-8 Simple example of breaking user stories down from acceptance criteria

I often get pushback from Scrum Teams that are just starting out. They insist that the story is way too complex to be broken down. Instead of pushing back too strongly, I've started instead to ask them about the acceptance criteria for the epic story. In no time at all, they rattle off a dozen different things that are important to the stakeholders and therefore have supplied a dozen different ways to break down the epic.

When do you break down epics?

Remember the Three Cs of user stories? The purpose of the card is to have a conversation. Epics that are far down in the Product Backlog are likely not being talked about too much. As the epics move further up the Product Backlog, more conversations happen about them and are captured as acceptance criteria on the back of the card. Once that card starts to fill up with acceptance criteria—a sign that an epic is getting closer to the top of the Product Backlog—you break it down. This could likely happen during refinement or even Sprint Planning.

Let's take a closer look at acceptance criteria.

ACCEPTANCE CRITERIA

Acceptance criteria define what the customer will see to approve the work as being complete. They can be written as test cases or something less detailed. Although acceptance criteria are owned by the Product Owner, it is crucial to involve the whole Scrum Team (and even some stakeholders) when defining them.

I never actually write acceptance criteria on the back of a physical card. It is far from practical as you keep turning the card over and over again. However, the mindset remains. I like to find a way to limit the number of acceptance criteria, either by number of items or amount of text. In Figure 7-9, you can see an example of a template that limits the number of acceptance criteria (to nine). One of my biggest issues with agile management software tools is that it does not limit the amount of text (space-boxing) for user story descriptions and acceptance criteria.

Product Backlog Item

Product Name:	AMP
User Story Name:	Renewal Notification
User Story Description:	As a sales manager I want to be notified by email of expiring contracts so that customers are not without coverage and we are not missing out on revenue.

Release:	1		Sprint:	1

Notification email sent to all Account Executives (AE) on the 15th and 30th of every month containing a summary* of all expiring contracts. • Summary email content outlined in <u>analysis doc</u>	Tested YES Accepted
AE summary email contains a clickable URL to AMP, which displays all expiring contracts (see Query User Story) for that AE.	Tested YES Accepted
Once a month, Account Sales Manager (ASM) receives an escalation email* containing all their team's contracts expiring within 60 days. • 60-day Escalation email content outlines in <u>analysis doc</u>	Tested YES Accepted
60-day Escalation email contains a clickable URL to AMP, which displays all Expiring Contracts for the ASM's team.	Tested YES Accepted
Once a month, ASM and VP receive an escalation email* containing all their region's contracts expiring within 30 days. • 30-day Escalation email content outlines in <u>analysis doc</u>	Tested YES Accepted
30-day Escalation email contains a clickable URL to AMP, which displays all Expiring Contracts for the VP's region or the ASM's team.	Tested YES Accepted
	Tested Accepted
	Tested Accepted
	Tested Accepted

Approved for Release:	YES		Date:	Jun 26, 2017	

Figure 7-9 Example of Product Backlog item with acceptance criteria

Here are three common ways of writing acceptance criteria:

Test That . . .

Start each acceptance criteria with the words "Test that . . ." This gets people into a testing mindset right off the bat. For each Product Backlog item, what will be tested to ensure the item is "Done"?

Demonstrate That . . .

Start each acceptance criteria with the words "Demonstrate that . . ." This gets people thinking about the Sprint Review and what they would want to show to stakeholders that demonstrates value. In a way, the Scrum Team is writing the script for the Sprint Review. You can hand out a list of acceptance criteria in the Sprint Review and go through them one by one. An example of this is in Figure 7-9, where we added "Demonstrate that . . ." to the acceptance criteria section.

Given, When, Then (Gherkin syntax)

Gherkin syntax serves two purposes—documentation and automated tests. The grammar is readable by anyone, yet it is also parsable by test automation tools, like Cucumber.[7]

Given	<a *precondition*>
When	<a *user action occurs*>
Then	<an *expected result*>

Good acceptance criteria should be SMART and SAFE:[8]

- **SMART**
  - **Specific**—what is the outcome?
  - **Measurable**—how can the outcome be measured?
  - **Attainable**—is it attainable with the current setup (skills, technology, etc.)?

---

7. Cucumber Ltd.'s homepage, accessed March 1, 2018, http://cucumber.io.
8. This acronym was first defined by Jef Newsom, one of the founders of Improving Enterprises.

- **Relevant**—is it aligned with the objective?
- **Time-Bound**—at which point in time can the outcome be measured?

- **SAFE**
  - **Success**—what is the success criteria for the Product Backlog item?
    For example, an ATM user receives a receipt of the transaction.
  - **Advance**—what has to happen before the success outcome can be reached?
    For example, an ATM user accepts the terms and conditions.
  - **Failure**—what could go wrong, and how can you cope with it?
    For example, an ATM user does not have enough money in his account—prompt for another amount.
  - **Error**—what are the error situations that are out of our control?
    For example, there isn't enough cash in the ATM machine—display "out of service" message.

Spikes

Every once in a while, usually in early Sprints, a Scrum Team will encounter a Product Backlog item that they cannot break down any further. This is typically because the team does not yet know enough about the technology or domain.

A *spike* is a research Product Backlog item whose goal is to learn more about what is needed to complete the requested functionality.

Spikes are typically very simple proof of concepts that are likely to be thrown away after they have served their purpose. The ultimate goal of a spike is to reduce risk through experimentation, allowing us to make better product decisions sooner.

> ## Caution
>
> The danger with spikes is that they may, like anything, become abused. Every Sprint ends up with a spike story, and before long teams start planning whole spike Sprints. As spikes do not produce any immediate value to the business, this is a slippery slope. Use them, but do not abuse them.
>
> *Good reason for a spike:* Download and install a candidate third-party API to see if it meets our performance needs. This would allow the Scrum Team to decide whether to attempt the feature or not.
>
> *Poorer reason for a spike:* Research a feature so that the Development Team can feel more confident with their estimates. This is likely more about fear of failure than experimentation and does not necessarily help the Scrum Team make decisions.

I have seen a waterfall approach hidden behind "analyze," "design," "implement," and "test" Product Backlog items instead of actual functionality being "Done" at the end of the Sprint.

Ralph

A preferred approach is to both research and implement the Product Backlog item in the same Sprint. If both cannot be completed within the Sprint, then the whole Product Backlog item goes back on the Product Backlog, and the Development Team completes it in a future Sprint. The team is no worse off than if they had preemptively separated the story into different Sprints.

It is worth repeating that this focus on completing valuable quality increments every single Sprint is essential to the agility of Scrum Teams and the business as a whole. Each Sprint results in an Increment, which from the stakeholders' point of view is "Done."

PRODUCT BACKLOG ORDERING

The 2011 *Scrum Guide*'s description of Product Backlogs replaces the word "prioritize" with "order." The reason for this was that "priority" was too often equated with business value and categorizations such as High, Medium, Low, or MoSCoW[9] (Must, Should, Could, Won't).

The last time I reviewed a company's "H-M-L prioritized" Product Backlog, I did a count of the categories. Eighty percent of them were High, 10 percent Medium, 10 percent Low. Rather than spend a lot of wasted effort prioritizing a long list in this manner, it is much simpler to just acknowledge that they are all important to the business and ask, "Which do we want to do first?"

While business priority is important, it is not the only variable that affects the order in which you pull things off the Product Backlog.

To properly order your Product Backlog, you need to consider many aspects:

- **Business Value**

  The value created from implementing the feature: revenue, cost saving, customer retention, prospect customers, and future opportunity. Features that map closest to the product vision likely rank highest here.
  Example: A "make payment" feature that generates direct revenue

- **Risk**

  The importance of a Product Backlog item in terms of exposure to a harmful situation. This includes both business and technical risk. The higher the risk, the higher it should be in the Product Backlog.
  Business risk example: A feature that must be implemented before a regulatory deadline
  Technical risk example: Implementing new technology on which a feature depends without knowing whether the technology solution will even work

- **Cost/Size**

  The cost of implementing a feature. This is mostly (but not exclusively) associated with the effort and time that the Development Team needs to build it.

---

9. "The DSDM Agile Project Framework (2014 Onwards)," chap. 10, Agile Business Consortium, accessed March 15, 2018, https://www.agilebusiness.org/content/moscow-prioritisation.

- **Dependency**

  Regardless of value, risk, and cost/size, sometimes a feature cannot be done before another. These can be both business and organizational dependencies.
  Business example: An authentication feature that must be completed before anyone can use the more valuable features
  Organizational example: A feature that depends on another downstream team creating a service for your team to use

As you can see, many forces are at play. Consider the following formula:

$$\textbf{(Business Value + Risk) / Size = Order Rank}$$

By finding a way to enumerate each of these variables, you can create an order ranking system in which the higher the number, the higher the item will be in the Product Backlog (see Figure 7-10). Then make adjustments based on identified dependencies.

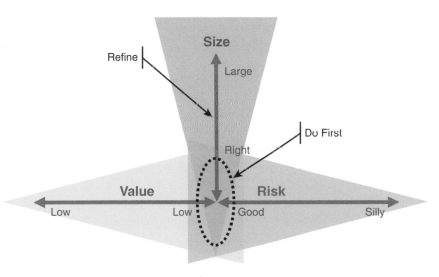

Figure 7-10 Value, risk, and size (cost) as dimensions for Product Backlog ordering

By focusing on smaller valuable features, you risk that the large yet valuable items get ignored. As these are likely the more strategic initiatives, identifying them and breaking them into smaller (right-sized) deliverables becomes an important part of refining the Product Backlog.

My family wants to renovate our kitchen. But because it is such a daunting task, we keep putting it off. It is important and strategic, but is just not getting done. The solution? Break it down into smaller tasks. Could we start with getting some people in to provide suggestions and cost estimates? That would get the ball rolling, and if we determine that the costs and risks are manageable, we will commit to the new kitchen and start to break it down into smaller tasks. Before you know it, we will have a new kitchen. Maybe.

Items that are low value, low risk, yet cost very little (left side of Figure 7-10) should not necessarily be ignored either. Consider these as "fun-sized" and work on them if there is extra capacity or they can be taken by newer Development Team members who are still getting comfortable working with the product. Some organizations even open-source these items to other groups within the organization or even to the public.

Obviously, the risky items that have little value (the right side of Figure 7-10) should be ignored.

This formulaic approach to ordering could be a good start. Just do not consider it a magic formula to which you are bound. Ordering the Product Backlog is more of a nondeterministic problem. You shouldn't strive for the best answer as it likely does not exist. Aim for a good answer and trust the empirical process of inspecting and adapting. A good Product Owner, with help from the Development Team, can use intuition and experience to order the Product Backlog just as effectively.

With this in mind, spending a lot of time ordering the bottom half of the Product Backlog can be considered somewhat wasteful. Focus instead on the order for the next few Sprints. Since you are refining as you go, the rest will work itself out.

Ordering the Product Backlog will open up many important conversations within your Scrum Team (and with stakeholders) that will clarify assumptions, misconceptions, and dependencies and thereby reduce accidental complexity. This process itself generates lots of value.

MEASURING VALUE, RISK, AND SIZE

In the previous section, this formula to consider when ordering your Product Backlog was introduced:

$$(\text{Business Value} + \text{Risk}) / \text{Size} = \text{Order Rank}$$

This formula may seem straightforward, but where do the numbers come from?

Value

If you can determine the monetary value amount of the Product Backlog item (e.g., this feature will make $300,000), then that would be ideal. However, it is rarely that easy.

Other approaches use somewhat arbitrary numbers to indicate value, much like with relative effort sizing. The number range does not matter as much as getting stakeholders engaged and using the wisdom of the crowd. There are plenty of facilitation techniques for this, such as:

- **Business Value Game**[10]

  Use planning poker to estimate value instead of size

- **Buy-a-Feature**[11]

  Innovation Game using money to purchase features

- **20/20 Vision**[12]

  Innovation Game for simple ordering of a Product Backlog

- **Thirty-Five**[13]

  Collaboration activity for ordering

10. "Business Value Game," agile42, accessed March 1, 2018, http://www.agile42.com/en/agile-coaching-company/agile-scrum-tools/business-value-game/.

11. "Buy a Feature," Innovation Games, accessed March 1, 2018, http://www.innovationgames.com/buy-a-feature/.

12. "20/20 Vision," Innovation Games, accessed March 1, 2018, http://www.innovationgames.com/2020-vision/.

13. "Thirty-five," TastyCupcakes.org, accessed March 1, 2018, http://tastycupcakes.org/2012/10/thirty-five/.

Using these democratic and inclusive processes with stakeholders for assigning business value to Product Backlog items has two main benefits for Product Owners:

1. They get a better overall sense of what their stakeholders are thinking.
2. Their stakeholders feel more included and heard.

Remember that business value is not the only factor when ordering a Product Backlog. Risk, cost, and technical dependency also play their parts.

Risk

The easiest way to measure risk is with a simple Low, Medium, High ranking provided by the Scrum Team. To use this system in the formula cited above, assign a number to each risk rating (e.g., L=1, M=5, H=10). Ultimately, the scale you use to represent risk depends on other factors: How important is risk for your product? What scale are you using for value?

Risk may not even need to be considered for certain products, while others may want to give risk more weight and more ranges.

Size

The most common scale to use when assigning relative size estimates to Product Backlog items is the Fibonacci sequence (1, 2, 3, 5, 8, 13, etc.). The next chapter on release management will get more into the reasons for relative estimation. For the purposes of ordering a Product Backlog, just know that the size of an item is a factor. However, what you name the unit that represents its size is not that important (often it is called a point or story point).

Imagine you have two Product Backlog items, PBI_a and PBI_b. PBI_a is more valuable to the business while PBI_b is cheaper but addresses a bigger risk. Which should you do first? Let's apply the formula:

$$PBI_a \rightarrow (25 \text{ value} + 5 \text{ risk}) / 8 \text{ size} = 3.75 \text{ order rank}$$

$$PBI_b \rightarrow (15 \text{ value} + 10 \text{ risk}) / 5 \text{ size} = 5 \text{ order rank}$$

In this case, PBI$_b$ ranks higher on the Product Backlog as it addresses a large risk and is relatively cheap to implement.

This can be a handy technique, but like everything it can be taken too far. As a Product Owner, are you now stuck with the order derived from this formula? Of course not. Like any tool, if it makes your job easier, then keep using it. If you want to move a few things around after the formula ranking, then feel free.

Keep in mind that this formula does not take dependencies into account. It may be a good idea to have your Scrum Team make a pass over the ordered Product Backlog to reorder based on technical and business dependencies.

Refinement is a great opportunity to revisit this ordering each Sprint.

"Done"

In this section, we define "Done" and then work through an example of "Done."

Definition of "Done"

When you get a bathroom remodeled, buy a new car, or dine in a nice restaurant, you have certain expectations about the end product. Despite the best intentions, if the customer expectations do not align with the producer's understanding of those expectations, then conflict and unhappiness generally follow. Whether a tile doesn't quite line up, the car is dirty, or the dinner plate is not prewarmed, you are disappointed.

A clearly communicated and shared set of expectations creates the transparency needed to avoid this problem.

Software is no different. Whether you purchase a software package, consume a product as a service, or implement against an external API, you have certain expectations about quality, performance, and support. These expectations define what it means to be truly "Done."

What should "Done" include? The answer depends on the context. Good candidates are:

- thoroughly tested
- integrated
- documented
- releasable

Sound good? Well, how much testing? How much documentation? Is there a difference if you are building a dating website or a vital medical product? There is not one universal definition of "Done" for all possible products. However, you need to ensure that "Done" allows for continuous releases without disappointing your customers and other stakeholders and is clearly communicated and understood by all people involved.

From the *Scrum Guide*

When a Product Backlog item or an Increment is described as "Done," everyone must understand what "Done" means. Although this may vary significantly per Scrum Team, members must have a shared understanding of what it means for work to be complete, to ensure transparency.[14]

This shared understanding, with the goal of transparency, is manifested in the definition of "Done."

When do you get to "Done"? Scrum indicates that the Increment must be "Done" by the end of the Sprint. However, waiting until the very end to get to "Done" can be risky. A Development Team can hedge their bets by getting each Product Backlog item to "Done" throughout the Sprint. The moment a Product Backlog item meets the definition of "Done," it is then considered part of the Increment. The sooner they can achieve this within a Sprint, the better (see Figure 7-11).

---

14. Schwaber and Sutherland, *Scrum Guide*, 18.

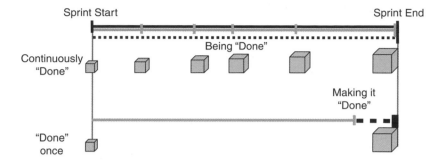

Figure 7-11 Continuously "Done" versus "Done" once at Sprint end

Consider this list of "Done" elements:

- Unit tested
- Code reviewed
- Matches code style guide
- No known defects
- Checked into main dev branch
- Public API documented
- Acceptance tests pass
- Product Owner approved
- Regression tests pass
- Release notes updated
- Performance tests pass
- User guide updated
- Support guide updated
- Security tests pass
- Compliance documentation updated

At what point could your Development Team realistically do these? Every time they complete a Sprint Backlog item? A Product Backlog item? At the end of a Sprint for the overall Increment? Or will it have to wait until just before a release?

What if you placed them in a chart like the one in Figure 7-12?

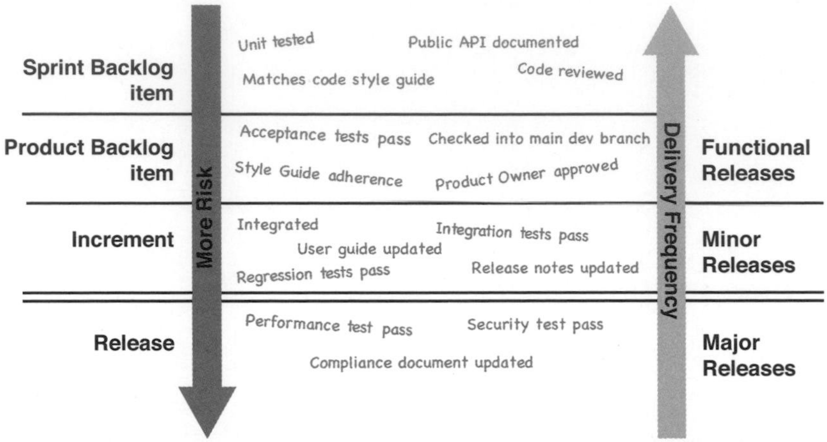

Figure 7-12 Being "Done" more often reduces risk and promotes continuous delivery.

In an ideal world, all of these items would be completed at the Sprint Backlog item level. The introduction of practices like automation and the elimination of wasteful bureaucratic activities could make it a reality, but likely the extra effort could reduce your ROI, at least in the short term.

The further down the line you go in Figure 7-12, the more risk you introduce. Anything in the "Release" level is a huge risk, as you are indicating that those items cannot be addressed within a Sprint and would have to wait until right before a major release. So how far up the line can you push these activities? What can you do to move them up a level? If it takes two weeks to do regression testing, then likely you cannot complete it within a Sprint. However, delaying regression testing to the very end is risky. Your Scrum Team should be focusing on all the elements in the "Release" level and asking what practices they can put in place to move them up. In the case of regression testing, automation can make a big difference. But do not just settle for doing regression testing once a Sprint for the Increment. What would it take to get all the regression tests running every time the Development Team completes a Product Backlog item? Or what about every time a programmer checks in code? This is how a Scrum Team gets closer to continuous delivery.

So what's the difference between acceptance criteria and the definition of "Done"? The definition of "Done" is for the whole Increment. Acceptance criteria are specific to a single Product Backlog item. To realize the value of a Product Backlog item, you must fulfill all of its acceptance criteria plus what is in the definition of "Done." If you throw out the Product Backlog item, you also throw out its acceptance criteria. The definition of "Done" stays. In other words, the definition of "Done" is the global acceptance criteria.

The definition of "Done" addresses two aspects. One is what is required from a good engineering point of view, the technical aspects of the Development Team. The other, albeit smaller, aspects are domain requirements like regulations, laws, and so on. The latter need to be communicated to the Development Team so that they can figure out a way to address them correctly from their point of view (see Figure 7-13).

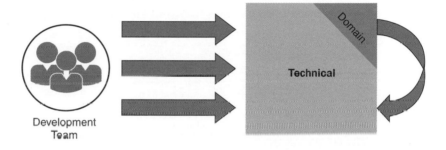

Figure 7-13 Division between technical and domain areas of definition of "Done"

How often does the definition of "Done" change? Again, it depends. Whenever there are new insights about the product and its quality, it is time to change the definition of "Done." Usually more changes occur in the beginning since a lot of learning happens in the first Sprints, especially on the technical side. The domain aspect often changes whenever marketplace or internal/external regulatory requirements are introduced. Nonfunctional requirements (performance, usability, legal, etc.) often find themselves on the definition of "Done." The definition of "Done" grows over time (see Figure 7-14).

Figure 7-14 Definition of "Done" growing over time

Think of the definition of "Done" as the code (as in rules, not programming) of quality that everyone commits to. Unlike professions such as doctors, plumbers, and accountants, the software development industry has no universally agreed-upon document to protect it when under pressure to deliver more, faster. At least when a Scrum Team (and the development organization) within a company sets its own standards of quality, they have something to point to when asked to do something that could compromise the quality of the product. As part of continuous improvement, the Sprint Retrospective is a good place to amend the definition of "Done."

EXAMPLE DEFINITION OF "DONE"

What "Done" means may vary wildly from team to team. Following are example definitions of "Done" from valued trainer colleagues:

- Barry Overeem:
  - Created design
  - Updated documentation
  - Tested
  - Approved by Product Owner
  - Clear on "how to demo" at Sprint Review
- Francois Desrosiers:
  - Code review done
  - Unit tests done

- BDD tests done based on the acceptance criteria
- Documentation done (based on the documentation that the client defined as essential and valuable)
- Features tested/approved by the PO or business analyst
- Features deployed in the staging environment
- Source code of the feature is in the proper branch
- Jeronimo Palacios:
  - It works
  - Passes the acceptance criteria
  - It is in production
  - Peer reviewed
  - Covered by tests
  - Passes all the tests
  - Merged into Master
  - No apparent bugs
  - Accepted by the PO
  - API documented
  - Anything not trivial commented
  - Argument for binaries documented
- Fredrik Wendt:
  - Everything is version controlled
  - Code reviewed
  - Automated tests setup
  - Solution shared with full team
  - Live/in production
- Vincent Tence:
  - All automated tests pass
  - The application supports the expected load

- Response time is within accepted limits
- Manual tests are conclusive
- Exploratory tests are conclusive
- Development Team is satisfied with test coverage
- The application has been translated to French and English
- The application is accessible and available on all supported devices
- Release notes are up-to-date and ready for publication
- Online help is up-to-date with latest features
- Ops diagnostic can be done efficiently and timely
- Ops Team is confident they can operate and support the application
- Revision history is exploitable
- Development Team can set up a new development environment automatically
- New key learnings and design decisions are documented
- Development Team is satisfied with the new user experience
- Codebase is in a better state than before
- Development Team is satisfied with new code quality
- Ops Team can roll back to a previous version retaining all data
- Application is available in Pre-Production environment
- No new security vulnerability has been introduced
- Development Team can reproduce identical deployment

- Ralph Jocham:
  - Compliant to development standards
  - Passes code analysis
  - Documented (Scenario, SAD, Test Case, Interfaces)
  - Reviewed or pair programmed

- Automatic Unit Tests (for non UI, i.e. tier containing business logic has a test coverage of 95 percent or higher)
- Automatic Selenium Tests; each usage scenario has at least one Selenium test
- Automatic Appium Tests on target device
- All text is internationalized
- No known bugs exist

Figure 7-15 shows a useful definition of "Done" template for multiple teams working on one product. It defines common elements across the teams, but also leaves autonomy in how they work within each Development Team.

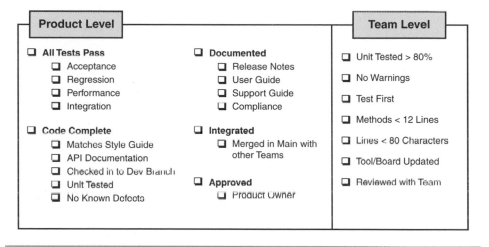

Figure 7-15 Definition of "Done" template

Why Is This Important for the Product Owner?

As a Product Owner, some of these "Done" elements are obvious. You need to have an integrated product, you need to have the required level of documentation and compliance, and you definitely want some degree of testing. But why should you be concerned about programming elements like coding standard adherence? Why is it important for you that a method is no longer than 12 lines and that lines do not have more than 80 characters? Why should you, as a Product Owner, be aware of these points or even enforce them?

Look at it this way: Why do you change the oil in your car on a regular basis? Why do you check the pressure in your tires on a regular basis or bring the car in for service? As a driver, you only want to get from point A to B; that's where the value is for you. However, if you do not pay regular attention to maintenance, eventually the negligence will catch up to you and will result in being broken down on the side of the road with high repair costs. It is the same for software. If you do not maintain it on a regular basis, you will accrue lots of technical debt—slowing development, reducing innovation, and costing far more in the long run.

For that reason, it is important for a Product Owner to understand the technical concepts of the definition of "Done" and be aware that they could have dire consequences in the long run. That is why you want to know about them and track them. If this is not already happening, then ask your Development Team to start measuring them and to maybe add the measurements into the automated continuous integration environment, which will let everybody know the moment the Development Team checks in any code that violates the definition of "Done."

This is like being notified from your car dashboard the moment something goes wrong. Ultimately, a good definition of "Done" creates transparency for the Product Owner, the Development Team, and the stakeholders.

"READY" IS A MINDSET

Working with a self-organizing Development Team is powerful, and you will be amazed at what they can deliver. However, even self-organization has its limits.

Garbage IN → Garbage OUT

If you feed garbage into the Sprint, you most likely will get garbage as output.

In other words, *if you are not "Ready" at the beginning of the Sprint, you won't be "Done" at the end of the Sprint.*

Mise en place is a French culinary phrase that roughly translates to "putting in place" or "everything in its place," which refers to organizing your kitchen before you start cooking. Essentially you make sure that you have all the required ingredients in sufficient amounts, the right equipment ready to go, oven preheated, and so forth. Imagine halfway through baking your grandmother's famous apple crumble pie you discover that you do not have enough apples. You would have to run out and buy more, but once you return the already cut apples may have turned brown. If you want raving reviews, that surely is not going to get you there. Once you put everything in its place and make sure you have the tools and infrastructure, you are *ready* to roll.

What is the equivalent in software product development? Well, it is not as simple as laying everything out in front of you. Software product development is complex, abstract, and less tangible. That means "Ready" is also less tangible. Even if the Product Backlog items have been broken down, estimated, and given clear acceptance criteria, you still may not know how to implement the Product Backlog item.

Jeff Patton includes a useful metaphor in his story-mapping book[15] that emphasizes the importance of "conversation" in the Three Cs (card, conversation, confirmation). He tells a story about showing a vacation picture to a friend, a picture like the one in Figure 7-16 showing Ralph and a few friends on vacation.

You see a photo of Ralph being surprised by a handful of colorful birds. For Ralph, it is more. It is a memory he can relive by looking at it. He was there to experience the moment, the location, the story about how the birds found him, the sound of the birds, the noise they made (they were deafening), their smell (they were pungent), and their rather sharp claws that left scratch marks on his skin that remained visible days later.

---

15. Jeff Patton, *User Story Mapping: Discover the Whole Story, Build the Right Product* (Sebastopol, CA: O'Reilly Media, 2014), *https://jpattonassociates.com/user-story-mapping/*.

Figure 7-16 Ralph on vacation with birds

For the rest of us, it is just a photo; for Ralph, it is a vivid memory. That is what Product Backlog items are. Think about them as memories you create for each Development Team member. Apart from the size, estimate, and acceptance criteria, it does not matter that much what is written on the card. What matters is the narrative behind the card. Put enough on the Product Backlog item card to remember, but make sure the narrative sticks so that it can be recalled if it becomes part of the Sprint Goal.

In other words, getting a Product Backlog item "Ready" is about communicating the story behind the picture in a way that the Development Team can act on it.

Getting to Ready

What exactly does "Ready" entail? There are three minimum needs that each Product Backlog item should meet before being tackled in a Sprint:

1. **Small** enough to be completed within one Sprint
2. **Sized** so that you can get an idea about the overall effort of the whole Product Backlog
3. **Just enough detail** (acceptance criteria) so that it can act as confirmation that the Product Backlog item is functioning as intended

On top of that, you may even refer to architectural constraints, business rules, UX designs, dependencies, and more, based on the needs of the product and the Scrum Team.

None of this has to be perfect. The Development Team just has to know enough to make a forecast in Sprint Planning. This may vary from Scrum Team to Scrum Team.

Scrum does not define the concept of "Ready." The *Scrum Guide* considers Product Backlog items that can be "Done" within one Sprint as "Ready." Why? "Done" is a black-and-white checklist; you can check each point off with a yes or a no. One or more no's mean that you are not fulfilling the definition of "Done" and are not releasable. "Ready," on the other hand, is not a checklist but a helpful guide during refinement that may not always be achievable. Defining "Ready" should not mean that a Development Team cannot attempt a Product Backlog item that is not 100 percent "Ready."

Definition of "Ready" warning: *I have worked with Development Teams that would refuse to accept a Product Backlog item into a Sprint if it didn't meet their definition of "Ready." While that seems reasonable at first, what I noticed was that this document started to become a gate or even a contract that shifted the mindset of the Development Team—a mindset that was less agile. Remember the third value from the Agile Manifesto, "Customer Collaboration over Contract Negotiation"? The definition of "Ready" cannot be used as a contract. If a Product Owner wakes up in the middle of the night before a Sprint Planning session with the greatest idea ever, shouldn't he be able to take it to his Development Team the next day to be considered for the upcoming Sprint? Even if it hasn't been fully vetted with the definition of "Ready"? The warning here is to treat "Ready" as a guideline, not a concrete contract that could decrease true collaboration.*

The important thing is that "Ready" is a mindset, a common understanding to be reached within the Scrum Team. It doesn't matter whether the content is in the form of a user story, a sentence, or a rough sketch. What does matter is that each Development Team member understands the intention of the Product Backlog item and feels good about starting it. So on top of the three points shown earlier: *small* enough for one Sprint, *sized*, and *just enough detail*, consider a fourth point:

  4. **Understood** by the Development Team

Once this state is reached, feel free to make the Product Backlog item part of your Sprint Goal.

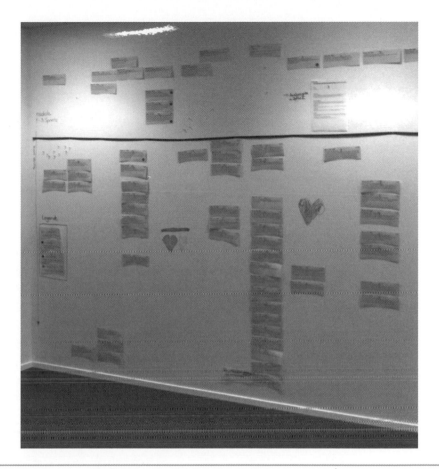

Figure 7-17 Using a "Ready" line for Product Backlog items

I once worked with a Scrum Team that had a great idea. They added a "Ready" line to their Product Backlog wall, which was arranged similarly to a story map. After each refinement session, Product Backlog items moved further up the wall as they were estimated, split into more cards, and had acceptance criteria added.

Ralph

At some point, the card was close but still underneath the black "Ready" line. Only after the Development Team and Product Owner considered it "Ready" was the card moved above the line to be brought into one of the upcoming Sprints. Figure 7-17 shows an example of this.

LEAN REQUIREMENTS MANAGEMENT

There is nothing worse than when a beautiful piece of hard work has to be thrown out.

I once had a project canceled after my team and I worked overtime for three months. We lived in the office, apart from going home to get fresh clothes and to kiss our families twice a week. After a "successful" beta-launch, the project was canceled the very next day because of fear about possible patent infringement litigation. What a WASTE!

Ralph

Instead of being driven by activities like planning, analysis, design, implementation, and testing, where your batch size is the whole product, it is good to have a Product Backlog that allows you to think in value. That is one reason it is important for the Product Owner to always keep the Product Backlog ready and ordered. The Product Backlog is emergent, so that the details come into focus as the Scrum Team works through it. The longer they can wait, the better decisions they will make.

This essentially means that the first reasonable moment to make a decision is the last responsible one.

Last Responsible Moment (LRM)

A strategy of not making a premature decision but instead delaying commitment and keeping important and irreversible decisions open until the cost of not making a decision becomes greater than the cost of making a decision.[16]

This enables you to keep the unknown-unknowns, the complexity, vague for as long as reasonable. But once the time is right, you go deep. You go from a "mile wide and inch deep" to "an inch wide and a mile deep." You do this just in time and then go ahead and create another Increment with exactly what you specified a little earlier. This way you delay to avoid creating waste.

---

16. Agile Glossary Definitions, s.v. "last responsible moment (LRM)," Innolution.com, assessed March 1, 2018, http://www.innolution.com/resources/glossary/last-responsible-moment-lrm.

In other words, have just enough of your Product Backlog "Ready" for the next few Sprints. Anything else is considered waste.

Lean manufacturing or lean production, pioneered by Toyota, is a systematic method that minimizes waste without sacrificing productivity.

Lean defines seven areas of waste. An easy way to remember them is by thinking of wasteful TIM WOOD, as outlined in Table 7-1.

Table 7-1 TIMWOOD Mnemonic Device

Transport	Moving work between phases. In software product development, this equates to handoffs between people and departments.
Inventory	Unnecessary storage. In software, this equates to any work—requirements, specifications, source code, tests—that has not yet been released and used by the customer.
Motion	Doing the same thing again and again, like manual regression testing. Task switching is another example of motion waste (e.g., on product index).
Waiting	Anything that causes idle time like waiting for people (skills), data, system availability; in short, it is related to dependency management.
Overproduction	Unused features (e.g., usage index).
Overprocessing	Work not adding value or helping the product. Unnecessary documents, unnecessary meetings, or shuffling people between teams so that they have to relearn over and over.
Defects	Bugs.

Anything that does not add value is considered waste. In Japanese this is called *muda*. Lean differentiates between two kinds of muda:

- Muda Type I—Non-value-added activity, necessary for product or customer.
  For example, compliance documentation.
- Muda Type II—Non-value-added activity, unnecessary for product or customer. *The aim is to eliminate this type of waste.*

STORY MAPPING

Typically, Product Backlogs are represented as one-dimensional priority queues. The enforced order is helpful as it requires you, the Product Owner, to make tough decisions because no one Product Backlog item can be as important as another. This provides valuable insight about how to proceed. However, sometimes it is helpful to add other dimensions to the Product Backlog for themes, customer segments, releases, and so on.

Story mapping, originally developed by Jeff Patton,[17] is a powerful tool to discover the right solution for your users and evolves as you gain insights. It is the process of visualizing your product from the initial vision, to user key activities, and viable releases (see Figure 7-26). A story map becomes a multi-dimensional map that tells the story of the overall product and provides a development strategy for fast learning.

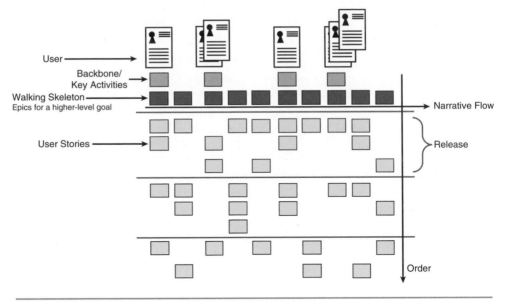

Figure 7-18 Structure of a story map

17. Patton, *User Story Mapping, https://jpattonassociates.com/user-story-mapping/.*

Steps to Creating a Story Map

The steps involved in creating a story map are covered in this section.

1. Key Activities—The Backbone

Try to see the whole picture from a bird's eye view, the backbone (see Figure 7-26). Identify your users and their high-level key activities. Look to your Business Model Canvas as a source for this information. *Customer segments* could identify users, and *value propositions* could be candidate activities. See the business modeling section of Chapter 2.

2. Epics—The Walking Skeleton

Break down these high-level activities into epics to form the walking skeleton of your story map (see Figure 7-26).

3. User Stories—The Map of Your Most Important User

Once you have the walking skeleton, take the most important user you can think of and map out the user stories for this user for a typical day with your product. The flow of the user stories is from left to right. Identifying your most important user should be straightforward if you have already crafted a product vision. See the product vision section of Chapter 2.

4. Discover Additional Key Activities

Often, many user stories belong together and can be grouped as an activity that folds back into your backbone. This is an iterative process as more and more stories and activities emerge over time (see Figure 7-18). Activities may come first or may be identified in retrospect by grouping existing user stories.

5. Enhance the Map with Additional Users

Once you have developed a story map for your most important and critical user, go ahead and do the same for other users based on their importance. There is no point in getting into detailed mappings for users whose needs you are not yet willing to address. Again, use the flow from left to right and add their activities and tasks. Make sure each "user" of a task is clearly identifiable.

EXPLORE THE STORY MAP

Next you want to engage in some exploration of the story maps.

1. Fill in and Refine the Story Map

Break down large user stories into smaller ones and add more detail. This splitting of user stories could be for different users, different flow alternatives, and more. Other cards get rewritten as understanding grows. All these changes mean that the story map is changing again and again.

2. Think Outside the Box

Try to come up with all great possibilities you can think of and try them out on your story map. Do not be restricted while you do this. Later will be the time to triage the story map. Also, do not forget to think about all the things that can go wrong.

- Think outside the box to come up with cool product ideas.
- What are the variations the users expect from the product?
- What are the exceptional paths for all the things that can go wrong, and how would the user recover?
- Are there other users, and how would they like to use the product?

3. Collect Feedback

Tell this story map to others who have experience in that domain and understand the needs of the users. Use their input to refine the story map. Also, run the story map by your Development Team to learn about risks, dependencies, and available technologies. Again, this process is iterative.

4. Group It by Releases

The whole story map is likely too much for one release. Move more important user stories higher up and move less essential stories further down to form groups by releases. Think about the resulting story map as a different kind of roadmap where the first release is your Minimal Viable Product (MVP).

STORY MAPS AND PRODUCT BACKLOGS

How do story maps tie together with a Product Backlog?

The short answer is perfectly. As described in the Product Backlog section, the Product Backlog reflects all the work the Development Team needs to do. The Product Backlog is a one-dimensional priority queue. The story map expresses the vast amount of work from the Product Backlog in more than one dimension. What the Scrum Team needs to do is to project the story map into your Product Backlog (see Figure 7-19). The resulting order has to reflect what best maximizes value generation, risk mitigation, and technical dependencies for fast learning.

You may also discover constraints, which is work that slows or halts other Product Backlog items (or user stories) from being completed. Constraints could be technical or something else.

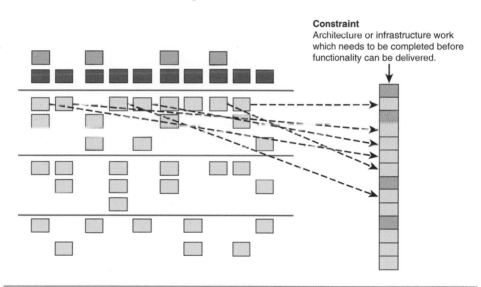

Figure 7-19 Story map projected into Product Backlog

THE PAST AND THE FUTURE

In certain situations, such as the replacement of an existing product, it is a good exercise to first map the current-reality story map and then the future story map. Contrasting both points of views helps to understand and frame the delta and resulting work for the desired outcome.

IMPACT MAPPING

Requirements can end up as an overzealous shopping list. If you feel that you only have one chance to voice your needs, you may try to prepare for all possible contingencies. This approach, when combined with a defined process in which the whole product is being delivered as one big batch, poses two big problems:

1. No big picture (vision)
2. No learning (validation)

How does impact mapping address these points? Impact mapping is a strategic planning technique that prevents companies from getting lost while building a product. Each assumption is clearly communicated. Each of the team's activities is clearly focused and aligned toward one of those clear business objectives. As each activity is clearly directed toward an objective, it can be measured and validated while working on it. This allows for more effective roadmapping.

On top of this, working in Sprints with "Done" Increments at the end of each Sprint facilitates ongoing learning about what the Scrum Team builds and how they work together. This covers customer feedback, scope, tests, integration, and many more elements. This feedback allows for validated learning. Those learnings in turn drive the scope and roadmap.

This approach of having a clear vision and thinking in value with the measurable business objectives based on continuous validation allows you to deliver even large interdependent products in an environment of constant change.

Also, as all decisions are being validated, this process leads to better choices regarding the roadmap and the scope within, which in turn causes less scope creep and waste along the way.

In his popular book *Start with Why*,[18] Simon Sinek makes the strong argument that you should always start with "Why" as described in his Golden Circle (see Figure 7-20).

What	Every company on earth knows "What" services or products they do.
How	Some companies know "How" they do it. This sets them apart from the rest and makes them somewhat special.
Why	Very few organizations know "Why" they are doing what they are doing. The "Why" is not about making money. Money follows result. The "Why" is the reason the company exists.

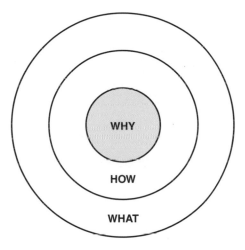

Figure 7-20 Golden Circle

18. Simon Sinek, *Start with Why: How Great Leaders Inspire Everyone to Take Action* (New York: Penguin Group, 2009).

Impact mapping builds and extends this thinking by using the "Why" to identify the right scope and how to validate it. This is achieved by adding the question of "Who" is going to benefit (see Figure 7-21).

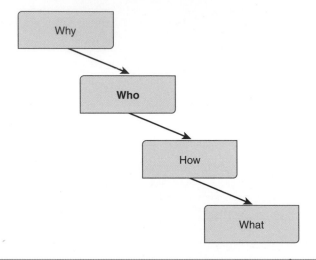

Figure 7-21 Impact mapping driven by the person being impacted

I like to think about it the following way: Because of what we do, we improve someone's life. It might not be much—having to click one button instead of two, say—but it is still an improvement. Try to think about "Who" this person is and "how" you will improve her life.

If "Why" is the goal you want to achieve along with a value metric to validate the business objective and the "Who" is the actor performing the act, you can identify "How" you can achieve this impact. Once the impact is identified, you can come up with "What" is needed. This is your deliverable. The resulting impact map allows you to compare the various options and measure the outcome (see Figure 7-22).

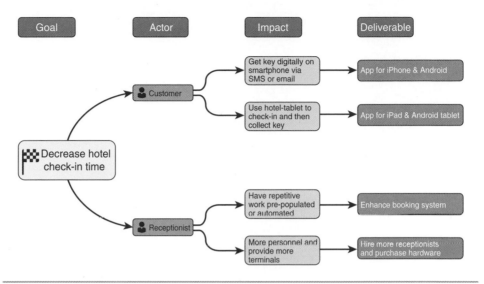

Figure 7-22 Impact map example

Each deliverable in turn can be broken down into tangible Product Backlog items, in the form of user stories, for example (see Figure 7-23). Given that the goal, the actor, and the deliverable are established, defining the Product Backlog items is more straightforward.

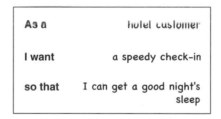

Figure 7-23 Product Backlog item as user story from impact map

SUCCESS CRITERIA

Impact mapping is a powerful way to come up with the right deliverables to achieve a specific goal. Still, wouldn't it be great to quantify upfront how success can be measured (see Figure 7-24)?

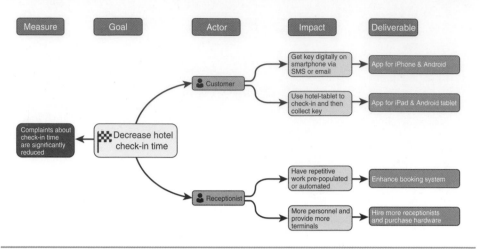

Figure 7-24 Success criteria as measure of impact validation

Think about a measure and how it will validate your targeted impact. This practice is useful as it enforces defining value validation measures and the resulting metrics upfront. This is a good mechanism to tie your measures back to your EBMgt metrics: in this case, customer happiness.

Figure 7-25 shows a way of making this transparent by creating a different view of your Product Backlog

1	2	3	5	8	13	21	Impact	Value Measure
▢ ▢		▢	▢	▢			■	■
▢	▢	▢ ▢		▢			■	■
							■	■
	▢		▢ ▢		▢	▢	■	■
▢	▢ ▢			▢	▢		NONE	

▢ Product Backlog Item

⑤ Size of Product Backlog Item

Figure 7-25 Assigning Product Backlog items to impacts

Each Product Backlog Item gets associated with an impact, and each impact has a clear measure for validation. By having the Product Backlog item sized, it helps to derive the anticipated overall effort and resulting cost.

The goal is to have each Product Backlog item associated with an impact. There may be some work that cannot be associated. That is acceptable as long as you can still justify its existence, which could lead to newly discovered impacts.

SPECIFICATION BY EXAMPLE

> *As formality increases, tests and requirements become indistinguishable. At the limit, tests and requirements are equivalent.*[19]
>
> —Robert Martin and Grigori Melnik

Let's break that quote down. Formality does not mean that you drill down with a big upfront design effort to specify everything in the Product Backlog. It means that you remove enough ambiguity from a Product Backlog item just in time to be "Ready" for it to be developed with minimal waste.

Requirements have a tendency to be abstract. At the beginning, this is a good thing as it leaves your options open while you are deriving scope from rather broad goals or a product vision.

However, the further a Product Backlog item moves up the Product Backlog, the more it needs to be "Ready" to be consumed within a Sprint. By the time a requirement has tests written for it, it becomes much more precise (see Figure 7-26). This is where tests and requirements become indistinguishable. Once there is something as precise as a test, why is the requirement needed anymore? The test is the requirement and the requirement is the test. Eliminating the need for separate requirements reduces waste. As tests are constantly being executed, they are much more likely to be kept up to date than a requirements document.

---

19. Robert C. Martin and Grigori Melnik, "Tests and Requirements, Requirements and Tests: A Mobius Strip, *IEEE Software* 25, no. 1 (2008): 54–59.

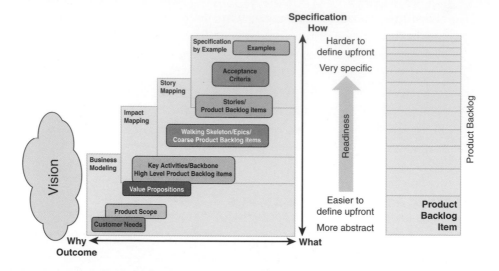

Figure 7-26 Different levels and granularities of "Ready"

At the same time, the human brain is not that great at dealing with lots of information at once. This means that when you do need more precision, it should be done just before putting the effort into developing it.

I was once a developer/architect for a large product. We were about five months in (five Sprints) when I found myself working on this one feature. I thought I understood it fairly well and knocked it out in a couple of days. I submitted it to our QA person through our tracking tool. Not 10 minutes later, I was notified that my feature failed the tests. Perplexed, I contacted the QA person who showed up at my desk to with a three-page test case in hand. She pointed to where I went wrong. My response was a common one from programmers like me, "What? I didn't know it was supposed to do that. Where did this come from?" She explained to me that she had met with the Product Owner weeks prior who helped her write the test case. I felt wronged since I had only started the feature days prior and asked, "Next time, can I have this before starting? Or can you just invite me to your meeting?" What I realized in that moment was that from my perspective, I wasn't looking at a test case, I was looking at the requirements. These were the answers to the test, which would have assured me passing and saved everybody a lot of time.

You get to that level of precision by breaking down a requirement into all possible scenarios and by illustrating them. Each scenario will be illustrated with at least one concrete example and more if needed. This process of illustrating is a team effort so that all relevant perspectives are considered. The resulting examples then guide the Development Team to implement the requirement—and these examples also guide the testing effort. Both development and testing get the information from the same source. You succeed in removing all ambiguity by having tests as requirements and requirements as tests. In other words, executable requirements.

Once you reach this level of precision, it is fairly easy to automate them in a meaningful way. Specification by Example exploits this formality and formulates requirements by writing automatable tests. These automated tests can then function as executable documentation (see Figure 7-27).

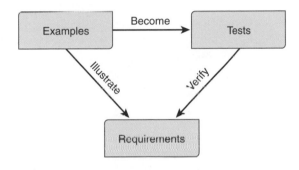

Figure 7-27 Examples driving requirements and tests[20]

Examples sound nice, but how do you get there? Get familiar with the concept of the Triad.[21] The Triad is made up of a representative for each the following domains:

- Business
- Development
- Testing

---

20. https://less.works/less/technical-excellence/specification-by-example.html.

21. The term "Triad," created by Ken Pugh, is a more common term for the "Three Amigos," created around 2009 by George Dinwiddie.

In Scrum, these roles would be covered by the Product Owner and/or a subject-matter expert for the business domain, and a programmer and tester from the Development Team. As you can see, these three domains can be easily covered by a cross-functional Scrum Team. Together, they will refine and illustrate the requirements and all acceptance criteria with specific examples.

Consider the Triad to be the amalgam between the why and the what from the business perspective and the how from the development perspective. Therefore, on the Agile Testing Quadrants, described first by Brian Marick[22] in 2003, they reside in Quadrant 2 (see Figure 7-28). With the evolution of agile, Quadrant 2 has emerged as the most important area for testing.

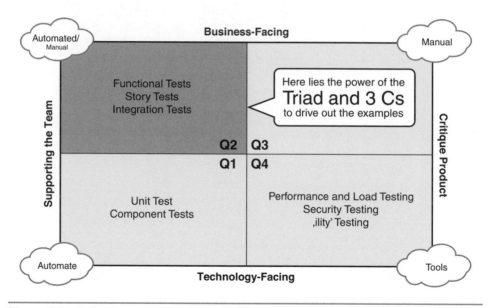

Figure 7-28 Agile Testing Quadrants and the Three Cs or Triad

The benefits of using Specification by Example and to illustrate the requirements with examples are numerous.

---

22. "My Agile Testing Project," Exampler Consulting, August 21, 2003, http://www.exampler.com/old-blog/2003/08/21.1.html#agile-testing-project-1.

This tight collaboration between the three domains is a great antidote for misunderstanding. It prevents bugs and subsequent bug fixes. This leads to less rework, higher product quality, and faster turnaround times.

Also, often not as obvious, it allows for concurrent work on Product Backlog items within a Sprint because of better alignment of the activities of the various roles like programmers, testers, and business analysts in the cross-functional Development Team.

Ultimately, Specification by Example gets all on the same page. Everyone may think they know what is meant by acceptance criteria such as:

"When users log in with invalid credentials, they should get a warning message."

In reality, that statement could mean entirely different things to different people. Invalid password? Invalid e-mail? Incorrect role? No password? Too many attempts? What message? The same message every time?

Simply asking, "Could you give me some real examples that you would try to prove this works?" could resolve much ambiguity. Table 7-2 presents such examples.

Table 7-2 Specification by Example example

Username	Password	Result	Message
suzieq	Wr0ngP@ss	fail	"Incorrect Password. Please try again."
suzieb	R1ghtP@ss	fail	"No user with name "suzieb." Please try again."
suzieq		fail	"Please enter a password."
bobbyg	R1ghtP@ss	fail	"You are not authorized for this system. Please contact your supervisor."

These examples are of data that you would need to gather at some point in the development of this particular feature anyway (while writing unit tests, adding test data, exploratory testing, etc.). Pulling at least some of this data together earlier in the development cycle is the essence of Specification by Example. These are no longer tests, they are executable requirements.

There are plenty of opportunities within Scrum to create and expand these examples. Product Backlog refinement, Sprint Planning, or even during the Sprint when the Development Team starts work on a new Product Backlog item.

Ralph

A while back, I was on a team that developed forensic software helping validate laboratories so that they could submit findings to court. As a laboratory, you have to prove that you will get the right and correct result over and over again. This also meant that the product we developed had to be FDA compliant. It had to consider all the applicable laws and other regulations and provide guidance for those laboratories in order to become validated. While it was an exciting product to be a part of, it was way above my pay grade. My uncertainty in programming certain features caused me to go and see our business analyst over and over again. "Gloria could you quickly explain once more how this works?" was my usual question. At some point Gloria, I guess she was fed up, handed me a spreadsheet which contained all the important information about certain calculations (see Figure 7-29). Instead of having only the abstract theory, I had concrete specific examples for all possible cases. These examples helped me, as a programmer, implement the functionality correctly the first time. Once I was done, our testers used the same spreadsheet to test the product.

In this project, we discovered Specification by Example the hard way. Once we came up with this approach—to illustrate our requirements with lots of examples in spreadsheets—our productivity and product quality went up by leaps and bounds.

Those spreadsheets were actually our documentation and placed in our version control system in which a small self-developed program read out the input values and performed and compared the results with the spreadsheet. Whenever parts of the spreadsheet created unexpected behavior of some of the assays, we received an updated spreadsheet. This spreadsheet then replaced the existing one, and we just reran all the tests. If something failed, we saw it immediately and could start to have conversations with the right people.

Quantitation Precision Study
Detector: **Quantifiler Human**
Sufficient Quanfiler Mix Produced? Yes

Prepare Quantifiler Human Reagent Mix:

Kit Items	Vol of Mix per rxn (ul)	Vol of Mix per rxn (ul) w/ overfill	Total Vol for mix (ul) w/ overfill
Quantifiler Human PCR Reaction Mix	15.7	12.34	424.44
Quantifiler Human Primer Mix	13.3	98.76	822.28
Total	29.00		1246.72

Prepare Standards:

Standards	Target Conc (ng/ul)	Target Vol Produced (ul)	DNA Extract Conc (ng/ul)	DNA Extract vol (ul)	TE Buffer (ul)	Vol of Std Produced (ul)	Conc of Std Produced (ng/ul)	Vol of Std Needed
Standards	50	200	200	50	150	200	50	54
Standards	16.7	150	50	50	100	150	16.7	54
Standards	5.56	150	16.67	50	100	150	5.56	54
Standards	1.85	150	5.56	50	100	150	1.85	54
Standards	0.62	150	1.85	50	100	150	0.62	54
Standards	0.21	150	0.62	50	100	150	0.21	54
Standards	0.068	150	0.21	50	100	150	0.069	54
Standards	0.023	150	0.07	50	100	150	0.023	4

Prepare Standards Master Mix (only include half of the designated overfill %):

Standards	Std Conc (ng/ul)	Vol of Std per rxn	Vol of Std per rxn w/overfill	Total Vol of Std w/ overfill	Vol of Quantifiler Mix per rxn	Vol of Quantifiler Mix per rxn w/overfill	Total Vol of Quantifiler Mix w/ overfill	Total Vol of MM w/ overfill
Standards	50	2	3.14	3.14	23	35.42	35.68	26.3
Standards	16.7	2	3.14	3.14	23	35.42	35.68	26.3
Standards	5.56	2	3.14	3.14	23	35.42	35.68	26.3
Standards	1.85	2	3.14	3.14	23	35.42	35.68	26.3
Standards	0.62	2	3.14	3.14	23	35.42	35.68	26.3
Standards	0.21	2	3.14	3.14	23	35.42	35.68	26.3
Standards	0.068	2	3.14	3.14	23	35.42	35.68	26.3
Standards	0.023	2	3.14	3.14	23	35.42	35.68	26.3
							Total:	284.64

Prepare Samples/Ctrl Master Mix (only include half of the designate overfill%)

Sample Name	Vol of DNA/Ctrl/Buffer per rxn	Vol of DNA/Ctrl/Buffer per rxn w/ overfill	Total Vol of DNA w/ overfill	Total Vol of Ctrl w/ overfill	Total Vol of TE buffer w/ overfill	Vol of Quantifiler Mix per rxn	Vol of Quantifiler Mix per rxn w/overfill	Total Vol of Quantifiler Mix w/ overfill overfill	Total Vol of MM w/ overfill
1001	2	3.14	9.2	0	0	23	35.42	81.4	78.8
1002	2	3.14	9.2	0	0	23	35.42	81.4	78.8
1003	2	3.14	9.2	0	0	23	35.42	81.4	78.8
1004	2	3.14	9.2	0	0	23	35.42	81.4	78.8
1005	2	3.14	9.2	0	0	23	35.42	81.4	78.8
1006	2	3.14	0	3.1	0	23	35.42	81.4	26.3
1007	2	3.14	0	0	3.1	23	35.42	81.4	26.3
								Total:	560.8

Figure 7-29 Life science Specification by Example example

Think about the Specification by Example development flow the following way: First you create the high-level Product Backlog item, a user story, for example. This user story then gets refined and illustrated with examples until it is considered "Ready" and becomes part of the Sprint forecast. Then each example gets turned into an automated functional test,[23] and for each of the tests, the functionality is developed, driven by unit tests (aka TDD—Test-Driven Development) as in Figure 7-30.

---

23. Often this is called ATDD (Acceptance Test-Driven Development).

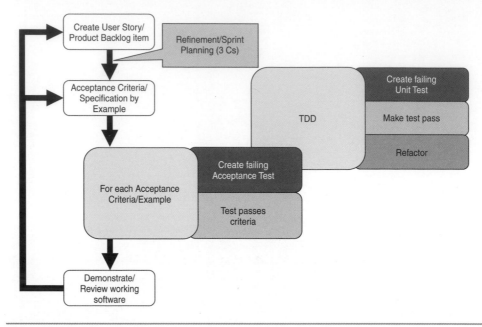

Figure 7-30 Putting Specification by Example and Test-Driven Development together

QUIZ REVIEW

Compare your answers from the beginning of the chapter to the ones below. Now that you have read the chapter, would you change any of your answers? Do you agree with the answers below?

Statement	Agree	Disagree
The Product Backlog replaces the need for any other requirement documents.	☐	✔
Agile requirements must be no more than a few sentences.	☐	✔
User story is synonymous with Product Backlog item.	☐	✔
Defects should not be in the Product Backlog because they are triaged by the Development Team.	☐	✔
The Development Team should not allow any Product Backlog items into the Sprint unless they meet a definition of "Ready."	☐	✔
A Product Backlog can be made up of tests.	✔	☐

RELEASE MANAGEMENT

8

QUIZ

To set the stage for this chapter, try answering each of the following statements with Agree or Disagree. Answers appear at the end of the chapter.

Statement	Agree	Disagree
With Scrum, you need to release at the end of each Sprint.	☐	☐
You cannot provide release dates with Scrum.	☐	☐
You can release multiple times within a Sprint.	☐	☐
Not allowing teams to release during important business periods (code freezes) reduces agility.	☐	☐
With Scrum, Product Backlog items must be sized using relative points.	☐	☐
A good release plan should include a buffer time period just before a release to stabilize the product (fix defects, regression test, document, etc.).	☐	☐

Customer collaboration over contract negotiation.

—Agile Manifesto

As Product Owner, you will undoubtedly have pressure from stakeholders (executives, managers, paying customers) for schedules and budget.

This is when you need to shift your stance to one of customer collaboration and partnership over contract negotiation and vendorship.

Easier said than done, right?

Instead, consider responding with "Based on historical data, this is when we forecast we can 'finish.' But as you know, these initiatives are complex and things will change. We will let you know as soon as they do. We also do not know how much our team can do until we try. How about we get a Sprint or two under our belts and revisit this plan when we have actual data?"

Otherwise, you are implying certainty at the moment you and your team know the least. An inflexible plan (scope, schedule, budget) at this early stage is doomed for failure and your 'real' stakeholders know this. Ultimately, it is your stakeholders who have the most to lose in this situation, and taking this more realistic stance is to look out for their best interests. Remember the product over project mindset from Chapter 1.

This chapter provides you with tools to help you convey this message more effectively.

REASONS TO RELEASE

By now it should be clear that the only way to create value is to release. Testing your products against the marketplace is crucial for the agility of your organization. However, not all releases are created equal. Releasing every day may sound great, but if all you are doing is making emergency maintenance patches, then it is not so great. Figure 8-1 lists a number of reasons for making a release.

Ideally, you are responding to customer requests. These types of releases are the closest thing you have to guaranteed value since the customer is saying they will pay for them. The next most important reason to release is to take advantage of a market opportunity. There is no guarantee of value, but there is a big upside if your hypothesis is correct and you are first to market.

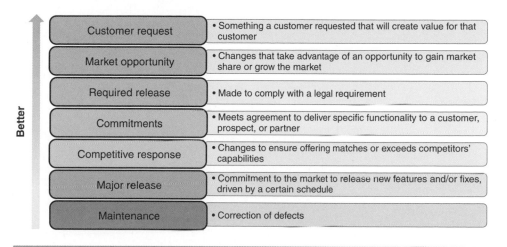

Figure 8-1 Some release reasons are better than others

The further down the list you go, the less agile you are in terms of time to market, innovation, and customer satisfaction.

Major releases are determined, often arbitrarily, by reasons that are in opposition to a product mindset. Maybe the act of releasing is long and expensive. Maybe you do not want to risk releasing during busy and crucial business operations. Maybe you are just following the terms of some contract.

Let's look at this in more detail.

RELEASE STRATEGY

How often should you release? The answer to this is often determined by reasons seemingly out of your control (e.g., process, technology, regulations, business needs).

Table 8-1 shows how the approach determines the type of release. The subsequent sections will expand on them.

Table 8-1 Mapping Approaches to Release Types

Approach	Commonly Used Process Term	Release	Validation
Phased	Waterfall	Major (every 6–12 months)	Once at the very end
Phased with agile development	Water-Scrum-Fall (or Hybrid)	Major (every 6–12 months)	Once at the very end
Scrum without releasing the increment until set release dates	Scrum	Major (every 6–12 months)	Once after the release date
Scrum with a release at the end of a Sprint	Scrum	Minor (every 1–3 months)	At Sprint boundaries
Scrum with multiple releases within a Sprint	Scrum	Functional (on demand)	As features are complete

MAJOR RELEASES

The waterfall model is obviously conducive to major releases. However, Scrum is not immune either. Many Scrum teams can go six months or more without an actual release to production. Likely these teams are using Scrum with more of a project mindset over a product mindset.

Major releases (see Figure 8-2) are still prominent within today's enterprises. With waterfall, a major release is the result of a long sequential phased approach. Each phase describes certain project activities like planning, analyzing, and designing. This is defined, linear thinking that may work when building simple and understood products. However, with complex products you do not know the solution, so batching up all your work and investing so much into each phase that culminates in a big release (big assumption) is tremendously risky.

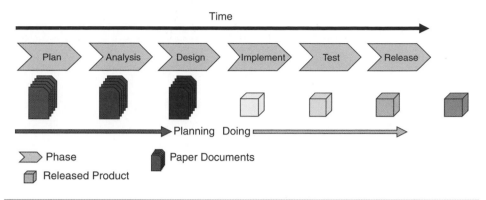

Figure 8-2 Major release because of sequential phase-driven development

Some teams set up what they believe is an agile approach by grouping the more technical phases into iterations (they may even call them Sprints: e.g., Analysis Sprint, Design Sprint, Test Sprint). Usually there is a prescribed planning and approval process, and then Scrum is used to implement the preset requirements, followed by some testing before finally releasing. This is nothing more than waterfall with some Scrum practices in between—in other words, Water-Scrum-Fall (see Figure 8-3).

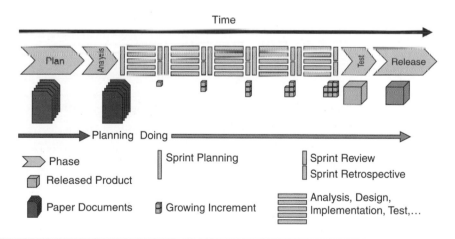

Figure 8-3 Water-Scrum-Fall

Using Scrum properly, you have a potentially releasable Increment each Sprint. You can minimize assumptions by showing the Increment to stakeholders in the Sprint Review. However, if you hold that increment back from a release to production until a much later date, you still have not eliminated the risk of building the wrong product.

I am going to repeat a story from Chapter 4 as it is very relevant to this section: I worked on a year-long initiative to create a first-of-its-kind online document printing product. Five months in, we had the ability to upload a file and set some minimal printing options, without the ability to pay or add more complex finishing options (tabs, inserts, bindings, etc.). At the time, management did not want to hear about going to production early as we were not yet "finished." Seven months later, after going to production, we realized that few customers actually used all the extra finishing options we painfully added to the product. Through a Special Instructions text area, we found out what customers really wanted: oddly sized posters and banners. Looking back, the ideal MVP would have been a simple upload with minimal printing options and an instructions text field. We could have then guided product development based on what our actual retail users were asking for — speeding up the feedback loop and generating real value more often.

What is holding teams back from releasing? This is an important question to ask. The answer should reveal some crucial strategic areas that need to be addressed.

Is it the technology? Consider investing in technology more conducive to releasing such as test automation, continuous integration, and virtualization.

Is it the internal processes? Consider streamlining these to get to "Done" more often.

Is it compliance? Consider making the governance people true stakeholders and find ways to meet compliance within each Sprint.

Is it customer absorption? Consider making it easier for your customers to consume the release. Sometimes this is a technical solution; sometimes it is through better communication and training.

Many times, it is the customers who do not want a release. Examining the reason behind this is important. If it is based out of fear because previous major releases were so painful, then you need to take the steps to make this less painful rather than just avoiding the pain. You need to work that muscle until it doesn't hurt anymore.

Scrum does not solve your problems, it reveals them.

Consider these other reasons that may increase the cost (and pain) of a release:

- **Additional hardware** and environments needed for production
- **Pilots** to test the release in production before rolling it out to customers
- **Data Migration** to update production databases
- **Training** for users on the latest features
- **Installation** that could be quite complex for some environments
- **Configuration** specific to different environments

Are major releases always bad? When you consider costs of a release and determine that those costs outweigh the value (negative ROI), then it may be justified.

Think about it long and hard, and do the work to justify and measure, before making the decision to use a major release strategy. If there is a way to instead reduce the cost of releasing, then that should be your focus.

During my time at a life-science company where we developed DNA sequencers, we had two types of customers: research institutions like universities and pharmaceutical companies as well as hospitals and validated laboratories.

Ralph

The former couldn't get a fix or new feature fast enough because they were living on the edge. In contrast, the hospitals and laboratories did their DNA analysis to help people, and since people were involved the product had to be FDA compliant and validated. Any change, even the smallest one, required a full-scale revalidation. This was time consuming and expensive.

Since we could deliver on an as-needed basis, we could cater to either customer: major releases for the hospitals, and functional or minor releases for the universities.

MINOR RELEASES

Organizations that are set on major releases quickly find that they need to make smaller releases for items that cannot wait until the next major release. These can be bug fixes and patches or stand-alone functionality that augments the major release.

Minor releases are likely aligned to Sprint boundaries when using Scrum. They have a smaller absorption cost and less risk for the customer, but are still somewhat arbitrary in terms of when value is delivered.

Major and minor releases are often distinguished by their version numbers: for example, v4.1, v8.3.2.

Many Scrum Teams consider releasing at the end of each Sprint as the ultimate goal. But can they do better?

FUNCTIONAL RELEASES

How do the big dot-com companies manage to move so fast? They are not phase-driven, they are value-driven. They are not smarter, they are faster. Delivery beats strategy every time. Whenever a feature is done, meaning releasable, it is released. Once the feature is live, the team can immediately start to measure and validate their assumptions. This is validated learning at its best. Amazon makes a release every 11.6 seconds. You read that right— seconds.[1] Think about it: A project is nothing more than a big bag of features to process and deliver. Why wait until some arbitrary date?

A Product Backlog is organized into independent valuable features. Once a feature is complete, why wait? Why grow your inventory? Why delay learning? You do not have to ship 7,500 times a day like Amazon, but being capable of releasing within a Sprint is a big leap forward, a graduation to the major leagues (see Figure 8-4).

---

1. Diego de lo Giudice, "Keynote: The State of Scaling Agile in the Age of the Customer," Scrum Day Europe, Amsterdam, 2014.

A popular misconception with Scrum is that releases happen only at the end of a Sprint. However, no Scrum rule bars getting an individual Product Backlog item to "Done" and releasing it within a Sprint. Effectively, this means adding "released" to the definition of "Done." The Sprint Review then becomes about inspecting an Increment that is already in production. Imagine the trust needed between the stakeholders, the Product Owner, and the Development Team to make that happen.

Functional releases have lower absorption costs and are often expected through explicit customer demands—the ultimate validation feedback loop—and equate to *continuous delivery* of value.

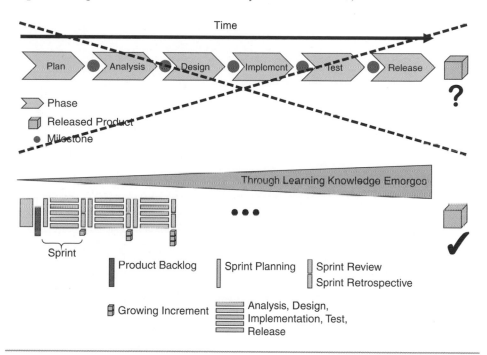

Figure 8-4 Continuous learning and improving through fast feedback loops

Keep in mind that any work you do before the customer actually receives the feature is considered inventory, a form of waste that needs to be maintained and managed (a cost).

Customer delight = Providing a **continuous** *stream of additional value to customers and delivering it sooner*

—Stephen Denning

Functional releases are an example of applying the three Vs (vision, value, validation) continuously.

In fact, the more often you release, the easier many of the decisions you need to make become.

When releasing every six months, logically it may make sense (at least on paper) that an organization could reserve the last month or so to decide to:

- have a separate group run all manual tests;
- fix all outstanding bugs;
- write up documentation;
- hand off to an operations team; and
- train the users.

Obviously these are all risky to leave to the very end. But risk aside, if that same company simply decides that it would like to deliver value to its customers more often, many of the above-mentioned decisions become harder or even impossible to stick with.

The further an organization moves from major releases toward functional releases (see Table 8-2), the more essential the following agile capabilities become:

- Bring testing into the Development Team
- Bring operations into the Development Team (DevOps)
- Automate tests
- Automate deployment
- Create cross-functional teams
- Create self-organized teams

- Engage stakeholders and users more often
- Do many of the other activities referenced in this book

Table 8-2 Comparison of Different Release Strategies

Major	Minor	Functional
• Many large changes	• Broad changes	• Individual functionality
• Infrequent (often aligns with organization timelines)	• Prescheduled (often aligns with Sprint boundaries)	• Continuous delivery (often during a Sprint, even daily)
• Freezes other work	• Often not cohesive	• Immediate value
• High customer absorption cost	• Often bug fixes and patches	• Low customer absorption costs
• High business risk	• Less business risk	• Minimal/no business risk

→ *The closer you get to functional releases, the more agile capabilities are needed.*

Increasing the release cadence even further to at least once per Sprint sets the stage for a more agile business, a business that runs experiments based on high-quality, self-testing code. The feedback loop of the three Vs tightens.

Notice that this approach also makes release planning easier. Customers tend not to ask for dates as often when you are constantly providing them valuable features. Budgets also become easier to acquire when customers are seeing a continuous return on their investments. We will cover more about budgeting later in this chapter.

ESTIMATION AND VELOCITY

If you were asked "How long does it take you to get from Zürich to Hamburg where the distance is 867 km (539 miles)?" your first question would likely be "What means of transportation can I use?" Good question. If the answer is a Porsche 911, your reply would be different than if you only had a bicycle. The distance remains exactly the same, but your velocity will vary.

Velocity represents your capability to make progress. This velocity is the determining factor for how long something will take. The Development Team's velocity will always vary: people fall ill, solutions change, conflict happens, hardware fails. This is the complex world you live in. If you had to make a forecast based on a Development Team's velocity, which would you choose? The velocity from a stable team, which has been working together for six months or more, or a newly formed group of people? The answer should be obvious: the stable team. A team that has been working together with minimal distractions will have a more consistent velocity and therefore predictability. This is the reason the on-product index introduced in Chapter 3 is so important for you as a Product Owner.

Which vacuum cleaner salesperson can give you a more reliable estimate on how many vacuums he will sell next month? The guy who has been doing the job consistently for ten years? Or that other guy who just transferred in from another region and sells vacuums cleaners part time? The senior guy will have a much easier time predicting next month's sales. He has empirical evidence that will allow him to make predictions well beyond the month. If he averages 20 vacuum sales a month, he can tell, with a fair amount of certainty, how many vacuums he will sell for the year.

20 vacuums per month (velocity) × 12 months = 240 vacuums (total sales)

What if you took the same approach?

Your stable Development Team has a history of producing eight Product Backlog items per two-week Sprint (velocity). The customer wants to know how much she will get for the release six months from now.

8 PBIs per Sprint (velocity) × 12 Sprints = 96 items off the Product Backlog

Conversely, if the customer wants to know how long it will take to get 50 items done, you can switch up the simple formula this way:

50 PBIs (total) / 8 PBIs per Sprint (velocity) × 2-week Sprints = 12.5 weeks

Just that easy, right?

While it would be nice to keep all your release plans this simple, there are three caveats:

1. *False sense of security:* Be careful showing any type of formula. It may give stakeholders the sense that there is precision and certainty when there certainly isn't any. Always remember that this is the complex world of product development, and anything can happen.

2. *Lack of empirical data:* If you hired a team yesterday and put a formula like this to use, you better not be implying any kind of certainty in the plan. In fact, there is no (honest) way to create certainty in that situation.

3. *Varying sizes:* What if there is a huge variance in size between the different Product Backlog items? A team may have achieved a velocity of 8 Product Backlog items in that last Sprint, but were they small items? Huge items? A combination?

All three of these concerns are ultimately about transparency. It is important to set the expectation that this formula will be run over and over as you gather more data. Things will change, and your forecast and plan should adjust accordingly. It is an ongoing calculation.

When it comes to dealing with the varying sizes of your Product Backlog items, there are more options.

You could take the time to break everything down into similar sizes, or you could weight them differently from one another.

A simple weighting mechanism is to assign t-shirt sizes (XXS, XS, S, M, L, XL, XXL) to each item. If you then equate each t-shirt size with a numerical value (points), you could use points instead of simply counting Product Backlog items. A popular number sequence in the agile community is Fibonacci (see Table 8-3).

Table 8-3 Mapping T-Shirt Sizes to Points

T-Shirt Size	Points
XXS	1
XS	2
S	3
M	5
L	8
XL	13
XXL	21

Ultimately, the number sequence used is somewhat arbitrary. The Fibonacci sequence has emerged as a favorite because the difference between numbers gradually increases. This works well as the bigger the estimate, the less accurate your estimate will be.

Revisiting the formula that ignored size variance:

50 PBIs (total) / 8 PBIs per Sprint (velocity) × 2-week Sprints = 12.5 weeks

When you take into account the size variance of the Product Backlog items by applying points, you end up with a revised end date:

160 points (total) / 19 points per Sprint (velocity) × 2-week Sprints = 16.8 weeks

Obviously, if the size variance between Product Backlog items is not that large, then the act of sizing each individual item could seem wasteful. You may want to ask yourself (and your Development Team) which activity will take more time: breaking all the Product Backlog items down to roughly even sizes or going through each item and applying points.

I was working with a Development Team that had been together fairly consistently for at least six months. During a planning poker[2] sizing meeting I heard one team member say to another, "I don't know why I bring my whole deck of planning cards with me, everything is just a 3 or a 5." Although it sounded like that team member was complaining, what he was unknowingly conveying was that the Scrum Team (including the Product Owner) had achieved consistency in how they were creating Product Backlog items. At some point, they stopped creating large Product Backlog items because they knew that they would need to break it down later anyway. It was then that I recommended doing away with point sizing altogether. Couldn't they save some time and just make everything a 1?

Notice that using these techniques, you can create release plans (with dates) without ever needing to estimate Product Backlog items in time units like weeks, days, or hours.

Studies have shown that human beings are pretty good at comparing things. For example, they do a good job at comparing building heights. However, they are not so good when asked to estimate how tall a building is with a unit like meters or feet.

By leveraging this skill and by harnessing past experiences, you can improve accuracy. Do not forget, it is still an estimate and not a 100 percent precise science. A study done by Rally,[3] where they analyzed more than 70,000 Scrum teams, found that by far the worst performing teams estimated in hours

---

2. James W. Grenning, "Planning Poker or How to Avoid Analysis Paralysis while Release Planning," Hawthorn Woods: Renaissance Software Consulting, April 2002.

3. Ken Schwaber and Jeff Sutherland, "Changes to *The Scrum Guide*," Scrum.org, July 6, 2016, https://www.scrum.org/About/All-Articles/articleType/ArticleView/articleId/1020/Changes-to-the-Scrum-Guide--ScrumPulse-Episode-14 (start watching at min 30:00).

followed by the ones using no estimates at all. The best performing teams used relative point estimation. Based on that, you could conclude that doing no estimations at all is better than estimating with days or hours.

A final warning about using points for velocity: Recall from Chapter 3 that velocity is still a circumstantial representation of value and is prone to Goodhart's law: "When a measure becomes a target, it ceases to be a good measure."

Velocity must be considered a value-neutral metric, and the Scrum Team should be the main audience for it. They should use it to bring awareness to their release plan so that they can inspect and adapt along the way. While being transparent on overall progress is important, the point values themselves should be considered meaningless to outside stakeholders such as management and customers. Chapter 3 provides many other options for metrics that can be used as a better indication of value delivered.

MANAGING MULTIPLE TEAMS

Assume that you have multiple stable Development Teams, each with an established velocity. The sum of all the resulting Increments is what your organization is capable of delivering each Sprint. This history of delivering "Done" Increments is your main determining factor for the future. You can plan for more, you can hope for more, but the chances that the velocity will increase on its own are slim to none.

Organizations often try to get more out of their Development Teams by throwing multiple projects at them, resulting in the problem described by Johanna Rothman in *Manage Your Project Portfolio*.[4]

---

4. Johanna Rothman, *Manage Your Project Portfolio: Increase Your Capacity and Finish More Projects* (Raleigh, NC: Pragmatic Bookshelf, 2009), 11.

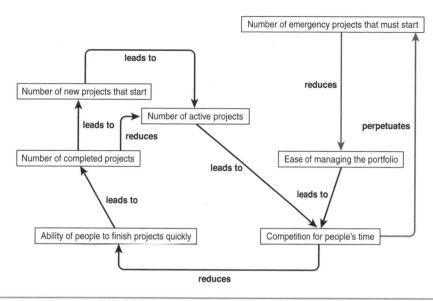

Figure 8-5 Low On-Product Index through multitasking or full-time equivalents (FTE)

Figure 8-5 shows that the number of active projects increases the competition for people's time. This reduces the ability to finish projects quickly, which lowers the number of completed projects. But all the projects are planned for the whole fiscal year, and you now need to start other projects. That is usually the moment when working on multiple simultaneous projects seems to make a lot of sense. In this complex adaptive system, this is called a positive reinforcement loop. This loop feeds on itself and worsens the situation with every revolution. Eventually you are so busy and so overloaded and doing so many things in parallel that nothing can be shipped.

The all-too-common fix? Instantiate an emergency project. Often they get fancy names like "Task Force," "Tiger Team," or "Alpha Team." These teams have to "just make it happen" and therefore have lots of freedom and are exempt from the normally enforced company governance. This, in turn, makes it harder to manage the company's portfolio. However, the people placed on the task force team do not appear out of thin air. They get pulled from other ongoing projects and are likely the higher performing team members. Now you have two closed loops speeding each other up. It is a vicious cycle.

The solution here is to stop thinking about long projects and start thinking instead about shipping value through products.

Then, the $64,000 question is:

How many concurrent products in your portfolio can your development organization's capacity support?

If that number is larger than the number of Development Teams, you are beyond your capacity (WIP limit), and everything and everyone slows down, as described above. A good practice is to work your portfolio backlog the same as you do your Product Backlog: ongoing refinement of value, size, risk (see Figure 8-6)

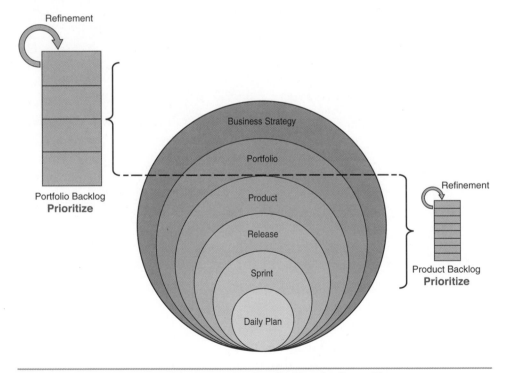

Figure 8-6 Products in a portfolio lead to Product Backlogs for Scrum Teams

Having an idea of the size of your portfolio backlog compared to the size of your capacity is crucial. As described earlier in the book, Development Teams cannot effectively support multiple products. So a development organization made up of ten Development Teams can support only ten or fewer products.

Having multiple teams work on a product is certainly an option for increasing velocity. However, throwing more people onto products is not always the answer. There is overhead to scale. As shown in Figure 8-7, if you are not careful, adding people can actually slow down progress (velocity).

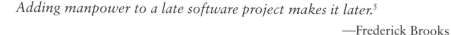

Adding manpower to a late software project makes it later.[5]

—Frederick Brooks

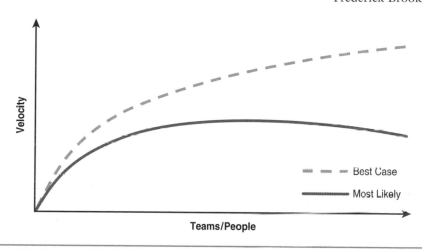

Figure 8-7 The cost of scaling

SCALING PRODUCTS

In today's agile community, there is a lot of buzz around scaling. But what does scaling even mean, and why do you need to do it? Are you scaling an agile adoption effort? Are you trying to increase velocity for a single product? Do you just have too many people who you need to keep busy? Let's break it down beginning with the 2×2 in Figure 8-8.

---

5. Frederick Brooks, *The Mythical Man Month* (Reading, MA: Addison-Wesley, 1995), 25.

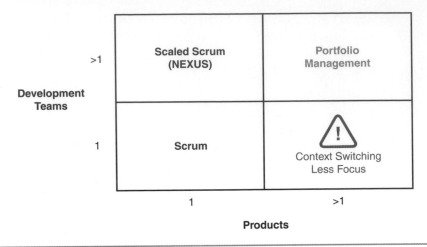

Figure 8-8 Number of Development Teams and products

Let's have a look at each quadrant.

ONE PRODUCT, ONE DEVELOPMENT TEAM

This is the sweet spot for Scrum: a dedicated Scrum Team focused on a single product. The rules of Scrum help the team members work out their communication and integration dependencies. They will likely have dependencies on outside people, environments, and other things outside of their immediate control, but they can usually manage them like any good self-organizing Development Team would.

Nail It Before You Scale It

When it comes to scaling, too many organizations attempt to scale Scrum to multiple Development Teams before they are even able to get just one Development Team to reliably create a "Done" Increment each Sprint. All they really end up doing is scaling their dysfunction and reducing their overall velocity (see Figure 8-7).

SEVERAL PRODUCTS, ONE DEVELOPMENT TEAM

This quadrant is not about scaling. It is about managing the Product Backlog in a way that minimizes context switching (see Figure 8-9).

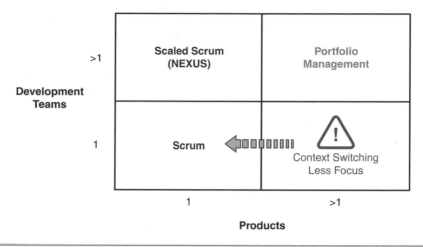

Figure 8-9 Moving only the work of one product into a given Sprint

As mentioned earlier in this chapter, if you have more products than you have Development Teams, you will lose effectiveness.

You might try to cheat your way out of this situation by having one Development Team work on only one product in a given Sprint. However, even if this seems tempting and a reasonable approach, be aware that this is a suboptimal solution and will work only if the Development Team is not disturbed during the Sprint with other "important" work from another product.

I have found that the only situation in which having one Development Team work on many products makes sense is with small companies that support multiple products but have budget for only one team. One Product Owner I worked with placed all the work across the products into one Product Backlog and had to determine which products took precedence each Sprint. It certainly wasn't as effective as having dedicated Development Teams for each product, but it was a price the company was willing to pay given its situation.

SEVERAL PRODUCTS, SEVERAL DEVELOPMENT TEAMS

Although this quadrant has many Development Teams and many products, it is not necessarily a scaling issue. One hundred dedicated Development Teams working on 100 products may have the odd dependency here and there, but they should be able to manage with pure Scrum and good engineering practices.

The real challenge here is determining which products are the most important and how much to budget for each, where budget equates to Development Teams. This is portfolio management.

Johanna Rothman describes this in *Manage Your Product Portfolio*: "Portfolio is an organization of projects by date and value, that the organization commits to or is planning to commit to."[6]

Even though we would have preferred Johanna had used the term "product" instead of "project," the spirit of this statement still applies.

An organization should have one product portfolio (see Figure 8-6), which represents all the products that it is committed to. Managing this backlog implies selecting, prioritizing, and killing your products.[7]

Essentially, the idea is to move the highest value product from the top right either into the Scaled Scrum (Nexus) quadrant or the Scrum quadrant depending on number of Development Teams dedicated to it (see Figure 8-10).

---

6. Rothman, *Manage Your Product Portfolio*, 23.
7. Craig Larman and Bas Vodde, *Scaling Lean & Agile Development* (Boston: Addison-Wesley, 2009).

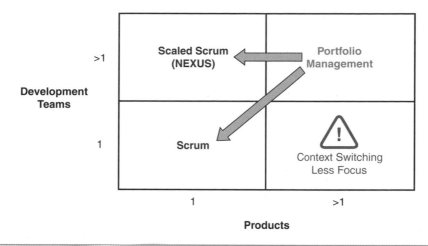

Figure 8-10 Prioritization of products into Scaled Scrum or team Scrum

ONE PRODUCT, SEVERAL DEVELOPMENT TEAMS

This is the domain of a large-scale product approach and ultimately defines scaling. Scaling is not about adopting agile or Scrum, managing your portfolio, or dealing with context switching. Scaling is about multiple Development Teams working on a single product.

When one single Development Team does not suffice, a scaling approach that still stays true to the values of Scrum may be needed.

There are many scaling frameworks (with lots of cool acronyms) available, like Large-Scale Scrum (LeSS), Disciplined Agile Delivery (DAD), Scaled Agile Framework (SAFe), Scrum@Scale, and Nexus. All have varying degrees of detail and approaches, most of which are outside the scope of this book.

Scaled Scrum Is Still Scrum

Ultimately, the core values and practices of Scrum apply at scale. Nexus, LeSS, and Scrum@Scale come closest to this as they were developed in accordance with the *Scrum Guide* and *therefore keep an empirical mindset and self-organization at heart*. Next we quickly review Nexus, the scaling framework we have the most experience using.

THE NEXUS FRAMEWORK

According to Merriam-Webster, a Nexus is:

> A connection or links between groups or series. Often in the context of providing focus.[8]

This section on Nexus highlights a few key points that are important for Product Owners to know when dealing with scale. For more details, take a look at the Nexus Guide[9] or *The Nexus™ Framework for Scaling Scrum.*[10]

In the same way Scrum is a framework for three to nine people to work more effectively together; at scale, Nexus is a similar framework for three to nine Development Teams to work more effectively together. The same challenges that people have communicating, dealing with dependencies, and integrating all apply between teams the same way they do between people on a team.

> *Nexus is the exoskeleton of scaled Scrum.*
>
> —Ken Schwaber

The Nexus framework (see Figure 8-11) scales up to nine Development Teams for one product with one Product Owner and one Product Backlog.

Unlike single-team Scrum, Product Backlog refinement is a mandatory event in Nexus since multiple Development Teams need to be aligned in the context of the larger product. Nexus refinement takes place on two levels:

1. As an activity across all Development Teams with the goal of increasing communication and minimizing dependencies between teams. This also allows for high-level relative sizing of the Product Backlog items. The top of the Product Backlog is then divided out between the Development Teams that will likely work on them.

2. Once a Development Team selects items from the Product Backlog, they will refine it as they would with single-team Scrum and then coordinate remaining dependencies with other Development Teams. Here they can apply their own estimates.

---

8. *Merriam-Webster*, accessed March 22, 2018, https://www.merriam-webster.com/dictionary/nexus.

9. "The Nexus Guide," Scrum.org, accessed March 3, 2018, https://www.scrum.org/resources/nexus-guide.

10. Kurt Bittner, Patricia Kong, and Dave West, *The Nexus™ Framework for Scaling Scrum* (Boston: Addison Wesley, 2017).

This provides relative estimation at two levels, possibly even with two different scales, where the higher-level describes the overall product development velocity, the velocity the Product Owner has to work and plan with. They can then append the progress from all Development Teams into one release plan for the one Product Backlog. From a stakeholder perspective, the workload separation between Development Teams (the magic behind the curtain) should be inconsequential.

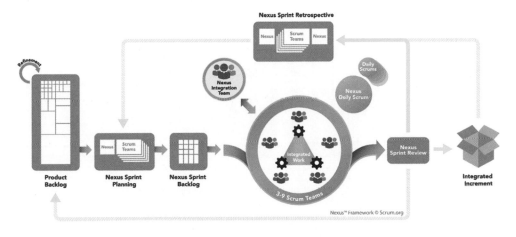

Figure 8-11 The Nexus framework

The ultimate goal of the Nexus Sprint is to have one integrated working product Increment across all Development Teams. When a Nexus can successfully achieve this along with a well-maintained shared Product Backlog, it provides excellent transparency for the Product Owner and stakeholders.

REPORTING

A well-kept Product Backlog contains all the information needed for reporting.

Because of the fact that Scrum provides you with the ability to actually complete a valuable product increment each Sprint, it opens up a wide range of possibilities when it comes to reporting.

The primary measure of progress is working software.

—Agile Manifesto

FORECASTING BASICS

As long as the Product Backlog is continuously refined and you only have one Product Backlog for your product, this Product Backlog is—along with the Development Team's velocity—all you need for reporting.

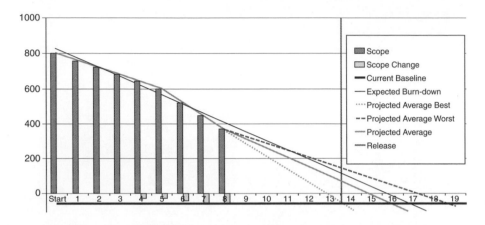

Figure 8-12 Release burn-down allowing for some forecasting

The release burn-down example in Figure 8-12 shows progress across Sprints for a large product with three Development Teams. The Product Backlog was fairly large, and as you can see, it took the Development Teams about five Sprints until they had enough learned—emergence—about the domain, technology, and how to work best as the Development Teams. Starting at Sprint 4, the size of the Product Backlog grew. This was either new functionality (Scope) or an updated estimate because of better understanding.

The thin black line is the expected burn-down trendline (based on the least squares[11] regression) over all known data points (all Sprints). The thicker gray line represents the average velocity extrapolated from the last known data point (last Sprint). The dashed lines are respectively the average of three lowest and highest Sprint velocities. The spread of these lines is often referred to as the cone of uncertainty, which has its roots in hurricane trajectory predictions. The further you look into the future, the less accurate your predictions will be.

---

11. "Least Squares Regression," Math Is Fun, accessed March 20, 2018, https://www.mathsisfun.com/data/least-squares-regression.html.

Cone of Uncertainty

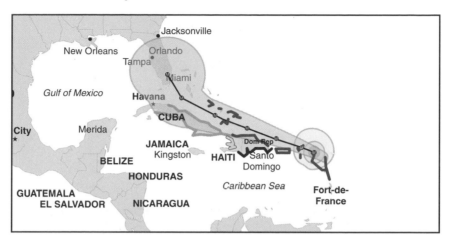

Figure 8-13 Hurricane forecasting with the cone of uncertainty

Predicting your product's progress is a lot like predicting hurricanes (see Figure 8-13):

From weather.com

Each *tropical system* is given a *forecast* cone to help the public better understand where it's headed.

The cone is designed to show increasing forecast uncertainty over time.

Based on previous forecast errors [over the previous five years], the entire track of the tropical cyclone can be expected to remain within the cone about 60 to 70 percent of the time. The cone becomes wider over time as the forecast uncertainty increases.[12]

Swap out "tropical system" with "Product Backlog" and "public" with "stakeholders" and most of the above statement translates to your world. Of course, there are no guarantees. Wild things still happen (unknown-unknowns) while

---

12. "Cone of Uncertainty: Facts and Myths About This Tropical Forecasting Tool," Weather.com, September 4, 2017, https://weather.com/science/weather-explainers/news/tropical-storm-cyclone-forecast-cone-hurricane.

predicting product development efforts, just like they do with weather systems. Hurricanes escape the cone 30 to 40 percent of the time. You never know for sure what path a hurricane will take until the storm happens. However, as you collect empirical data from where the hurricane has been, you develop a narrower landing area. In the same way, using Scrum properly, you can collect data about what has actually been "Done" to narrow the landing area of where you will end up.

Use the cone of uncertainty as a way to remind stakeholders of uncertainty, not to imply certainty.

The project management world often cites a "cone of uncertainty" that implies the more you analyze, the more precise your predictions will be. Introduced in this context by Barry Boehm[13] and later picked up by Steve McConnell,[14] this idea has largely been debunked.[15] We use the hurricane "cone of uncertainty" with customers all the time and find it a great tool for showing what has been "Done," communicating the uncertainty of the future, and moving away from more traditional status reports, such as Red-Amber-Green (RAG) traffic light reports.

This is also a good time to remind you that this forecasting, while useful, is only circumstantial evidence of any value delivered. Think of it instead as miles traveled (progress). It does not indicate whether you are traveling in the right direction (or even in circles). For more direct evidence of value, stick with the measurements described in Chapter 3.

13. Barry Boehm, *Software Engineering Economics* (Upper Saddle River, NJ: Prentice-Hall, 1981).

14. Steve McConnell, *Software Estimation: Demystifying the Black Art* (Redmond, WA: Microsoft Press, 2006).

15. Laurent Bossavit, *The Leprechauns of Software Engineering*, Leanpub, last updated June 27, 2017, https://leanpub.com/leprechauns.

Forecasting

As shown in Figure 8-14, the end of Sprint 13 is the scheduled release date. Since this release burn-down chart was created after Sprint 8, the team has five more Sprints to complete the Product Backlog. How likely is this, and what options are available?

- **Change the release date** → What are the implications of moving the date? Can we set expectations now about this possibility? Can we put a contingency plan in place?
- **Increase velocity to complete all scope** → Can we add people to the Development Team? Is it too late for that to make a difference? Can we move other distractions off the Development Team's plate? Can we improve tooling and infrastructure? Can we bring in another Development Team to help?
- **Work with scope** → What is absolutely necessary for this release—Minimum Viable Product (MVP)?

Figure 8-14 shows a situation where scope was adjusted as the date was non-negotiable.

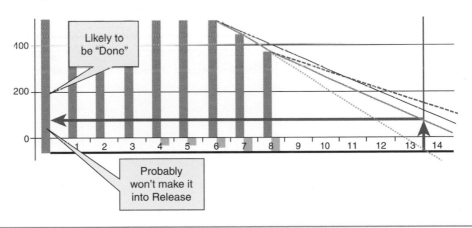

Figure 8-14 Scope projection based on burn-down chart

Inspecting the release burn-down chart, you could decide that the gray line is a reasonable forecast. Since the date is fixed at the end of Sprint 13, you can draw a vertical line from the current bottom of the scope until you touch the gray line. From this intersection, you then draw a horizontal leftward until you touch the Product Backlog. Scope above is likely to be completed ("Done") by the release date. Scope below likely won't.

This is good information for the Product Owner to make conscious scope decisions. For example, functionality in the "Done" part could be "simplified" to require less effort, thereby creating room for "currently won't make it" functionality. Another option would be to descope less urgent functionality until a future release. This is hard work for the Product Owner, but like most things in life, it boils down to tradeoffs.

Overall, the value in using release plans such as these is to visualize and communicate the level of uncertainty that exists (transparency). It allows the Scrum Team as well as stakeholders to face the reality of their situation sooner rather than later (inspect) and then start making plans to adjust (adapt).

FORECASTING ACROSS MULTIPLE PRODUCTS

How can you compare Scrum Teams working on separate products?

Well, this depends on intent. If the intent is to find out which Scrum Teams are better in terms of velocity, the answer is "You can't and you shouldn't try." Each Scrum Team has its own unique scale for estimating their Product Backlog, not to mention different levels of complexity and capacity. As mentioned in Chapter 3, doing this will also result in extrinsic motivation that may lead to fudging the numbers.

However, if the intent is to compare progress in a way to better distribute capacity and work, then there may be a way.

Acknowledging that each team has its own relative way of estimating, you can remove the actual numbers and instead focus on the slope of the velocity to get a progress overview. Regardless of what each individual Development Teams base unit is, the slope stays comparable.

Assume you have several connected subproducts, each with its own Scrum Team. You could create a release burn-down per subproduct and overlay them as in Figure 8-15. This makes it transparent which one has the highest risk of not being done on time and which one is on the critical path.

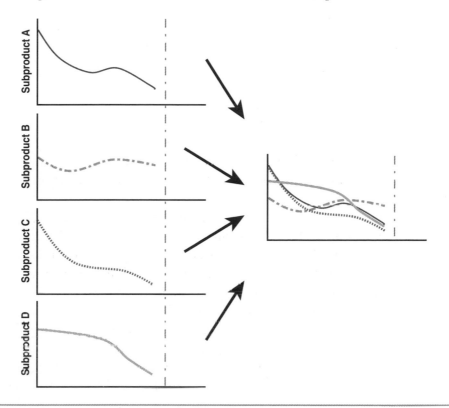

Figure 8-15 Using unitless release burn-down slopes to compare progress

With this value-neutral data, you can make decisions accordingly and actively steer development. You may decide to move people from subproduct C to subproduct B or Product Backlog items from subproduct B to subproduct C as C is doing fine right now. You might decide to hire an extra person to help with testing. The options are endless, and in the end it depends on your context. Regardless of what you decide to do, the next Sprint provides the transparency you need to inspect and adapt once more.

It is worth repeating that this information can be abused if associated with the performance of a Scrum Team. It can be valuable if treated in a transparent and neutral way with the purpose of inspection and adaptation.

PERCENTAGE OF COMPLETION

A simple-to-understand but not always simple-to-calculate metric is Percentage of Completion (PoC).

If you have to pack 120 jars of pickles, then it is reasonable to estimate that you are 50 percent complete once you pack the 60th jar.

However, when your project is made up of a series of interdependent steps, each one different from the next, then this becomes more difficult.

Imagine you have to make a large dinner, with many sequential and unique tasks, the only real way to estimate PoC is based on time spent/remaining. If you gave yourself two hours to make dinner and you are one hour into it, what is your PoC? If you have made the same dinner many times before, then you can assume you are 50 percent complete. However, if you are making the dinner for the first time and have no real confidence in your initial two-hour estimate, then that 50 percent PoC metric is misleading.

With more traditional waterfall processes, PoC is much more like the dinner example above, which only represents time spent. Figure 8-16 shows an example in which analysis is complete and design is 80 percent complete, putting the overall "project" at 37 percent completed.

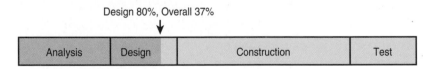

Figure 8-16 Percentage of completion measured by time spent

This kind of reporting is made without even having started any development work and rarely represents accurately how much is truly complete, especially when building something unknown and complex.

When using Scrum, PoC can be a more meaningful metric. Like the jars of pickles example above, the Development Team is actually completing features each Sprint. Saying that you are 72 percent complete should have more meaning: as in, 72 percent of the features are completed and ready for production, if not already in production.

You can also do this at a more granular level with individual initiatives. Figure 8-17 shows an example in which the "Online auctions Initiative is 67 percent complete." How do you know? Six of the nine Product Backlog items are actually "Done."

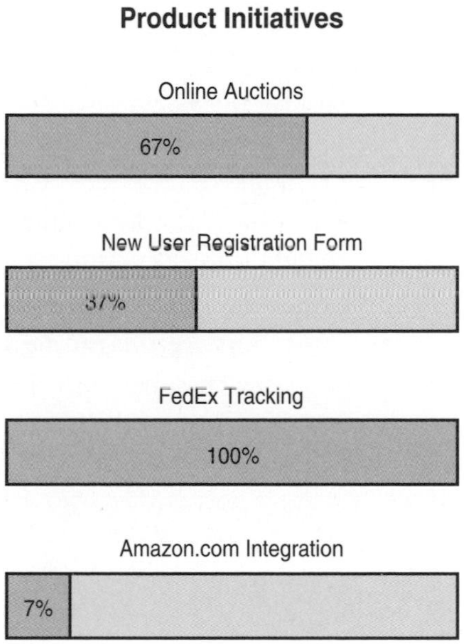

Product Initiatives

Online Auctions

67%

New User Registration Form

37%

FedEx Tracking

100%

Amazon.com Integration

7%

Figure 8-17 Percentage of completion by Initiatives

Consider adding metrics like these to your reports. They are more meaningful to your stakeholders, who likely think more in terms of valuable Initiatives than analysis, design, construction, and so on. A Sprint Review is an excellent opportunity to present them.

MONTE CARLO SIMULATION

Monte Carlo simulation is a risk mitigation technique for problems that require a numerical answer but are too complex to solve analytically. It instead applies random numbers and probability statistics to explore the likelihood of every possible outcome of a decision from one extreme to the other.

This technique has been used in physics, chemistry, research, business, and medicine, and even in the creation of the hydrogen bomb.

When applied to estimating Product Backlogs, Monte Carlo simulation works on the premise that each Product Backlog item has a range between an optimistic and a pessimistic estimate.

It simulates reality by assigning a random value between the optimistic and pessimistic range for a Product Backlog item. This is repeated across the whole Product Backlog, and the random Product Backlog values are added up. The resulting sum represents a point on the x-axis (see Figure 8-18). The y-axis represents the frequency of sums with the same value. This simulation is done at least 10,000 times.

The resulting plot is a distribution over time where the area is the likelihood of being done by that time.

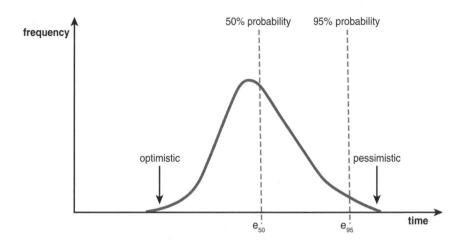

Figure 8-18 Probability distribution based on Monte Carlo simulation

There are two points on the horizontal time axis that are of statistical interest: e_{50}, where you have a 50 percent chance of being done; and e_{95}, with a 95 percent percent chance of being done.

There are several online tools available to help with running simulations like these. I developed a simple Ruby script that does the job for me.

You can even run a Monte Carlo simulation with Microsoft Excel.[16]

How does this help you with customers demanding a date/cost prediction?

You can apply this same technique when using relative sizing of the Product Backlog items by replacing time with effort/size. With that, you acknowledge that the total effort/size is not yet known even if the scope is understood.

---

16. "Introduction to Monte Carlo Simulation," Microsoft, last updated August 21, 2014, https://support.office.com/en-us/article/introduction-to-monte-carlo-simulation-64c0ba99-752a-4fa8-bbd3-4450d8db16f1.

Figure 8-19 shows a Monte Carlo simulation with 100,000 runs over a Product Backlog with 72 Product Backlog items between 1 and 21 story points.

The distribution assumption per Product Backlog item is as follows:

- The likelihood of the size estimate being correct is 75 percent.
- The likelihood of it being the next higher size is 20 percent and the next lower size is 5 percent (e.g., for a 13 story point item, the range is (5%) 8, (75%) 13, or (20%) 21; for a 1 story point item, it would be 1, 1, or 2).

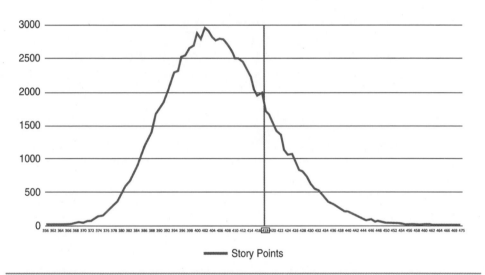

Figure 8-19 Real Monte Carlo simulation for Product Backlog size

In this case, let's say you choose an 80 percent probability of the total Product Backlog effort/size being at most 418 story points. If there are no changes to the Product Backlog, then there is still a 20 percent probability that the Product Backlog is larger.

Now you assume to have a total of 418 story points and an average velocity of 33 story points per Sprint.

Velocity has a variance as well, as shown in Figure 8-20 where the last eight Sprints reveal a variance between 29 and 37 points.

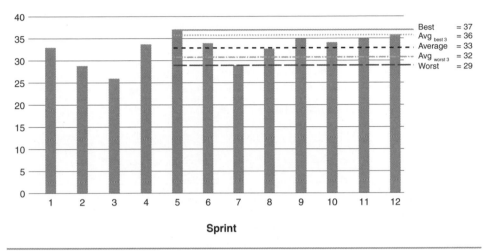

Figure 8-20 Velocity variance over time

With the Product Backlog effort distribution and the velocity average, you have a formula to calculate a possible completion date:

$$\text{Time} = (\text{Story Points}_{total} / \text{Velocity}_{avg}) \times \text{Sprint Length}$$

Now you can do a Monte Carlo with 100,000 simulations using random numbers between 29 and 37 story points. You subtract this velocity number from the total Product Backlog effort—418 in this case—until you are at or below zero. You count the frequency for the resulting number of Sprints. This distribution gives you a Sprint range for when the Product Backlog will be completed (see Figure 8-21): 50% probability in Sprint 14 and 95% probability in Sprint 15.

Will this work? It all comes down to your Development Team as they are doing the estimation and the work. The less stable the Development Team, the less precision, resulting in a higher variance in the estimates and velocity.

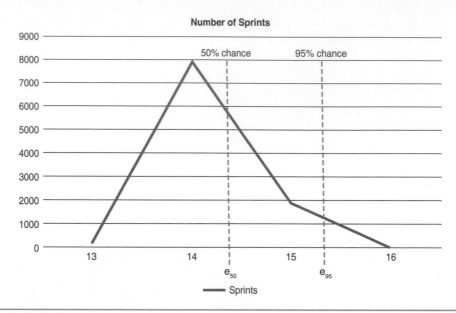

Figure 8-21 Monte Carlo simulation for number of Sprints

Do not let these statistics fool you with a false sense of precision. Every time the Product Backlog or the Development Team changes, the calculations need to be voided and redone. This becomes almost impossible with a volatile Development Team. No technique can guarantee you certainty when your team is in constant flux.

The more time a Development Team gets to collaborate, to emerge good practices, to learn from their past mistakes, the more they understand the product domain, the more reliable they will be. Rather than sponsoring a product, instead think of it as sponsoring a Development Team building the best possible product with the highest possible value within the given constraints.

> *Our tool will not estimate how long your project will take; all it will do is tell you how much uncertainty ought to be associated with whatever estimate you come up with.*[17]
>
> —Tom DeMarco and Timothy Lister

---

17. Tom DeMarco and Timothy Lister, *Waltzing with Bears: Managing Risk on Software Projects* (New York: Dorset House, 2003), 91.

WHICH COLOR IS YOUR VELOCITY?

Assume that over the last two years, you had a stable Development Team that had a consistent velocity of 100 points. As a Product Owner, could you assert that this Development Team generated the same amount of value each Sprint over that time?

The answer should be no. Your Development Team may have done the same amount of work, but is the output the same? Did your team's innovation rate change over time?

This can be visualized by categorizing (with colors if you aren't stuck with black and white, as in the print version of this book) your Product Backlog items and the resulting velocity (see Figure 8-22).

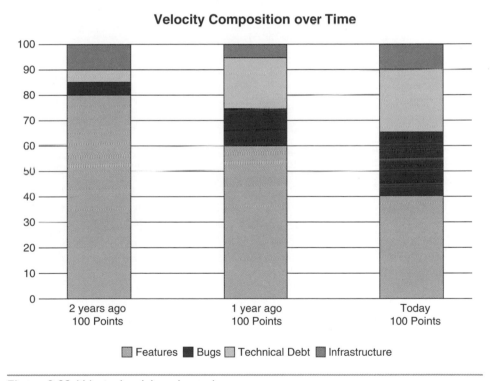

Figure 8-22 Velocity breakdown by work type

Features are good. This is what creates value by attracting new customers or keeping old ones.

Technical debt is not so good. However, the bad decisions made in the past still need to be dealt with. Addressing technical debt should help to have less rework in the future so that you can focus on more innovative features.

Infrastructure is work you have to do that fits neither into the feature nor technical debt category. It could be setting up a clustered load balanced database or upgrading environments. Again, these should help to create more value down the road.

Bugs are always bad. They are the manifestation of the inability to deliver a high-quality product. Bugs bridge the whole delivery life cycle from initial creation, refinement, implementation, testing, and releasing. A bug can be attributed to having made a mistake in any of these steps.

In the above example, the Development Team performs as well as it did two years ago. It still delivers around 100 points worth of output.

However, the value produced has decreased dramatically. It went from 80 points two years ago to only half of that, 40 points, today. Fighting technical debt and bugs went up accordingly.

Infrastructure is often higher in the beginning and decreases over time; it never vanishes completely. It is important to keep infrastructure and architecture sound.

The important take-away here is to monitor these numbers carefully, as this pattern is commonplace and can too easily be masked. The number value itself is not as important as its trend over time, which can indicate whether you are improving or getting worse. Consider the data in your given context, create transparency around them, and drive your decisions from there.

BUDGETING

At some point, an idea for a product initiative is proposed by someone. This initiative has prospective revenue generation or cost savings for the organization. Maybe a business case is created to show this potential ROI. The next step is budgeting.

In a defined phase-driven organization, the budgeting process is typically handed off to project managers and follows the following four steps:

1. **Prepare the Budget**

   Find out what is needed, create plan for initiative, and then send to decision makers.

2. **Approve the Budget**

   Determine whether the budget still aligns with the purported ROI of the initiative. Is it still worth doing? This can often be a political activity in which changes and cuts are expected before approval, which often bleeds into development time.

3. **Execute (and Control) the Budget**

   Doing the work and controlling costs. This is where scope creep is managed and change requests are made to adjust the budget.

4. **Evaluate the Budget**

   Making sure the money was spent and used correctly. This is the moment of truth when you find out whether the money was spent effectively.

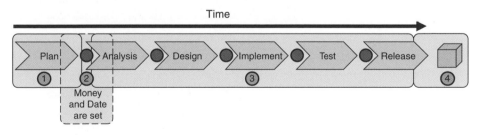

Figure 8-23 Setting date, time, and budget when the least knowledge is available

The problem with this approach is that money and date are set before the actual work has started, exactly when everyone knows the least about what is being built (see Figure 8-23). No real learning and no contact with complexity has happened yet. And for a project manager, their job is to deliver the specified project on budget, on schedule, and within scope.

The initial business case likely has merit. However, the lengthy budgeting process itself can add to layers upon layers of planning and handoffs that end up masking the original product vision. Think back to the product management vacuum described in the first chapter.

Instead of putting on these shackles before getting a chance to learn, you should leverage emergence by collecting real data—empirical evidence—by building a small part of the planned product. This part of the product should address anticipated features or technical risks as you want real data to drive a go/no-go decision. The cost of this learning is relatively easy to calculate: It is the number of members of your Development Team for the length of the learning period (see Figure 8-24). Usually, just a few Sprints should allow for enough empirical data to drive an informed decision. This time (and cost) may even be less than the time needed to create a comprehensive plan and budget.

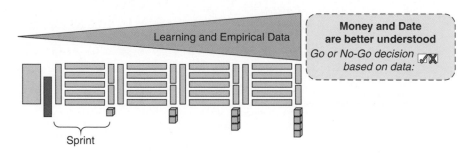

Figure 8-24 Two-phased budgeting: commitment after real knowledge is acquired

If the data shows that the risks are not manageable and the resulting uncertainty is therefore too high, this may be a good time to pull the plug. You lose some money, but you knew upfront how much it would be.

If the data shows that there is a realistic chance to build and ship the product, then go ahead and do it. It might even be a good time to speed up delivery by scaling up your Development Teams.

Be wise enough not to be reckless, but brave enough to take great risks.

—Frank Warren

Even better than building the first part of the product to gain data for making a go/no-go decision is to actually release the product before the next budgeting phase. It is much easier to make a case for a budget when you can demonstrate actual ROI. Remember the MVP we introduced in Chapter 4.

I was on a Scrum Team for an internal call center application. Those of us on the Development Team had no idea that our budget was almost up. However, a few Sprints earlier, when we were demonstrating some new functionality, one of the users convinced us to give them the functionality sooner, saying it would save him time during his daily tasks. When it was later announced that our budget was up, that user was able to show how much time (money) the team saved with the new functionality, which made acquiring new budgets much easier.

Five steps for agile budgeting (FEED-ME):

1. Fund products and their *visions* instead of projects

   Rather than thinking in terms of project funding, think about products. Having a product costs money. A two-week Sprint that costs $50,000 translates to an annual run rate of $1.3 million. How many people and Development Teams can that fund?

2. Empower the Product Owner

   Instead of assigning scope, schedule, and budget to a project manager, allow the Product Owner to become more of a sponsor with an entrepreneurial mindset for her product. Give her the fiduciary responsibility.

3. Establish transparency

In lieu of thinking and acting in a defined linear approach, establish empirical feedback loops that allow for continuous measurements. Keep asking, "Are we still on track? Are we still on the *right* track?"

4. Demonstrate *value* sooner

The more often you release, the more often your stakeholders will see a return on their investment, making them much more eager to continue or increase funding.

5. Manage stakeholder expectations

Ensure that your stakeholders are consistently informed on where the money is being spent and what they are getting in return. Remind them about the uncertainty of building complex products and that directions may need to change. Be on the lookout for new stakeholders as the work progresses.

6. Employ empirical budgeting through *validation*

Instead of being driven by fixed budget (and scope and schedule), recognize that budgets will need to vary to deal with the evidence gathered while validating your assumptions. Budgets may need to be reassigned, decreased, increased, or even killed. Plan to revisit the budget every time you validate and new evidence is collected.

Certainly all this is easier said than done, and moving to a more agile budgeting approach is not an overnight initiative. In the end, you need to play the cards that you are dealt. Just know that however the funding happens, an agile approach can still work.

If your organization is still demanding an upfront budget and . . .

. . . you have some say in the budgeting process:

1. Build a Product Backlog.
2. Determine a potential velocity with the Development Team.
3. Determine the number of Sprints.
4. Multiply the number of Sprints by the cost of a Sprint.

5. Realize that as you release functionality that provides a return, getting more funding will be much easier (if needed).

. . . you have no say in the budget and it is handed to you:

1. Build a Product Backlog.
2. Determine a potential velocity with the Development Team.
3. Determine how far down the Product Backlog you can get with the potential velocity.
4. Realize that as you release functionality that provides a return, getting more funding will be much easier (if needed).

. . . you are asked for a fixed budget for a fixed scope:

1. Realize that you have been asked to take on all the risk. Therefore communicate that the cost will be higher to effectively manage this risk.
2. Build a Product Backlog.
3. Determine a potential velocity with the Development Team.
4. Determine the number of Sprints.
5. Increase the cost of the Sprint by an extra member or two per Development Team for risk mitigation. Consider this a buffer to handle the overhead of scope changes.
6. Multiply the number of Sprints by the cost of a Sprint.
7. Realize that as you release functionality, customers will want changes. Accept any changes if there is capacity or if they can be swapped with equally sized items. Increase the cost for all other changes; otherwise the quality of the product will suffer.
8. Ensure that the budget includes a maintenance period following the end of the Initiative as there will always be unforeseen work after a release.

As you can see, a fixed budget and scope limits agility. Ultimately, it creates a vendor management situation where the customer is asking for a product as though he were buying it off the shelf. The difference is that the product does not yet exist and the vendor needs to account for that uncertainty.

I work for a software development company called Improving. As a vendor building products for our customers, we want to collaborate with them as much as possible to build the right product. Unfortunately, many clients ask for a fixed price for a fixed scope. We have learned the hard way that when we do not account for the risk by adding extra people, then accommodating the client with changes along the way ultimately decreases our profit and sometimes even puts us in the red. As this does not help us or the client, we like to provide them with two options: (1) time and material costs, which allows the client to increase or decrease budget as they see value along the way; or (2) a higher fixed cost, when they shift the risk to us.

Ultimately, the best thing you can do to manage all this risk is to build a working "Done" product at the end of every Sprint.

By putting yourself in a position to produce value throughout, the fundamental discussions around budgets and timelines change. The question is no longer about "Are we going to make it?" Instead it becomes "Are we getting the best ROI out of each Sprint?"

Not only will this approach make budgeting decisions easier, it will help with other important factors such as meeting stakeholder's expectations and complying with governance and regulatory requirements.

GOVERNANCE AND COMPLIANCE

The first two values of the 2001 Agile Manifesto are:

Individuals and interactions over *processes and tools*

Working software over *comprehensive documentation*

Both of these reflect the potential waste within governance activities that are implemented with the intention of mitigating risk. Agile teams mitigate risk by creating working software; therefore compliance documents, sign-offs, and audits are often seen as redundant.

But does this mean that all governance and compliance activities are wasteful?

To better answer this, let's take a look at some common documents in product development (Table 8-4)

Table 8-4 Comparing Common Documents in Product Development

Requirements	User Guides
Business Rules	Training Materials
Test Cases	Legal Compliance (Sarbanes-Oxley)
UI Mock-ups	Support and Maintenance Guides
Designs	Security Compliance
Coding Style Guides	Legal Traceability-Matrix (FDA, FAA, etc.)

Notice a difference between the documents on the left versus the documents on the right?

The documents on the left are consumed by the Development Team, while the documents on the right are consumed by stakeholders outside of the Scrum Team. Therefore, who should determine which documents are needed? Ideally, the Development Team should get to select the documents that help them (left), while the Product Owner should select the documents that help the stakeholders (right). Therefore, the documents on the left should find themselves either in the Sprint Backlog and/or in the Definition of "Done." The documents on the right should find themselves in the Product Backlog or also as part of the Definition of "Done."

This is a good way to look at governance. There is internal governance for the documents on the left and external governance for the documents on the right. External governance may be considered wasteful, but it is necessary. You treat it like you would any other stakeholder request. Internal governance, however, may be a good opportunity to reduce waste.

There are two main reasons internal governance is implemented.

The first is that there is a lack of trust with the Development Teams, so they are asked to document their work to ensure they do not get off track. In case they get off track, they are likely asked to provide even more documentation, outlining a plan to get back on track.

The second is that the organization may want consistency between teams, products, and departments to ultimately lower costs.

The first reason, lack of trust, is addressed with Scrum by creating working increments each Sprint. Therefore, the only real reason for internal governance should be to achieve consistency across the organization.

The larger the enterprise, the more governance is necessary to maintain oversight and stay in control. With waterfall, the governance checkpoints are aligned with milestones between development phases (see Figure 8-25). Until something is built, there is nothing but paperwork governance.

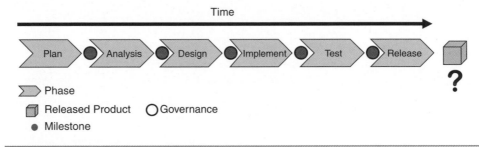

Figure 8-25 Governance at milestones

When things go wrong, governance usually grows, slowing the release down even further.

The myth is that without governance, there is chaos; the more governance there is, the more order there will be (see Figure 8-26).

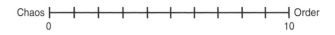

Figure 8-26 Governance spectrum

Governance is at its highest right before a release since releasing presents the most risk. This presents a problem with organizations that are attempting to be more agile and releasing more often.

I was coaching several teams within e-commerce for a large retail chain. The organization typically used 6- to 12-month release cycles and had an internal governance regulation of needing 17 signatures when planning a release and again before the release. Since we had planned on releasing every 2-week Sprint, this became an obvious bottleneck. It may have been possible for a major release strategy, but we were trying to deliver value more often. Getting 17 signatures at Sprint Planning and then again after the Sprint Review was impossible. Bringing this to the attention of the governance group and management stakeholders resulted in changes to their practices.

With a clear focus on value through continuous product delivery, you have all you need to govern.

Any paperwork describing progress is futile—no customers will pay for that. They pay money only for a working product. How do you get this working product? Leave it to the people doing the work by providing a clear vision and empower them to release frequently. Don't bury them in bureaucracy.

John Kotter describes this well:[18]

---

18. John Kotter, "Accelerate!," *Harvard Business Review*, November 2012.

> *The old methodology simply can't handle rapid change. Hierarchies and standard managerial processes, even when minimally bureaucratic, are inherently risk-averse and resistant to change.*

> *[Th]e absence of bureaucratic layers, command-and-control prohibitions, and Six Sigma processes, . . . permits a level of individualism, creativity, and innovation that not even the least bureaucratic hierarchy can provide.*
>
> —John Kotter

Once you have a "Done" working product at the end of the Sprint, you have all the feedback and learning to "govern" right (see Figure 8-27).

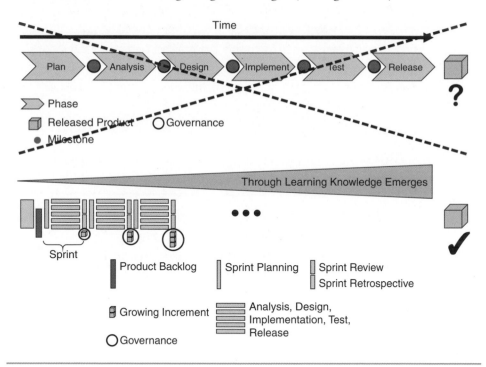

Figure 8-27 Agile governance based on working product

I am a big fan of the Toyota A3 Reports as described by Durward Sobek and Art Smalley.[19] So I was wondering how you could use them for reporting when using Scrum. The result is what I call the "Agile A4 Sprint Report" as it fits nicely on a page (see Figure 8-28). The top left describes how the past Sprint went and whether there were any learnings or difficulties. Just below, we see the Development Team's happiness index. Below that are all the risks that cannot be handled by Scrum itself. Each risk is described by its probability and impact if it materializes.

Top right is the burn-down over our Product Backlog. At the bottom right, we see the number of open bugs.

In the center is where the Development Team indicates whether the product is "Done" and can be released.

This report is updated every Sprint and made visible. That way it is easy to compare Sprint to Sprint and discover trends. This was all the governance we needed.

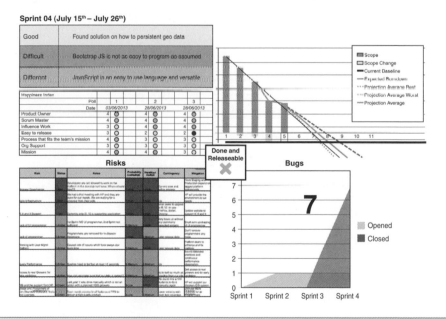

Figure 8-28 Agile A4 Sprint Report

19. Durward K. Sobek II and Art Smalley, *A3—Understanding A3 Thinking* (New York: Taylor and Francis, 2008).

KICKOFF

When planning a release, getting off on the right foot is important.

According to Sandy Mamoli and David Mole,[20] 30 percent of the success depends on how the team is launched. Even though the kickoff is not the most important ingredient, it still has the potential to ruin just about everything.

I do enjoy running for recreation and actually competed in a couple of marathons. Training is the most important aspect of what your final time will be. It is not all, though. Once you are in your starting block and ready to give your best, many things have been done in preparation. Simple things like clipping your toenails, selecting the right socks, pants, and shirt to avoid skin shavings, which could become rather painful over the 26.2 miles (42.195 km) distance. Calculating how often to drink which liquid, the target pace needed to reach your anticipated time. How much to eat of the right food the day before, to drink enough to be hydrated but not too much as you want to avoid a bathroom break. After you start, it is about finding your rhythm, your breathing, your pace. It is tempting to join the group that is starting like they are on a 100m dash. If you stick to your principles, however, I guarantee that you will pick them up about a third of the distance. Once the first 3 miles are completed, it is all about inspection and adaptation of time, pace, heart rate, and distance.

How to launch your product development initiative is sadly too often a second thought. It seems more important to get started instead of starting right. The "just start now, you will be told exactly what we need later" mantra is common. Basically, not enough developers with not the right skills will do

---

20. Sandy Mamoli and David Mole, *Creating Great Teams: How Self-Selection Lets People Excel* (Dallas: Pragmatic Bookshelf, 2015).

their best chasing a nonformulated vision. This is frustrating on many levels and does not create a buy-in or commitment from the Development Team(s).

Diana Larsen and Ainsley Nies describe how they like to kick off their product development efforts in their book *Liftoff*.[21] Figure 8-29 is a brief primer for a kickoff.

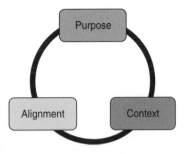

Figure 8-29 Kickoff with Purpose, Context, and Alignment

Purpose is about putting a stake in the ground, clearly formulating the vision, and deciding how you think you can get there (see Figure 8-30).

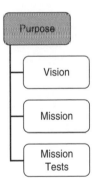

Vision
- What is the vision of the product? This is addressed in Chapter 2.

Mission
- Often the vision cannot be reached in one step but requires a sequence of smaller missions leading to the vision. What is your first/next step toward your vision?

Mission Tests
- How can you measure that you are on the right track toward your mission? See Chapter 3 on evidence-based management (EBMgt).

Figure 8-30 Purpose

---

21. Diana Larsen and Ainsley Nies, *Liftoff* (Hillsboro, OR: Onyx Neon Press, 2012).

I once worked on an agronomic product. The vision was to increase the harvest yield by 20 percent by a smarter usage of water, a scarce resource in that area. Our first mission was to have at least 100 farmers sign up and participate in the pilot as we wanted to validate our math model. The mission tests were rather simple: 100 farmers to see the benefit of using the product.

Ralph

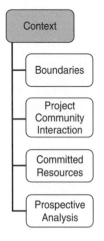

Boundaries

- What are our dependencies to other components or teams?
- Physical working environment

Project Community Interaction

- Who are our stakeholders?
- Customers
- Sales
- Marketing
- Users

Committed Resources

- Travel
- Infrastructure
- Hardware/Software

Prospective Analysis

- What are our assumptions?
- Are we realistic with what we have available and our goal?
- What are known threats and major risks?
- What is going to give when things turn bad?
- What are our opportunities and benefits?

Figure 8-31 Context

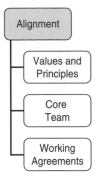

Values and Principles

- What are our values?
- How do we work and interact (Scrum values are commitment, openness, focus, respect, and courage)?

Core Team

- Who is on our cross-functional team?
- How much are the developers available (think about the On-Product Index)?

Working Agreements

- Do we have core business hours?
- Do we encourage remote working?
- When is our Daily Scrum?
- What is our definition of "Done"?
- How should we handle conflict when it arises?

Figure 8-32 Alignment

Following the steps in Figures 8-30, 8-31, and 8-32 and working out an answer for each of the points is a kickoff done well. Yes, this is a team effort; nothing you do is in isolation. Get everybody in the same room (see Figure 8-33) and have them, through strong facilitation, work it out for themselves.

How long does this take? In general, plan for at least one day. If one day is not enough, then do some team prep work upfront and do the kickoff as the big event. Or you might even go offsite for two days and build in some team-forming activities.

Figure 8-33 Kickoff at Swiss Postal Services in the VIP Lounge at Stade de Suisse

QUALITY

Let's begin with a few definitions of quality.

DEFINITIONS

Everyone wants quality service or a high-quality product. What exactly is quality, though? If the product is of high quality, shouldn't it be a success? Here are a couple of definitions:

- **Original ISO 9000 Definition of quality:** Degree to which a set of inherent characteristics fulfills requirements
- **Philip B. Crosby**[22] (well respected for his work on quality management): Conformance to requirements

---

22. https://en.wikipedia.org/wiki/Philip_B._Crosby

Quality is all about doing what you specified in the beginning, probably a long time ago when you knew the least. It focuses on process conformance and not on value and end user happiness.

Johan Laurenz Eveleens and Chris Verhoef[23] look at the definition of project success based on the definitions of the Standish Group:

Resolution Type 1, or project success

The project is completed on time and on budget, offering all features and functions as initially specified.

Resolution Type 2, or project challenged

The project is completed and operational but over budget and over the time estimate, and offers fewer features and functions than originally specified.

Resolution Type 3, or project impaired

The project is cancelled at some point during the development cycle.

Jørgensen and his colleagues show that the definitions do not cover all possibilities. **For instance, a project that's within budget and time but that has less functionality doesn't fit any category** (see Table 8-5, fourth row).

Table 8-5 Possible Definition of Successful Project

#	On Time	On Budget	All Features	Status	Happy Customer
RT1	Yes	Yes	Yes	Success	?
RT2	Over	Over	Less	Challenged	?
RT3	?	?	?	Cancelled	? (No)
4	Ok	Ok	Less	?	Yes

---

23. Johan Laurenz Eveleens and Chris Verhoef, "The Rise and Fall of the Chaos Report," *IEEE Software* 27, no. 1 (2010): 30–36.

What if the missing functionality is of low value and not missed by the customers? Does it reduce product quality? Not necessarily, because it is known that around 50 percent of the features are hardly ever used. Consider the most important quality criteria to be a satisfied customer with an okay budget usage and an okay timeline. With "okay" it is meant that the spent money and time was right in the given context; it could mean that either more or even less was used. However, this judgment call has to come from the Product Owner based on collaboration with the stakeholders.

Also, since you are "Done" after each Sprint, it is absolutely okay to spend less money and less time as originally planned and release more frequently to collect real feedback from the market, possibly for each feature to gather real value metrics.

TYPES OF QUALITY

Types of quality include product quality and technical quality.

Product Quality

The Product Quality is all about creating the right product—the right set of features and functionality. This responsibility lies with the Product Owner and has to be addressed through the right scope, which is represented through the Product Backlog.

In a regulated environment this is called *validation*—doing the right thing.

Technical Quality

The technical quality resides with the Development Team. It is the Development Team's responsibility to make sure that the developed product is always in good shape without technical debt and in a "Done" and releasable state.

In a regulated environment, this is called *verification*—doing it right.

Figure 8-34 summarizes quality.

Figure 8-34 Iron triangle of quality and relation to quality with the Scrum roles

In the end, it is all about doing the right thing right.

KEEPING QUALITY

The software product grows incrementally. Think about playing Legos, where you put one brick on top of another until you have what you want. This would work if you knew everything upfront, but since you operate in the complex domain, you will discover required changes to the existing Increment. The Increment grows, but existing functionality is being adapted throughout. That is the iterative part of iterative and incremental.

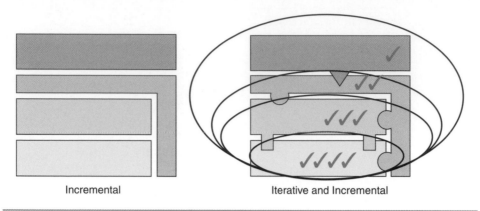

Figure 8-35 Keeping quality over time

Quality needs to be built into the product from day one; quality cannot be tested into the product at the very end. Testing after the fact is about stability and not about quality. Quality needs to be built into the product and you have to make sure that it stays (see Figure 8-35). You have to make sure that the achieved quality—product and technical—does not vanish over time (see Figure 8-36). Having it once doesn't guarantee its presence in the future.

Therefore, there has to be a full regression test of what was added and what was there already. For that, you need test automation. Manual testing will not scale for a large number of Sprints. If your only test strategy is manual, before you know it your regression tests will take up more of your Sprint than actual development. That is when you have a big problem. You will no longer be able to guarantee a quality product as you won't be able to get to "Done" as easily.

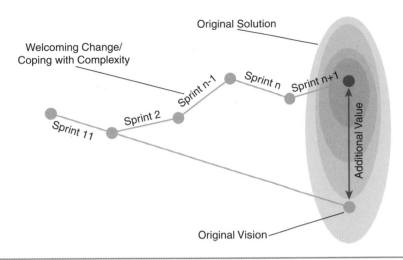

Figure 8-36 Maximizing and keeping value by ensuring quality

Let's revisit the Agile Testing Quadrants (see Figure 8-37), which were introduced in the "Specification by Example" section earlier in the chapter.

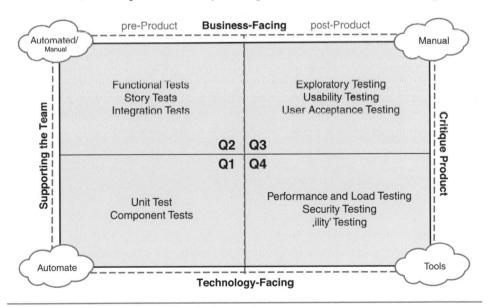

Figure 8-37 Agile Testing Quadrants with a product view

Quadrant 1

This quadrant is all about solid craftsmanship: good design, good engineering, good programming, and discipline. Quadrant 1 builds the foundation on which the product is going to be built. It is based on hundreds or thousands of automated unit tests. This is where testing frameworks like JUnit,[24] which was originally developed Kent Beck, come into play. This is where individual functions and classes are tested. Those tests ensure a big part of the technical quality.

A unit test does not touch the file system, database, or any other system; it is in memory only. That is what makes unit tests so fast and allows thousands of tests to run in a short time. Simulating the environment requires that you understood the behavior of the environment. It is exactly this understanding that drives better design decisions.

Furthermore, those tests are executable documentation, exactly describing the behavior of the used systems. Even better, this kind of documentation does not ever lie. It is either green for a successful test or red when something is wrong.

Quadrant 1 is all about the **How**.

Quadrant 2

This quadrant was put into the forefront through agile software development as it brings together the business, engineering, and testing points of view. This quadrant is an essential part for bridging the product management vacuum by having the crucial conversations to drive out all abstractness of the requirements. The tests in this quadrant make sure that the business quality is ensured. Tests in this quadrant should be automated with the occasional exception. If test automation seems unrealistic in this quadrant, it is often a sign of bad architectural decisions; this often shows that the business logic can be tested only through the user interface because it is not decoupled enough from the presentation layer.

---

24. "About," JUnit.org, accessed March 3, 2018, http://junit.org.

Since Quadrant 2 is also about integration, this is the place where integration with all other systems takes place. Simulations are being replaced by the real thing, and tests are not only in memory any more—this is where the rubber meets the road.

If done right, you can actually reuse most of your unit tests from Quadrant 1 by redirecting the test from the simulation to the real thing. Again, this should be straightforward assuming you have the right architecture and design patterns in place.

Quadrant 2 is all about the **What***.*

Pre-product

Quadrants 1 and 2 are pre-product. All the tests in these quadrants lead to the product. If one of the tests fails, you do not have a product. These two quadrants are your quality sentinels; if all of these tests are successful, you have a product. They perform the grunt work on a continuous basis and this is why these tests have to be automated.

This automation does not come cheap, but it pays back in spades in the long run. What can be better than to have a product that tests itself?

This is why continuous integration, along with automated builds and tests, is a must these days. If your Development Team does not have a continuous integration system up and running, they are putting you at risk. Make sure they have enough capacity each Sprint to implement the right infrastructure, or you will be paying for it eventually down the line (with interest) in the form of technical debt.

These two quadrants are all about supporting the Development Team in their daily work to deliver "Done" Increments of product continuously and build the foundation for emergent architecture.

Quadrant 3

Once you have the product, it is time to make sure it does exactly what the user wants in a usable way. This is when you provide the chance for hands-on playing around either from a testing side by exploratory testing or by real end users doing real target-driven work. Expect one of two feedbacks: Works for me/us or doesn't work for me/us. If it is the later, you declare the functionality as not "Done" and put it back into the Product Backlog for future evaluation. If it is the former—yay! Automate the UATs (User Acceptance Tests) and move them into Quadrant 2. This way, the pre-product tests ensure that you keep the quality.

As this quadrant is all about the human aspect, it is clear that these tests are manual. Those tests are enough work to keep testing busy, which is another reason for automating Quadrants 1 and 2.

Quadrant 3 is all about the **User***.*

Quadrant 4

How do you make sure your architecture is scalable, reliable, and performs well under load? Sure, you can test for many of those aspects in Quadrant 1 and possibly Quadrant 2, but in the end the only true measure for those quality attributes is with the final product. Once you have the product, you get the chance to make sure that system and underlying architecture afford all those nonfunctional requirements. These tests are often tool based, either through a purchased tool or custom development. Again, you have to automate as many of these tests as possible.

Quadrant 4 is all about the **Nonfunctional Requirements***.*

Post-product

Quadrants 3 and 4 are post-product. All the tests are performed on the existing product to appraise, assess, and comment the product. This validation is still on premise, meaning it is not yet the market feedback. However, doing this continously and frequently improves the likelihood of releasing a successful product and therefore shrinking the product management vacuum.

QUIZ REVIEW

Compare your answers from the beginning of the chapter to the ones below. Now that you have read the chapter, would you change any of your answers? Do you agree with the answers below?

Statement	Agree	Disagree
With Scrum, you need to release at the end of each Sprint.		✔
You cannot provide release dates with Scrum.		✔
You can release multiple times within a Sprint.	✔	
Not allowing teams to release during important business periods (code freezes) reduces agility.	✔	
With Scrum, Product Backlog items must be sized using relative points.		✔
A good release plan should include a buffer time period just before a release to stabilize the product (fix defects, regression test, document, etc).		✔

THE PROFESSIONAL PRODUCT OWNER

9

Now that the role of Product Owner has been addressed in depth, let's summarize by examining what it means to be a professional Product Owner. What traits does he have? How does she know when she is successful?

Let's start by revisiting an image from way back in Chapter 1.

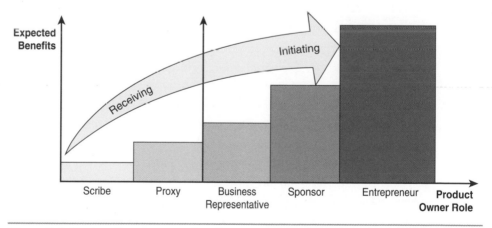

Figure 9-1 Product Owner personality affects outcome

The most successful Product Owners find themselves further along the line in Figure 9-1. Recall that these are more about attitudes and mindsets than titles.

UNDERSTANDING PRODUCT OWNER SUCCESS

Consider the two Product Owner extremes outlined in the next two sections.

THE RECEIVING PRODUCT OWNER

This type of Product Owner often works for a larger corporation and is responsible for an existing product. Upper management provides him with Key Performance Indicators (KPIs) against which he is measured, often in connection with set requirements. This limits being proactive and visionary. Traps of complacency (e.g., "This is just how we do things around here") make the situation even worse, turning the receiving Product Owner into more of a project manager. Because the strategic aspects of the Product Owner role are not well understood, many organizations equate the role with project management.

If this describes your role, then move toward truly owning the product and step up to do the right things. For example, fight for the right to build a strong dedicated Development Team (or teams) because you will need to rely on them. Make sure that you have enough bandwidth for being a good Product Owner; consider it a full-time job. Move your desk and sit with the Development Team and build a real relationship with them, which will result in a leap forward in productivity.

I once coached at a large insurance company that had a Product Owner who was allowed to do product work for 50 percent of his time. The remaining 50 percent was for other work. He did a really good job as Product Owner, but the 50 percent proved too little. When I tried to convince his boss to change this, I was told no and that the Product Owner would be assessed at year's end on the non-Product Owner work. He found himself between a rock and a hard place. Doing good product ownership on 50 percent was not possible, and the remaining 50 percent was more like 100 percent of the workload anyway. In the end, this employee pulled the cord and quit the company for another insurance company.

Ralph

If you are not an expert of the domain for which the product is being developed, then become an expert. Practice Toyota's approach of *Genchi Genbutsu* (go to where the work is done). Identify all your stakeholders and go and talk to them, even if it means leaving the building. You need to understand their needs, their fears, their frustrations, and their hopes, so that you develop true customer empathy. Solidify that relationship by using the feedback loop of the Sprint Review. Show that you listen and care about them. For stakeholders who cannot attend the review on a regular basis, find other ways to collect their feedback to show how important their opinion is to you.

THE INITIATING PRODUCT OWNER

This type of Product Owner has all the freedom, even budgetary, to do whatever is needed to realize the product vision. This level of entrepreneurship is most likely at odds with typical technology departments because they won't have enough connections with management and Development Teams. Talking to people, making deals, networking, spreading the vision, and plowing the field for the product doesn't allow an initiating Product Owner to spend enough time with the people on the ground.

If this describes your role, then find trusted lieutenants and empower them to assist you wherever needed by providing them with clear goals and insight. Let them find answers and work out the details on their own. Work and its related responsibility can be delegated, but you still stay accountable for the product as only you possess the visionary authority. Take the time to build relationships with the Development Team(s) by relentlessly sharing the product vision and providing feedback.

YOU

These two kinds of Product Owners are at opposite ends of the spectrum and often reflect totally different personalities. Your reality is most likely between these two extremes. Use the guidance provided in this book to tailor your own approach to become a great Product Owner. Try out ideas and measure the results to see whether they are helping or hindering; be empirical.

SKILLS AND TRAITS

When we teach Product Owner courses, the course finishes with an exercise that reflects on the Product Owner role. Participants are asked for the skills and traits of a good Product Owner.

What is a skill and what is a trait?

- Traits are who you are; skills are your abilities.
- Skills are easier to learn whereas traits require a change in personality.
- Performance reviews and interviews are too often focused on skills, such as experience doing something, knowledge of procedures, and quality of output.

With this description in mind, the participants are asked to list the skills and traits of an ideal Product Owner.

The charts in Figures 9-2 and 9-3 show how often a skill or trait was identified after hundreds of classes and thousands of students.

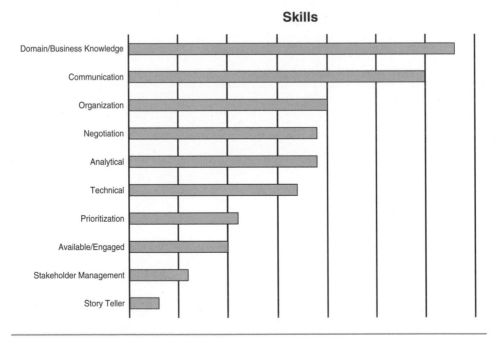

Figure 9-2 Skills of a good Product Owner

The most important skill is domain and business knowledge followed closely by strong communication skills.

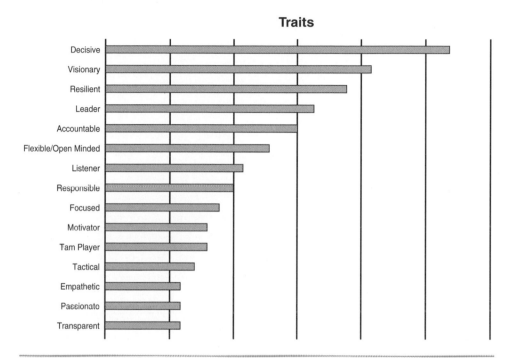

Figure 9-3 Traits of a good Product Owner

The most important trait is being decisive—having the power and ability to make decisions and putting an end to debate—followed by being a visionary.

If you plan to work as a Product Owner, these two charts essentially describe your job.

Example Product Owner job description:

> *We are looking for a visionary person with excellent business and domain understanding. In your role, we expect you to be a decisive leader displaying strong negotiation skills with all stakeholders and people involved. Your passion for the product and your ability to listen helps you to cope with changes and the occasional setback.*

This description is a tall order for sure. Being a Product Owner is not a walk in the park. The Product Owner is a keystone role in Scrum.

Use this list to assess yourself and start working on yourself. There is always room to grow.

In Barry Boehm and Richard Turner's book, *Balancing Agility and Discipline: A Guide for the Perplexed*,[1] appears an interesting mnemonic to describe an ideal customer: CRACK.

This mnemonic does a good job at summarizing the skills and traits of a Product Owner as well.

Keep Product Owners on **CRACK**:

- Collaborative:

  Work closely with Development Teams and stakeholders. Get to know them. Hand out your cell phone number. Ask them to text or call at any time. Get involved during the Sprint. Don't wait until the end to provide feedback. See yourself as part of the team.

- Representative:

  Build empathy with your stakeholders and customers. Be their voice when they are not around. Establish and communicate a product vision that accurately reflects their needs. Also represent the Scrum Team by standing up to management that is increasing pressure to deliver.

- Authorized:

  Be empowered to make any product-related decisions regarding scope, schedule, and budget. Make the final call when stakeholders cannot reach agreement while having confidence that you can adjust your path later when you know more information.

- Committed:

  Product Ownership is a full-time job. Stay committed to the product, the Development Team, stakeholders, and quality. Stay true to the vision, value, validation (the three Vs), and the empirical process that is Scrum. Do not let anything steer you off track.

---

1. Barry Boehm and Richard Turner, *Balancing Agility and Discipline: A Guide for the Perplexed* (Boston: Addison-Wesley, 2003).

- Knowledgeable:

  Know your domain and never stop learning. Work closely with users and subject matter experts to fill in any gaps in your knowledge. Stay on top of the latest technology trends. Examine the marketplace and competition to stay in front.

MEASURING SUCCESS

Ultimately, success of a Product Owner, and consequently the product, comes back to the three Vs (see Figure 9-4).

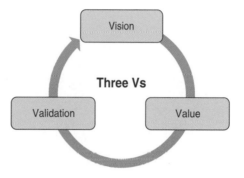

Figure 9-4 The three Vs

How clear is your product vision? Do the people creating the product know it? Do your stakeholders? Does your Product Backlog reflect the vision? Are your release plan and Sprint Goals in line with the vision?

How are you measuring value? How often are you measuring it? Are you maximizing return on investment? Are your customers happier? How about your Development Team? How much of your budget is being spent on new innovative features that your customers are asking for rather than maintenance?

Are you validating the product with your stakeholders and the marketplace? How often are you doing it? Are you adjusting the product's direction accordingly? Is the quality of the product consistent enough to release whenever needed?

If you can show positive trends for each of these questions, then congratulations: you are a true professional Product Owner.

Index

CREDITS

Frontmatter: "A successful child has many parents. A failure has none." Based on Tacitus, Agricola, ~ 98AD.

Chapter 1: "We didn't do anything wrong but, somehow we lost". Nokia CEO.

Chapter 1: "Gen. Helmuth von Moltke ... of innovative culture". Michael J. Gunther. *Auftragstaktik: The Basis for Modern Military Command?* (School of Advanced Military Studies, United States Army Command and General Staff College, Fort Leavenworth, Kansas, 2012).

Chapter 1: "If everything is important, then nothing is." Patrick M. Lencioni, *Silos, Politics, and Turf Wars: A Leadership Fable about Destroying the Barriers That Turn Colleagues into Competitors* (San Francisco: Jossey-Bass, 2002).

Chapter 1: "Product: A product is anything that can be offered to a market that might satisfy a want or need". Philip Kotler, Linden Brown, Stewart Adam, Suzan Burton, Gary Armstrong, *Marketing,* 7th Edition. (Frenchs Forest, New South Wales: Pearson Education Australia/Prentice Hall. 2007).

Chapter 1: "Organizations which design systems ... are constrained to produce designs which are copies of the communication structures of these organizations". Melvin E. Conway, (April 1968), "How Do Committees Invent?", *Datamation*, 14, no. 5 (April 1968): 28–31

Chapter 1: "1. Sequential lifecycle ... issues in the long run". Cesário Ramos. "Scale your product NOT your Scrum," Scrum.org Whitepaper, February 2016.

Chapter 1: "Many, many practices." Screenshot of Scrum © Scrum.org.

Chapter 2: "Whatever you can do or dream you can, begin it. Boldness has genius, and magic and power in it. Begin it now." Goethe.

Chapter 2: "A vision is a ... has on our staff". Ari Weinzweig, Zingerman's Co-Founder https://www.zingtrain.com/content/why-and-how-visioning-works.

Chapter 2: "Inspiring: To all that will be ... have to tell people about it too." Ari Weinzweig, Zingerman's Co-Founder https://www.zingtrain.com/content/why-and-how-visioning-works.

Chapter 2: "We continually foster world-class ... sources to meet our customer's needs". Dilbert's Mission Statement Generator.

Chapter 2: "Our challenge is to assertively network ... negotiate performance based solutions". Dilbert's Mission Statement Generator

Chapter 2, Figure 2-3: Boilerplate Product Vision/Mission statement. Dilbert's statement.

Chapter 2, Figure 2-4. Ceralios Product Box. Image from Don McGreal.

Chapter 2, Figure 2-5: Crunchy Flakes Product Box. Image from Don McGreal.

Chapter 2: "Technology skills do not necessarily ... in a way that you can make exceptional decisions." Venkatesh Rao, "Great CEOs Must be Either Technical or Financial," forbes.com, May 15, 2012.

Chapter 2: "Technology changes suddenly expand the strategy canvas and offer new ways of doing old things, or entirely new things to do." Venkatesh Rao, "Great CEOs Must be Either Technical or Financial," forbes.com, May 15, 2012.

Chapter 2, Figure 2-10: "Strategic Alignment Index". *Measuring the Business Value of Information Technology,* Intel Press.

Chapter 3, Figure 3-6: "Value Metrics based on EBMgt™". Adapted from "Evidence-Based Management for Software Organizations [EBMgt]," http://www.ebmgt.org/.

Chapter 3: "The mind is the laboratory where products, both fake and genuine are manufactured. People grow wild weeds, others grow flourishing flowers!" Israelmore Ayivor.

Chapter 3: "If for any reason you are dissatisfied with your Domino's Pizza dining experience, we will re-make your pizza or refund your money". https://biz.dominos.com/web/public/about-dominos/history.

Chapter 3: "Current Value reveals the organization's actual ... ability to sustain value in the future". Evidence-based Management Guide.

Chapter 3: "Autonomy: the desire ... something meaningful beyond than ourselves" Daniel H. Pink, *Drive: The Surprising Truth about What Motivates Us* (Edinburgh: Canongate, 2010).

Chapter 3: "The purpose of business is to create and keep a customer" Peter Drucker.

Chapter 3: Direct Feedback from Microsoft Office Product. Screenshot of MS-Office © Microsoft 2018

Chapter 3: "Time to market evaluates the software ... to sustainably deliver value in the future is unknown." Evidence-based Management Guide.

Chapter 3: "The ability to innovate is necessary but often a luxury.... available capacity to innovate." Evidence-based Management Guide.

Chapter 3: "Netscape's project to ... the same obstacles" Joel Spolsky, "Things You Should Never Do," April 6, 2000, Retrieved 2008-09-11.

Chapter 3: "When a measure becomes a target, it ceases to be a good measure." Campbell's and Goodhart's law.

Chapter 3: "slavishly imitates the working methods of more successful development organizations" New World Encyclopedia, s.v. "cargo cult," accessed March 5, 2018, http://www.newworldencyclopedia.org/entry/Cargo_cult.

Chapter 4: "Plans are useless but planning is indispensable". Dwight D. Eisenhower.

Chapter 4: "No plan survives contact with the enemy". Helmuth von Moltke.

Chapter 4: "Everyone has a plan until they get punched in the face". Mike Tyson.

Chapter 4: "Eighty percent of the time you/we are wrong about what a customer wants". Online Experimentation at Microsoft, 2009.

Chapter 4: "Forty percent of businesses....sweat, I should be." http://uk.businessinsider.com/chambers-40-of-companies-are-dying-2015-6.

Chapter 4, Figure 4-1: Transparent sneeze guard at a sandwich bar. Photo by Don McGreal.

Chapter 4, Figure 4-3: Audi "magic" bird's eye car view. Photo by Don McGreal.

Chapter 4: "The problem is that we do not understand the problem." Paul McCready.

Chapter 4: "Customer Feedback is the basis for ideas, customer data is the basis for decisions." Roman Pichler.

Chapter 4: "For MacCready, he had no ... or is it the courage to fail?" "A willingness to fail solved the problem of human-powered flight," *Financial Review*, October 2015.

Chapter 5, Figure 5-7: "Nothing but a pack of cards. At this whole pack rose up into the air, and came flying down upon her...", *Alice's Adventures in Wonderland*. Illustration from John Tenniel, published in 1865. Morphart Creation/Shutterstock.

Chapter 5: "If there's no risk on your next project, do not do it." Tom de Marco.

Chapter 5: "a late change in requirements is a competitive advantage." Mary Poppendieck.

Chapter 6: "Scrum is a framework for developing, delivering, and sustaining complex products." ScrumGuides.org ©2017 Ken Schwaber and Jeff Sutherland.

Chapter 6: "Scrum is founded on empirical process ... predictability and control risk." ScrumGuides.org ©2017 Ken Schwaber and Jeff Sutherland.

Chapter 6: "Significant aspects of the process ... common definition of "Done." ScrumGuides.org ©2017 Ken Schwaber and Jeff Sutherland.

Chapter 6: "Scrum users must frequently ... inspectors at the point of work." ScrumGuides.org ©2017 Ken Schwaber and Jeff Sutherland.

Chapter 6: "If an inspector determines ... Sprint Retrospective". ScrumGuides.org ©2017 Ken Schwaber and Jeff Sutherland.

Chapter 6: "The Product Owner is responsible ... from a different set of requirements". ScrumGuides.org ©2017 Ken Schwaber and Jeff Sutherland.

Chapter 6: "Vision without execution is hallucination." Thomas Edison.

Chapter 6: "The Development Team consists of professionals ... belongs to the Development Team as a whole." ScrumGuides.org ©2017 Ken Schwaber and Jeff Sutherland.

Chapter 6: "The Scrum Master is responsible for promoting … of Scrum in the organization."
ScrumGuides.org ©2017 Ken Schwaber and Jeff Sutherland.

Chapter 6: "The Scrum Team consists of a Product … version of working product is always available."
ScrumGuides.org ©2017 Ken Schwaber and Jeff Sutherland.

Chapter 6: "The Product Backlog is an ordered list … the work make the final estimate."
ScrumGuides.org ©2017 Ken Schwaber and Jeff Sutherland.

Chapter 6: "The Sprint Backlog is the set of Product Backlog … solely to the Development Team."
ScrumGuides.org ©2017 Ken Schwaber and Jeff Sutherland.

Chapter 6: "The Increment is the sum … release that occur during the Sprint." ScrumGuides.org ©2017 Ken Schwaber and Jeff Sutherland.

Chapter 6: "When a Product Backlog …work done on it." ScrumGuides.org ©2017 Ken Schwaber and Jeff Sutherland.

Chapter 6: "At any point in time…looking decision-making". ScrumGuides.org ©2017 Ken Schwaber and Jeff Sutherland.

Chapter 6: "The heart of Scrum …calendar month of cost." ScrumGuides.org ©2017 Ken Schwaber and Jeff Sutherland.

Chapter 6: "A Sprint would …rarely makes sense." ScrumGuides.org ©2017 Ken Schwaber and Jeff Sutherland.

Chapter 6: "The work to be …within the Sprint". ScrumGuides.org ©2017 Ken Schwaber and Jeff Sutherland.

Chapter 6: "The Daily Scrum is a 15-minute time-boxed … a key inspect and adapt meeting."
ScrumGuides.org ©2017 Ken Schwaber and Jeff Sutherland.

Chapter 6: "A Sprint Review is held at the end of the … overall to meet new opportunities."
ScrumGuides.org ©2017 Ken Schwaber and Jeff Sutherland.

Chapter 6: "The Sprint Retrospective is an opportunity … to focus on inspection and adaptation."
ScrumGuides.org ©2017 Ken Schwaber and Jeff Sutherland.

Chapter 6: "Product Backlog refinement is the act of … Product Owner or at the Product Owner's discretion."
ScrumGuides.org ©2017 Ken Schwaber and Jeff Sutherland.

Chapter 6: "Increment: \ 'i?-kr?-m?nt, 'in- \ noun the action … from the stem of increscere
"grow"." By permission. From Merriam-Webster.com © 2018 by Merriam-Webster, Inc.
https://www.merriam-webster.com/dictionary/word.

Chapter 6: "The problem with quick and dirty … is that dirty remains long after quick has been forgotten".
Steve C. McConnell, *Software Project Survival Guide* (Redmond, WA: Microsoft Press, 1998).

Chapter 6: "Agile Manifesto for... the left more." http://agilemanifesto.org/.

Chapter 6: "The problem with my proposal … we value craftsmanship more." https://www.infoq.com/news/2008/08/manifesto-fifth-craftsmanship.

Chapter 7: "requirement : a : something wanted or needed : NECESSITY b : something essential to the existence or occurrence of something else : CONDITION". Merriam-Webster Dictionary.

Chapter 7: "The Product Backlog is an ordered … its content, availability, and ordering".
ScrumGuides.org ©2017 Ken Schwaber and Jeff Sutherland.

Chapter 7: "Card: Legend has …broken into smaller stories". http://ronjeffries.com/xprog/articles/expcardconversationconfirmation/.

Chapter 7: "Independent: Stories are easiest to work with … know whether this goal is met."
William C. Wake, *Extreme Programming Explored* (Boston: Addison-Wesley, 2002).

Chapter 7: "Detailed Enough acceptance criteria to get started … value, risk, cost, dependencies, etc." Roman Pichler and Mike Cohn.

Chapter 7: "SMART: Specific—what is the outcome? … display "out of service" message." This acronym was first defined by Jef Newsom, one of the founders of Improving Enterprises.

Chapter 7: "The Product Backlog is an ordered … the lower the order, the less detail."
ScrumGuides.org ©2017 Ken Schwaber and Jeff Sutherland.

Chapter 7: "When a Product Backlog item … work to be complete, to ensure transparency."
ScrumGuides.org ©2017 Ken Schwaber and Jeff Sutherland.

Chapter 7, Figure 7-16: Ralph on vacation with birds. Photo by Ralph Jocham.

Chapter 7, Figure 7-17: Using a "Ready" line for Product Backlog items. Photo by Ralph Jocham.

Chapter 7: "Last Responsible Moment (LRM) … making a decision." http://www.innolution.com/resources/glossary/last-responsible-moment-lrm.

Chapter 7: "As formality increases … requirements are equivalent". Robert C. Martin, and Grigori Melnik, "Tests and Requirements, Requirements and Tests: A Mobius Strip," *IEEE Software*, 25, no. 1 (2008): 54-59.

Chapter 7: "Triad: Business, Development, Testing". The term 'Triad' is by Ken Pugh, and is a more common term for the 'Three Amigos' created around 2009 by George Dinwiddie.

Chapter 8: "Customer collaboration over contract negotiation". Agile Manifesto.

Chapter 8: "Customer delight = Providing a continuous … customers and delivering it sooner". Stephen Denning.

Chapter 8: "Adding manpower to a late software project makes it later". Frederick Brooks, *The Mythical Man Month* (Reading, MA: Addison-Wesley, 1995), 25.

Chapter 8: "Portfolio is an … planning to commit to." Rothman, *Manage Your Product Portfolio*.

Chapter 8: "nexus –noun \'nek-s?s\: a relationship or connection between people or things". By permission. From Merriam-Webster.com © 2018 by Merriam-Webster, Inc. https://www.merriam-webster.com/dictionary/word.

Chapter 8: "Nexus is the exoskeleton of scaled Scrum". Ken Schwaber.

Chapter 8: "The primary measure of progress is working software". Agile Manifesto.

Chapter 8: "Each tropical system is given … the forecast uncertainty increases." https://weather.com/science/weather-explainers/news/tropical-storm-cyclone-forecast-cone-hurricane.

Chapter 8: "Our tool will not estimate how long … estimate you come up with". Tom DeMarco and Tim Lister, Waltzing with Bears: Managing Risk on Software Projects (New York, NY: Dorset House Publising, 2003).

Chapter 8: "Be wise enough not to be reckless, but brave enough to take great risks." Frank Warren.

Chapter 8: "Individuals and interactions over processes and tools; Working software over comprehensive documentation". Agile Manifesto.

Chapter 8: "[...] the absence of bureaucratic … hierarchy can provide". John Kotter, "Accelerate!" *Harvard Business Review*, November, 2012.

Chapter 8, Figure 8-33: "Kick-Off at Swiss Postal Services in the VIP Lounge at Stade de Suisse". Photo by Ralph Jocham.

Chapter 8: "Resolution Type 1, or project success … point during the development cycle." Johan Laurenz Eveleens and Chris Verhoef, "The Rise and Fall of the Chaos Report," *IEEE Software*, 27, no. 1, 2010.

Chapter 9: Collaborative: Work closely with Development … competition to stay in front. (216 words) Barry Boehm and RichardTurner, Balancing Agility and Discipline: A Guide for the Perplexed (Boston, MA: Addison-Wesley, 2003).

Cover: "This book presents a method of communicating our desires, cogently, coherently, and with a minimum of fuss and bother." Ken Schwaber.

Cover graphics, art: Sabrina Love/Scrum.org.

Continuously Deliver an Integrated Product with Multiple Scrum Teams

- Understand the challenges of delivering working, integrated product increments with multiple teams, and how Nexus addresses them

- Form a Nexus around a new or existing product, and learn how that Nexus sets goals and plans its work

- Run Sprints within a Nexus, provide transparency into progress, conduct effective Nexus Sprint reviews, and use Nexus Sprint Retrospectives to continuously improve

The Nexus Framework is the simplest, most effective approach to applying Scrum at scale across multiple teams, sites, and time zones. Created by Scrum.org—the pioneering Scrum training and certification organization founded by Scrum co-creator Ken Schwaber—Nexus draws on decades of experience to address the unique challenges teams face in coming together, sharing work, and managing and minimizing dependencies.

This concise book demonstrates how Nexus helps teams to deliver a complex, multi-platform, software-based product in short, frequent cycles, without sacrificing consistency or quality, and without adding unnecessary complexity or straying from Scrum's core principles.

informit.com/nexus

Pearson

informit.com
the trusted technology learning source

O'REILLY
Safari

Register Your Product at informit.com/register

Access additional benefits and **save 35%** on your next purchase

- Automatically receive a coupon for 35% off your next purchase, valid for 30 days. Look for your code in your InformIT cart or the Manage Codes section of your account page.

- Download available product updates.

- Access bonus material if available.*

- Check the box to hear from us and receive exclusive offers on new editions and related products.

Registration benefits vary by product. Benefits will be listed on your account page under Registered Products.

InformIT.com—The Trusted Technology Learning Source

InformIT is the online home of information technology brands at Pearson, the world's foremost education company. At InformIT.com, you can:

- Shop our books, eBooks, software, and video training
- Take advantage of our special offers and promotions (informit.com/promotions)
- Sign up for special offers and content newsletter (informit.com/newsletters)
- Access thousands of free chapters and video lessons

Connect with InformIT—Visit informit.com/community